Management, Valuation, and Risk for Human Capital and Human Assets

Management, Valuation, and Risk for Human Capital and Human Assets

Building the Foundation for a Multi-Disciplinary, Multi-Level Theory

Edited by Meir Russ

palgrave
macmillan

MANAGEMENT, VALUATION, AND RISK FOR HUMAN CAPITAL AND HUMAN ASSETS

First published in 2014 by
PALGRAVE MACMILLAN®
in the United States—a division of St. Martin's Press LLC,
175 Fifth Avenue, New York, NY 10010.

Where this book is distributed in the UK, Europe and the rest of the World, this is by Palgrave Macmillan, a division of Macmillan Publishers Limited, registered in England, company number 785998, of Houndmills, Basingstoke, Hampshire RG21 6XS.

Palgrave Macmillan is the global academic imprint of the above companies and has companies and representatives throughout the world.

Palgrave® and Macmillan® are registered trademarks in the United States, the United Kingdom, Europe and other countries.

ISBN: 978–1–137–36094–6

Library of Congress Cataloging-in-Publication Data

Management, valuation, and risk for human capital and human assets : building the foundation for a multi-disciplinary, multi-level theory / Meir Russ, Ph. D., editor.
pages cm
Includes bibliographical references and index.
ISBN 978–1–137–36094–6 (hardcover : alk. paper)
1. Human capital—Management. 2. Knowledge management. 3. Organizational change. I. Russ, Meir, 1968– editor of compilation.
HD4904.7.P377 2014
658.3—dc23 2014015542

A catalogue record of the book is available from the British Library.

Design by Integra Software Services

This book is dedicated to my children Ira, Yaara, Maytal, Yifat, their spouses, and their children, who have added so much joy and happiness to my life.

Contents

Figures and Tables

Figures

Tables

Acknowledgments

A call for chapters challenged potential authors to consider a unifying, multilevel theory of human capital arriving from different academic traditions and perspectives. The authors were invited to contribute to the book based on approved proposals. Each complete chapter received external, blind review in addition to the editor review. The author thanks Kelly Anklam for her assistance in editing this introduction and also wishes to that the Frederick E. Baer Professorship in Business and the Philip J. and Elizabeth Hendrickson Professor in Business at UW-Green Bay for partial financial support. The author also thanks Leif Edvinsson for his comments on the earlier version of this chapter. Finally, the author hopes that the discussion of creating a unifying, multilevel theory of human capital will continue based on the chapters presented in this volume.

Introduction—What Kind of an Asset Is Human Capital, How Should It Be Measured, and in What Markets?

Meir Russ

Introduction

The effective employment and deployment of intellectual capital and human assets in organizations is widely recognized as a critical characteristic of successful economies and establishments. Their abilities to respond to changing environments, to "learn," and to be efficient and competitive all depend, to some extent, on the individuals within their boundaries. The leading and management of those individuals in a way that is consistent with the goals and policies of the organization creates value for it and results in the developement of human capital as an asset, which is the focus of this book. Many organizations and their executives realize that the most critical (if not the only) source of competencies, capabilities, and sustainable competitive advantage is having the ability to attract, retain, develop, and manage their human assets and talent.

The study of human capital and assets originated in economics (Becker, 1962, 2009; Fisher, 1906; Romer, 1989; Schultz, 1961; Smith, 1776) and was later advanced by accounting, human resource, behavioral perspectives, and management, among many other disciplines (e.g., Lev & Schwartz, 1971; Snell & Dean, 1992; Wright, McMahan, & McWilliams, 1994). Being a multilevel construct that is studied from multiple perspectives (e.g., Coff & Kryscynski, 2011; Ployhart, Nyberg, Reilly, & Maltarich, 2013), it is not surprising that there is no agreement on the definitions of human capital (e.g., Mahroum, 2000) or on a method to measure, report, and value it (e.g., Gavious & Russ, 2009).

Market Failure and the Need for a New Comprehensive Theory

In the early twenty-first century, a number of developments are making the management and measurement of human capital and assets increasingly salient and challenging to executives. These developments include the changing characteristics of the labor force, the rapidly growing pace of technological innovation, greater international competition, new experiments with organizational structures, and greater attention to relationships with customers. From the macroeconomic and legal perspectives, the prominence of human assets might be even greater. The limited ability of the financial markets to monetize human (or for that matter any other intellectual) assets results in major market failure. More than 80 percent of the economies of developed countries (as measured by their gross domestic product [GDP]) are composed of intangibles (e.g., Nakamura, 2001). At the end of the twentieth century and the beginning of the twenty-first century (1995–2007), "intangibles had over-taken tangibles to become the largest systematic source of economic growth" (Corrado & Hulten, 2010, p. 102). Intangibles were found to play a major role in allowing national economies hit by the financial crisis of 2007–2009 to regain their competitiveness (Lin & Edvinsson, 2010). Still, the present accounting and legal systems in those countries recognize the value of very few intangible assets (patents, trademarks, etc.) or do so only in special and limited circumstances (e.g., goodwill at sale; Corrado, Hulten, & Sichel, 2009), resulting in disputed accounting and/or the development of new standards (e.g., Financial Accounting Standards Board (FASB) Statement 142 in the United States). Fortunately, financial markets recognize this issue by providing minimal returns on financial and capital assets and practically no insurance vehicles for intellectual assets and by searching urgently for new sources of income and/or opportunities for value monetization. The increasing pace of economic bubbles; the growing economic, educational, and political inequalities; and the high level of unemployment and underemployment, especially of the younger generation, are further indicators of a desperately needed solution for this major market failure (and others; see, e.g., Kümmel, 2011, p. 172). Despite this urgent need, the effectiveness of these embryonic attempts to develop monetizing and valuation methods is still questionable. As such, it has become painfully clear that there is an absence of a comprehensive, unifying theory and, more importantly, a reliable, transparent, and widely accepted measurement system for the valuation of human capital and assets. Research should be done at the macro, meso, and micro levels (including at multiple levels in each of them), from diverse perspectives and disciplines, focusing on different and distinct units of analysis (countries, regions, cities, organizations, groups, and individuals) and their relative contributions (Barney & Felin, 2013, p. 146; Nyberg, Moliterno, Hale, & Lepak, 2014). This book is intended to be a small step in that direction.

Markets External to the Firm

Five markets (discussed below) play a major role while providing for the external environment, thereby forming the context for the discussion of human capital and assets. All markets are structured and framed by legislation (e.g., Asher, Mahoney, & Mahoney, 2005; Macey, 1989). The *financial* markets and the *product/service* markets are the two traditional markets customarily discussed by the business and economic literature (e.g., Grant, 1991; Jacoby & Skoufias, 1997; Ulrich & Ulrich, 1997). The next three markets (*labor*, *skilled labor*, and *talent*) are presently amalgamated into one market, the labor market, by the traditional economic literature (e.g., Goldin & Katz, 2009), where human capital is augmenting the effective units of labor (Acemoglu & Autor, 2012, p. 427) when capital, labor, and technology are the factors driving the economy (e.g., Acemoglu & Autor, 2012). This traditional literature differentiates between high- and low-skilled labor (e.g., Philippon & Reshef, 2012) or high-, middle-, and low-skilled labor (Acemoglu & Autor, 2011, 2012; Katz & Margo, 2013). Also, within this framework, regardless of the original perspective, all employees are considered either as an expense (as in current accounting standards) or as an asset (as the more progressive academic literature suggests).

I am advocating going beyond the distinction used by the present economic literature and separating the three labor markets: *labor*, *skilled labor*, and *talent*. Each one of the three is different, and even though today there is still some fuzziness at the margins and blending at the edges, technology-accelerated development is reducing such amalgamation and making the boundaries between the three sharper. This may require some explanation.

First, why is this happening and why now? The new knowledge-based economy and the continuous stream of technology-driven revolutions are creating an economy (and society) different from anything else the human race has ever faced (Arora & Gambardella, 1994; Leydesdorff, 2006). Kurzweil (2005) captured it best with a captivating title when he suggested "Singularity is near." Knowledge is a very unique product, production factor, and outcome (Gherardi, 2000; Grant, 1996; Lewin & Baetjer, 2011; Tang, 2005), and somewhere in the 1980s knowledge started to become a dominant factor in the global economy. Examples to illustrate why the transition from one labor market to three is occurring now are discussed next (different experts and different perspectives identify different time frames). The time interval between the most prominent events in human history is decreasing exponentially (Schmidhuber, 2007), rapidly shrinking the half-life of knowledge (Siemens, 2005). As early as 1970, companies with higher debt ratios started hiring more part-time employees, paying less, and responding more aggressively to economic downturns, and this trend has strengthened over time (Hanka, 1998). In the early 1980s, a separation became apparent between productivity gains and wages (Fleck, Glaser, & Sprague, 2011; Sachdev, 2007). The ratio of market-to-book value changed significantly in the 1990s (Lev, 2001). The average net debt ratio of US firms has fallen significantly since 1980 into negative territory (Bates, Kahle, & Stulz, 2009). The explanatory power of educational attainment for earning increased distinctly in the early 1980s, corresponding with the increase of returns from skills (Acemoglu & Autor, 2011). US productivity and earning by capital went up, and global GDP growth accelerated since the mid-1990s (Haskel, Lawrence, Leamer, & Slaughter, 2012).

Now let us turn to the labor markets and start the discussion with the basic four quadrants (see Figure I.1) differentiating between employees who have low and high uniqueness (to the firm and/or to the market) and low and high value (to the firm and/or to the market), which suggests that

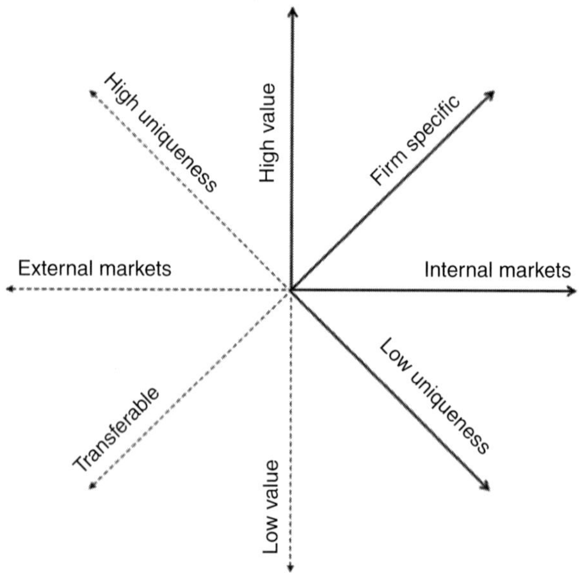

Figure I.1 Human capital taxonomy

not all employees of the firm should be seen as identical internally (to the firm) and/or externally (by the market) (e.g., Chen & Lin, 2004). I identify the low-uniqueness/low-value cell as *labor*; the high-uniqueness/low-value cell and the low-uniqueness/high-value cell as *skilled labor*; and the high-uniqueness/high-value as *talent*. Two additional dimensions should be added to the framework in regard to the value of human capital. The first dimension is the specificity of the knowledge: Is the knowledge held by the employee *firm specific* or *transferable* (or a mix)? The second dimension is the point of view of the evaluator: Is the perspective (or the "market") *internal to the firm* or *external*?

The Three "Labor" Markets

Next, I suggest why what is presently referred to as "labor" should be treated separately as three different and separate markets. The transition from one labor market T_1 to three markets T_2 could be seen as gradual, resulting mostly from technology and globalization pushes, but, at this point in time, my contention is that we have enough evidence to treat the three differently and separately and that preserving them as one market does more harm than good to public discussion and academic research. I will leave the discussion about the transit period from one market to three open at this time.

I propose to view labor as a human assets commodity with very little differentiation in skill, with a monopsonistic competition where a small number of buyers (firms, governments, not-for-profits, small and medium-sized enterprises (SMEs), etc.) can dictate the employment terms (within the legal framework) to a powerless mass of little-differentiated employees (e.g., Bidwell, 2013). The value created by *labor* is minimal at best (see also Kümmel, 2011), and the salaries and wages are mostly dictated by legislation and social norms regarding employment, unemployment, minimal wage, and so on, resulting from a dysfunctional labor market (see Figure I.2, A at time T_2). One should be careful though not to oversimplify this market, since the legal structure and economic and business forces allow for multiple arrangements to match the supply and demand of labor (see interesting discussions in Cappelli & Keller, 2013; Leoni & Gritti, 2013). Examples of the uniqueness of this market are present in studies regarding the base-of-the-pyramid (BOP) markets and their mechanisms, such as changing the nature of the classic principal–agent relationship by making the agent a principal (Kistruck, Sutter, Lount, & Smith, 2013, p. 663). Another example is what Autor and Dorn (2013) identify as the service occupation (versus the service sector). In their analysis, they identify growth in numbers of both employees and wages, trends that are significantly

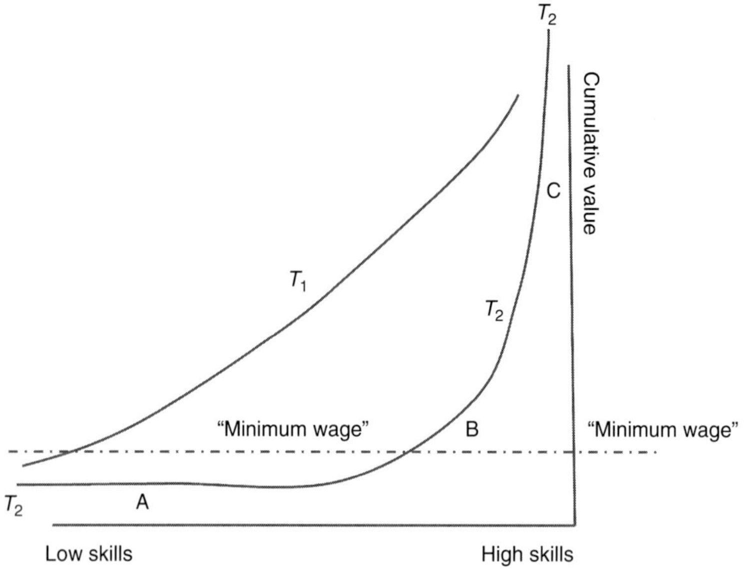

Figure I.2 Labor markets

different from those for the middle- and higher-skill percentile (between 1980 and 2005). If this proposition could be validated, there will be enormous implications. One implication is that the higher education of this sector (*labor*) cannot be entirely seen as a human asset when high school or vocational education might be sufficient for the tasks at hand (Autor & Dorn, 2013). For example, a study conducted in Italy based on 2004 data found about 14 percent of the employees to be overeducated (Cainarca & Sgobbi, 2012). A similar study done in China based on 2003 data reported that about 20 percent of higher education graduates were overeducated (Li, Morgan, & Ding, 2008). Sattinger and Hartog (2013) summarize the penalties for overeducation in wage consequences to be between 1.7 and 7.7 percent.

The value/reward of *labor*'s product and services is minimally dictated by economic and business supply and demand and is mostly dictated by the labor laws, social norms, and/or political pressure. As such, *labor* income is primarily dictated by minimum wage legislation or alternative unemployment benefits and is subject to distinct dynamics (see recent example in Krueger, Cramer, & Cho, 2014). Actually, seen from a narrow economic perspective, such an investment in higher education might appear to be a human assets debt, since economic benefits from the unemployment or underemployment of those individuals are minimal, if not negative (Bivens, Fieldhouse, & Shierholz, 2013; Leoni & Gritti, 2013). This may also suggest that education (like health care) should be alternatively framed as a right (Oakes, Rogers, Blasi, & Lipton, 2008; Yamin, 1996) and not as a product, since if delineated as a product, the majority of the population will not be able to afford it, and, as such, it should be more of a social and political issue and not an economic one.

The economic aspect of human capital discussed previously has in the *labor* market discussion gone above and beyond the credence attribute aspects of the value of a service as a product (Walker, Johnson, & Leonard, 2006; Yadev & Berry, 1996) and the public good aspect (Stiglitz, 1999), which were always inherent in the discussion of service valuation and have become even more entangled with the attributes and characteristics of knowledge as product and/or production factor (Gherardi, 2000; Grant, 1996).

The vast and fast-shrinking middle ground of labor markets (see Figure I.2, B at time T_2) is presently occupied by *skilled* employees, who have mostly codified skills (causing the potential for future job eliminations) (e.g., Chipulu, Neoh, Ojiako, & Williams, 2013; Frey & Osborne, 2013), are better paid (than *labor*), have some unique skills, and create some value. This market resembles more of the classic market where the supply and demand of labor and skills play their classic roles. In this market, capital investment and technology can potentially replace most of the jobs (most of them in services). Such a replacement will occur due to effectiveness, efficiencies, and financial profitability concerns, and the wages and value will go up and down in response to market, technology, skills, costs, and investments (Acemoglu & Autor, 2012). This middle ground, as suggested by Acemoglu and Autor (2012), includes the low-, medium-, and high-skilled labor, and the distinction between the three is a function, changing over time, of technology and investment in human capital (education, training, etc.), but it is fast shrinking due to technological advancements, global competition, and profitability pressures (e.g., Canon & Marifian, 2013; Kolev & Saget, 2010). The ongoing pressure on this market is also the result of the discrepancies between the productivity and costs share of labor and energy and the low cost of the combination of energy and capital in comparison to the high cost of labor (Kümmel, 2011, p. 245).

The *talent* market (see Figure I.2, C at time T_2) as defined here is an inefficient market, a market failure (Bator, 1958; Ouchi, 1980) where the value of the product is not captured by its pricing, either because the skills or tasks required to produce it are not codifiable or because the uncertainty, risk, and value are difficult, if not impossible, to ascertain (e.g., Cattani, Dunbar, & Shapira, 2013; Martin, Gomez-Mejia, & Wiseman, 2013). The *talent* market has a very different characteristic from the previous two markets and tends to operate more like an increasing-return economy (Maier, Pfeiffer, & Pohlmeier, 2004) where winner takes all (Arthur, 1989), either because of imperfect (asymmetry of information, risks) internal and external markets (see, for example, the exuberant incomes of CEOs: Bertrand & Mullainathan, 2001; or of financial executives: Philippon & Reshef, 2012) or because of an external networking effect (see the extremely high earnings of star performers, athletes, etc.: Ertug & Castellucci, 2013; Rosen, 1981). As a result, for example, in the United States, the income of the highest-earning (1 percent) workers almost doubled between 1991 and 2007 (Haskel et al., 2012). The inefficiency of this market comes at a stringent price. From a different perspective, Kümmel (2011, p. 212, table 4.5) estimated output elasticities for labor (for Germany, Japan, and the United States, for the second half of the twentieth century) to be between 0.09 and 0.15 and for creativity to be between 0.10 and 0.19, in comparison to output elasticities for capital and energy, estimated to be between 0.18 and 0.51, and 0.35 and 0.73, respectively.

One of the least discussed questions in the human capital and assets literature is that of risk and insurance (Hartog, Ophem, & Bajdechi, 2007). Since companies (and individuals) cannot monetize knowledge as an asset and since companies do not own (they may lease: e.g., Lev & Schwartz, 1971) human capital, what is the form of insurance they use to monetize the risk of losing human capital or keeping the human capital they have (Jaaskelainen, 2011; Mäenpää & Voutilainen, 2012; Ostaszewski, 2003)? Lambrecht and Pawlina (2013) recently proposed that companies are using cash (or negative debt) as an insurance policy to protect themselves from losing transferable (i.e., not company-specific) human capital, and since more of the knowledge created is now transferable, the amount of cash accumulated by companies is increasing, resulting in less hiring and investing. Others (e.g., Berk, Stanton, & Zechner, 2010; Pratt, 2011) suggest that due to the need to insure firm-specific knowledge (due to lack of other alternatives), companies are taking on less debt, resulting in slower growth. Again, if this contention is supported, it may explain why American (but not only) companies are holding trillions of dollars in cash (Sánchez & Yurdagul, 2013) while refraining from hiring new full-time employees.Social and geographic mobility could be used as one way for validating such a drastic proposal. If the three markets are indeed different and separated, then the "rules of the game" in each will be different. The lack of (or minimal) social and geographic mobility in the *labor* market (Bosker, Brakman, Garretsen, & Schramm, 2012; Gill, Koettl, & Packard, 2013; Machin, Salvanes, & Pelkonen, 2012; Partridge, Rickman, Olfert, & Ali, 2012) and the ease of social movement and global mobility of the stars and *talent* are well documented (e.g., Currid-Halkett & Ravid,

2012; Filatotchev, Liu, Lu, & Wright, 2011; Haskel et al., 2012), and the externalities go far beyond the traditional returns (e.g., Oettl & Agrawal, 2008). The professionals (the middle, *skilled labor*) seem to follow their own mechanisms (see examples in Cohen & Broschak, 2013; McGinn & Milkman, 2013).

I have to accept that this labeling (*labor*, *skilled labor*, and *talent*) and its implications might be controversial for some readers since it might have emotional, political, and societal connotations and implications (e.g., Reich, 2013). But such a development of the labor market is supported by current legislation and technological frontier developments (see also Kümmel, 2011). The present discussion of raising the minimum wage (e.g., Laliberte, 2012) can only be understood when one realizes that market forces (labor supply and demand of unskilled labor) will push the cost of labor as close to zero as possible because of unlimited supply and very limited (and I may add temporary) demand. The situation of the oversupply of labor is so damaging that more people are dropping out from the labor force today than they were in the last 30 years (e.g., BLS, 2013), and, more than ever, employees are taking jobs that they are overqualified for (the economists call that underemployment: Howell, 2010). All this is happening when companies lament that even in the worst economy they had jobs that they could not fill and a huge demand for talent, which also they could not fill (e.g., Quintini, 2011).

I would postulate that the cumulative curve of value from (and for) the firm (internal market/firm specific not transferable) and the individual (external market/transferable) as a function of skill percentile is not only exponential but as a function of time, the gaps, inequality, and polarization (winner takes all) is growing (see Figure I.2). Also, artificial intelligence and robotics, and the accelerating shrinking of the half-life of knowledge are mostly putting pressure on *skilled labor* because of the potential benefits and increased returns to the firm and to the producers of the alternative solution delivered through artificial intelligence and robotics. Replacing *talent* is still too expensive (even though IBM's Watson is getting smarter; Kroeker, 2011), so the most practical approach is to confront the middle (e.g., Autor, 2010; Canon & Marifian, 2013; Kolev & Saget, 2010). So, (the low-cost) *labor* is artificially maintained by the government (for political reasons—the people still can vote) and the dominant elite (buying social peace—see Anonymous, 2014) (it is cheaper to keep people working than keeping them in prison—even the United States realized that recently); the high-end (*talent*) market is not efficient, and the only economically efficient (but shrinking) labor market is the middle one. Accepting this perspective, as difficult and controversial as it could be, could illuminate the present (February 2014) discussion in the United States about the minimum wage. It seems that increasing the minimum wage could result in hundreds of thousands losing jobs while increasing income for millions (CBO, 2014). A question not asked yet is how many potential employees who are presently out of the employment statistics since they dropped out from the labor force will come back and look for jobs, which could paradoxically increase the rate of unemployment. The other less-discussed aspect is the impact this could potentially have on the *skilled labor* market (marginal at best in my opinion), which could be seen as additional evidence of the two markets being (almost completely) disconnected.

Now let us grant that new technologies (nano, bio, media, 3D printing, etc.) create new opportunities, and, given time, new jobs will be created as well (e.g., Brynjolfsson & McAfee, 2014; Levy & Murnane, 2012), but most of them will require a much higher level of skills (graduate education) or a mix of skills and creativity that only the star/talent employees might have; however, even this is changing (e.g., Banks & Humphreys, 2008; Rotman, 2013). Adding to this is the mostly negative (or nonexistent) role that legislation is playing for the intellectual property and intangible assets (including of course human capital and assets). On one hand, there are a few areas that are too restrictive. For example, patents are granted for too long to support innovation, and this creates opportunities for patent trolls, etc. On the other hand, many areas are not regulated at all, not allowing new markets to be created, and, as such, this limits the possibilities for ownership and capital investments or insurance protection. One interesting implication of this analysis is that, in light of such a legal and economic environment, we have to change the way we look at the majority of SMEs. The current economic and business literature sees them as drivers of innovation and job growth, and, I do grant, some are. But the vast majority of them are part-time or full-time, single- or less-than-five-employee firms. I would suggest seeing them not as an entrepreneur's venture trying to benefit from future opportunities, but as an attempt to capture and capitalize on one's (specifically the middle-ground individuals mentioned previously) human and social capital (Baumol, 2010, p. 156; Kaul, 2013). So, the large number of women and minorities hitting the glass ceiling are not leaving their present place of employment because they identified a business opportunity, but because they identified the ownership option as the best choice to capitalize on their experience and social capital, "biting" the working-for-a-corporation or unemployment option. Unfortunately, the vast majority of *labor* (see above) does not own or control the capital (financial, human, or social) needed for such venturing, and as such they are "stuck" in their job (underemployed) or are unemployed.

Human Capital and Assets Framework

Dimensions

Going back to the framework mentioned earlier (Figure I.1), I propose to add four additional dimensions, incorporating time (short, mid-, and long term), uncertainty (low and high), risk (low and high), and the degree of asymmetry of information (low and high) between players (see Figure I.3).

First, clearly, the changing nature of knowledge supporting the value of human capital and assets must be captured by the discussion on human capital and assets emphasizing the importance of *time*, time flow, and time horizon (e.g., Russ, 2010).

Next, the two dimensions of uncertainty and risk are related but different (Jarvis, 2011; Knight, 1921; Langlois & Cosgel, 1993).

Also, if the shrinking half-life of knowledge and the accelerated pace of change in the industry matter, resulting in higher uncertainty, then *time* and *uncertainty* dimensions must be captured as framing the discussion about human capital and assets (Alessandri, Ford, Lander, Leggio, & Taylor, 2004; Eaton & Rosen, 1980; Fama, 1977).

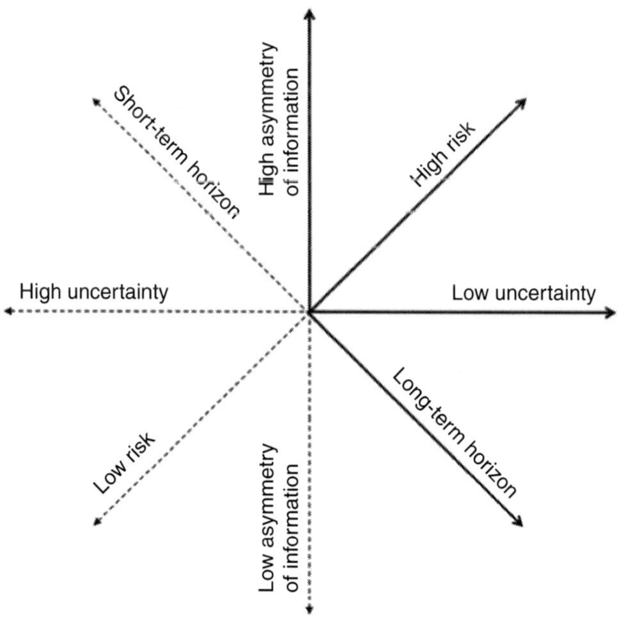

Figure I.3 The four-dimensional framework for human capital

Similarly, the importance of the *asymmetry of information* and its impact on *risk* is all too accepted in economic investment, agency theory, theory of the firm, and other literatures, and its impact on the different talent markets (executives vs. performers) cannot be overstated (Levhari & Weiss, 1974; Miller, 1977; Sapienza & Gupta, 1994).

Finally, specifically for human capital valuation purposes, the tools provided by "real options" and game theory allow for considering the four dimensions for valuation purposes (Chevalier-Roignant & Trigeorgis, 2011—see chapters 8 and 13 for discussion and examples).

Reporting

Also, using the distinction mentioned above between employees who have low and high uniqueness (to the firm/to the market) and low and high value (to the firm/to the market), as well as high and low uncertainty and risk, advocates that not all employees of the firm should be seen internally (to the firm) and/or externally (by the market) identically (e.g., Chen & Lin, 2004) and submits that some employees should be considered and reported as an expense and some as an asset (see a comparable discussion about intellectual capital in Ståhle & Ståhle, 2012, p. 169), thus questioning the uniform accounting treatment of such assets. There are some generalities here (allowing for standardization of reports, at least at the industry level). For example, it is clear (as mentioned above) that employees who have low uniqueness and create little value in an industry that is highly uncertain and risky should be considered as an expense, while employees who have high uniqueness and create high value in an industry that is low on risk and uncertainty should be considered as an asset. This eight-dimensional framework mentioned above should also allow for the strategy of the company to be communicated more clearly with different stakeholders. So, for example, one company might consider employees as assets while another company, having a different strategy, such as in a case where the employees have high uniqueness but at present create little value in an industry that is uncertain but less risky, will consider them as expenses. This framework could also be used to enrich the discussion within the human capital and assets literature regarding the aspects of value creation versus appropriation (e.g., Bowman & Swart, 2007; Carpenter, Sanders, & Gregersen, 2001), as well as that regarding the valuation of human capital (e.g.,Eaton & Rosen, 1980; Eiling, 2013; Fulmer & Ployhart, 2014; Levhari & Weiss, 1974) and the potential for insurance coverage (De Santis & Giuliani, 2013; Garcia-Parra, Simo, Sallan, & Mundet, 2009; Harvey & Lusch, 1999; Jaaskelainen, 2011; Mäenpää & Voutilainen, 2012; Ostaszewski, 2003).

The Book Framework and Chapters

This book goes beyond the current literature by providing a platform for discussion to broaden the scope of human capital and assets theory building and, more importantly, by encouraging a multidisciplinary fusion between diverse disciplines, similar to Itami and Numagami's "logical compound synthesis" (1992). The original call for chapters solicited proposals from a multidisciplinary array of scholars who could contribute to one or more of the following theoretical perspectives/disciplines: economics, economic development, finance, accounting, systems networks, behavioral, human resources, and social. Multilevel and multidiscipline theoretical breakthrough chapters were strongly encouraged. When appropriate, plurality of empirical methods from diverse disciplines that can enhance the building of a holistic theory of human capital and assets was also strongly furthered. Viewing the subject of human capital and assets from the traditional academic perspectives (listed above), the reader will notice that this collection of chapters focuses more on the accounting and human resource perspectives and that there is limited representation of the financial, social, behavioral, and systems networks perspectives. But investigating the subject of human capital and assets from the traditional academic perspective's prism will not promote the breaking of the silos between the perspectives and will not contribute to the development of a new research paradigm. A number of alternative frameworks were considered to outline and structure this book (e.g., Nonaka, Umemoto, & Senoo, 1996; Srivastava, Shervani, & Fahey, 1998). The adopted framework was chosen due to its academic validity and its relevance to practitioners. The framework for this book expands and adds to the intellectual capital schema proposed by Marzo (2013) and forms the content of this book around three out of the five major issues grounded in the praxis of human capital and assets while providing for a triangulation opportunity to analyze human capital and assets issues from diverse academic traditions, perspectives, and theories (see Figure I.4).

The five issues are as follows: definitions, origins; management; valuation, risk; value creation; and reporting, signaling. This book focuses on the first three. Let us briefly discuss each one.

Definitions, Origins

As mentioned earlier, there is no one accepted and shared definition for human capital. Different academic traditions and perspectives have different definitions and use different methodologies for the study of human capital and assets. For this book, I requested every author to be explicit about the definitions and perspectives they used for their chapter.

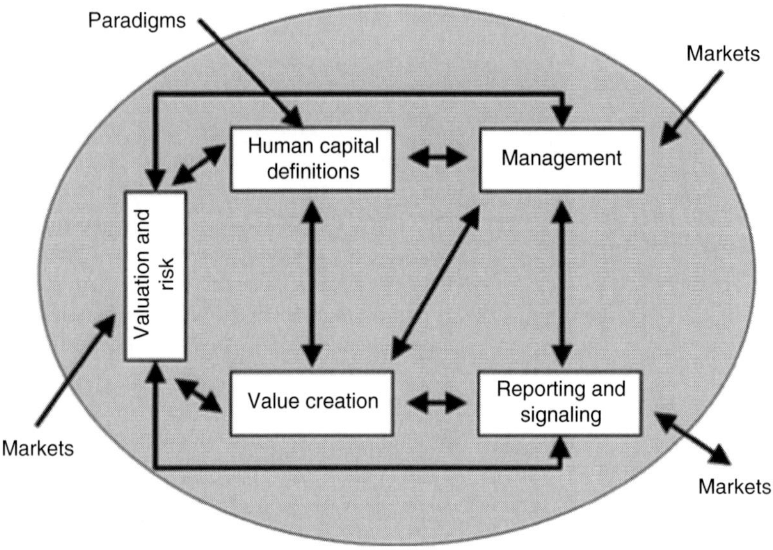

Figure I.4 Human capital: Major issues
Source: Based on and modified from Marzo (2013).

Management

Human capital management has a number of alternative definitions and scopes, and some are broader (e.g., Baron, 2007) than others. Here the focus will be on a more specific definition, one that includes, for example, the operational (e.g., recruiting, acquisition, retaining), cultural (e.g., rewarding), and developmental (e.g., training) aspects of human capital management and the alignment (e.g., planning, leading, implementing) between them for present value creation and future, potential value creation (Hayton, 2003; Van Marrewijk & Timmers, 2003), as well as employment relationships and human resource configurations (Lepak & Snell, 1999).

Valuation, Risk

The scope of human capital valuation and risks converges on estimating and monitoring the financial value of, and the risks and liabilities associated with, the value of human capital and assets, the effects that nonfinancial merits of human assets as antecedents have on financial valuations, the impact that the lack of standardized financial measures has on the workforce and financial outcomes, and the potential for insurance coverage (e.g., Fulmer & Ployhart,

2014; Garcia-Parra et al., 2009; Jaaskelainen, 2011; Mäenpää & Voutilainen, 2012; Ostaszewski, 2003).

Next, a brief overview of the chapters will be provided.

Part I—Management

Chapter 1, "Team composition and project-based organizations: New perspectives for human resource management," by Francesca Vicentini and Paolo Boccardelli, presents a multilevel analysis of human capital from the human resource perspective. The chapter analyzes the project-based Italian TV series industry at the individual and project team levels, using a cross-level model. The findings suggest that team reputation positively affects the project value, while at the individual level, team reputation is affected more by individuals with higher experiential task diversity than those with role diversity. This chapter is a significant addition to a small but profoundly needed literature of human capital at the project unit of analysis and presents a worthy example of the rigor needed when conducting a multilevel analysis. For practitioners and academics, the chapter suggests an interesting insight into the importance of the selection of team members and the mechanisms by which human capital translates into an effective outcome.

Chapter 2, "The effect of virtual work environments and social systems on human capital and assets," by Eugene Pierce and Sean Hansen, presents a grounded theory analysis from the behavioral perspective, exploring the factors that drive the effectiveness of virtual teams within a distributed work environment. The authors, utilizing semi-structured interviews and a quantitative survey instrument, explore how technology and managing the social framework as well as critical project management control structures facilitate the generation and maintenance of trust to drive the performance of distributed teams in the Web 2.0 technological context. The chapter describes how the establishment of trust has both direct and indirect effects on human capital development and the specific mechanisms of how to leverage those resources to enhance the performance of teams. This chapter, in a similar vein to the first one, adds to the discussion of virtual teams in a project context, this time from a team perspective, as well as provides an exemplary addition of research method triangulation. For practitioners and academics, the chapter suggests a noteworthy understanding of, and tools useful for, the leadership of virtual teams to achieve the expected outcomes.

In Chapter 3, "Perspectives on human capital initiatives," Alyssa Danielson places the subject of human capital initiatives at the focus of her dynamic human capital strategy from the human resource perspective. Applying a number of theories, the author presents a multilayered framework of criteria for selection of the preferred initiatives within the organizational context of outcomes and constraints. The framework discusses macro-strategic, meso policies and micro-practice human resource activities in support of the initiatives. For researchers, the chapter provides a potential focus area of research in the micro-foundation perspective from the dynamic viewpoint to human capital. For practitioners, the author suggests a well-defined map of connecting daily human resource routines to policies and strategies supporting organizational goals.

Part II—Valuation and Risk

Chapter 4, "Models of human capital valuation: A review with examples," by Franko Milost, reviews valuation models of human capital from the human resource perspective. The author reviews both nonfinancial and financial models with focus on the latter. The nonfinancial models include the Michigan, Flamholtz, and Ogan models. The financial models examined are the replacement costs model, the opportunity costs model, the discounted wages and salaries model, and two models (with examples) originally developed by the author: the dynamic model and the net value added model, which the author sees as a major step toward developing a general model for human capital valuation. The chapter offers an in-depth review of existing models for human capital valuation and provides an important addition for academics and practitioners to the human resource accounting literature, in light of the growing importance of talent management in the global economy.

Chapter 5,"Investments in human capital: Elements of investments, their valuation, a true and fair view of financial statements compiled by using the classical approach, and the related financial performance ratios," by Franko Milost, proposes a system of integrated financial performance indicators of human capital from the systems perspective. The author discusses the elements of investments in human capital and different methods used to valuate these investments. Specifically, the author focuses on the effects on employees that the treatment of investments in classical accounting has on the true and fair view of financial statements. The notion for valuating investments in employees via human resource accounting is founded on the economic concept of value, based on the present and future benefits associated with the asset. The chapter presents a number of basic and derivative financial performance ratios related to investments in employees, culminating in a system of integrated ratios. Complementing the earlier chapter, the author provides an additional model of human capital valuation, incorporating financial and accounting perspectives into a comprehensive system that could be very constructive to both researchers and practitioners.

Chapter 6, "Intellectual capital efficiency and corporate performance: Some empirical evidence," by Domenico Celenza, Marco Lacchini, and Fabrizio Rossi, presents empirical results from Italy of using the Value Added Intellectual Coefficient (VAIC^{TM}) indicator and studies the relationship between this indicator and the financial performance of the companies. As expected, the results support the positive and statistically significant relationship between VAIC and its components. However, the authors did not find the expected positive relationship between VAIC and companies' financial and equity performance indicators. They conclude that in Italy, similar to other countries, there does not seem to be a statistically significant relationship between VAIC and the financial performance of the company. Specifically, for human capital, its coefficient is positive but never significant with regard to return on investment (ROI) and return on equity (ROE). The authors suggest that in this study this might be a result of the Italian context with rigid labor regulations. Probably the most important contribution of the chapter is the "no significant relationship found," which is rarely reported and published. This chapter suggests that researchers and practitioners must be careful in assuming, *a priori*, a positive relationship between intellectual capital and its components, including human capital, and the financial performance of the organizations, as presently measured and reported.

Chapter 7, "An assessment of the Accounting Perspective on Intellectual Capital and some results from the European Union," by Michele Di Marcantonio and Marco Mattei, reports the use of two financial indicators of intellectual and human capital and their empirical findings from the study of European Union companies. The authors use the VAIC indicator (similar to the earlier chapter) and the impact intellectual and human capital have on firm financial performances. They report that the impact is not consistent among samples and business performance indicators in terms of both the significance and sign of coefficients. The second model used is a modification of, and a partial repetition and validation of, a method originally developed by Olhson. The authors report that the indicators of structural capital and human capital are always significant, suggesting that this information is relevant for investors who operate on the European stock markets. This chapter is a worthy example of the use of two quantitative methods when conducting a rigorous financial analysis of intellectual capital and human capital, suggesting to researchers and practitioners that different methods and tools have very different validities for predicting future outcomes.

Chapter 8, "Human capital assessment: A labor accounting or a management control perspective?," by Paola Demartini and Paola Paoloni, uses action research from two accounting perspectives—labor and management control—discussing two case studies to understand the role of intellectual capital and human capital assessment within an organization. As such, the major issue addressed in this chapter is how firm-specific information on intellectual and human capital will help managers to intervene into processes of organizational knowledge management. Two research streams are cognized by the authors: ostensive versus performative; consequently, two complementary roles of measurement are identified: essence versus convention. The authors suggest, following their case studies, that the most important role of measurement and control is to provide the information needed for management decisions so that it is integrated into the narrative of efficient knowledge management and intellectual and human capital management. This chapter is a major contribution to the developing literature on human capital accounting in practice, focusing on enablers and boundaries for implementation of intellectual capital models within the companies, thus filling a major gap between academic theory and practitioner practices.

Conclusion

Two final thoughts about, and a definition of, human capital will conclude this introductory chapter.

Final Thoughts

The following eight chapters in this book use and cover an impressive number of theories, models, tools, and research methods. Not surprisingly, no one dominant theory or perspective has emerged from this collection of chapters regarding "the theory" of human capital and assets. While considering the present state of the subject (see also recent reviews by Fulmer & Ployhart, 2014; Nyberg et al., 2014), it seems that the science of human capital is at the pre-paradigm phase (Kuhn, 1962), far from being a reference discipline (Serenko & Bontis, 2013; Wade, Biehl, & Kim, 2006).

Two ideas to advance the field of human capital will be introduced next: the need to identify a unifying paradigm, and the need to identify measures complementary to the unifying paradigm. A human capital definition, consistent with the discussion, will close this part.

Paradigms

Three leading paradigms are presently well established for framing the discussion of human capital, knowledge, and knowledge management: the cognitivist, the connectionist, and Maturana and Varela's (1980) autopoiesis (see examples at Jelavic, Tan, & Nya, 2011; Magalhães, 2004; Russ, Fineman, &

Jones, 2010). An extended, multilayered, transdisciplinary perspective of autopoiesis was added by Luhmann (1997), which recently was embraced into the study of management (Seidl, 2004), knowledge management (Vines & Hall, 2011), and information theory (Di Prodi, 2012) literatures. This will be considered a fourth paradigm for the purpose of starting this discussion (see Figure I.5). These four paradigms will be situated on two dimensions: (a) single-actor (e.g., Bertrand & Mullainathan, 2001) versus multi-actor (e.g., Currid-Halkett & Ravid, 2012), and (b) open (e.g., Cornelissen, de Jong, & Kessels, 2012; Katz & Kahn, 1978; Koskinen, 2013) versus operatively closed (Blyler & Coff, 2003; Seidl, 2004) systems. A third dimension will be added to this framework as well: the linear systems theory (e.g., Weiss, 1995) versus dynamic systems theory (e.g., Hazy, 2012; Schneider & Somers, 2006). It is worth noting that different perspectives are using different paradigms to drive their theories and analyses, and, while some of the perspectives use them systematically over the years (e.g., the economic, financial, and accounting perspectives), some perspectives are transitioning and/or transforming to different paradigms (e.g., organizational behavior,

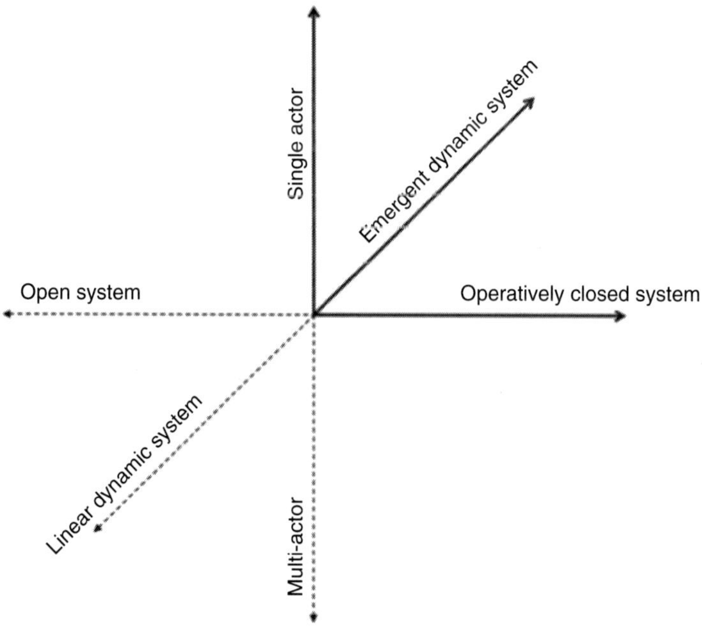

Figure I.5 Human capital paradigms

human resources) and even modifying their units of analysis and their relevant measures (e.g., from individuals to organizations: Reilly, Nyberg, Maltarich, & Weller, 2012).

Indicators

It has become obviously and painfully clear, during and since the last economic crisis, that financial and economic data are at best a weak indicator about the present, and predictor of the future, state of an organization and of the economy. That is the best that we presently have, but it is probably not good enough. Could information be the key? And if yes, for what? Information is seen as a critical aspect in physics (e.g., Davies & Gregersen, 2010; Zuse, 1982), in complex systems and life sciences (e.g., Farnsworth, Nelson, & Gershenson, 2013; Gershenson, 2012; Haken, 2006), and in economics (e.g., Stiglitz, 2002). Should information be used as a unifying measure (Zeleny, 1997) in place of, or complementing, money as the basic unit of economic reality? Some academics think so (e.g., Leydesdorff, 2006; Luhmann, 1997, as referenced in Jalava, 2006).

There are two ways to look at information: as meaning and as Shannon information (Haken, 2006; Leydesdorff, 2006; Menant, 2011). Russ et al. (2010) differentiated between the two by defining the latter as data and the former as data plus metadata, when the metadata provide for the context and the meaning needed for decisions. Menant (2011) refers to the context as goals, actions, and constraints. Russ et al. (2010) refer to the action, with a purpose of creating value as knowledge, and different from the "meaning" of information. Regardless, an autopoietic organizational system, in order to survive, must make decisions, communicate, and evolve, in the context of goals and constraints, considering at least three dimensions: social, temporal, and factual (Luhmann, 1997, as referenced in Jalava, 2006, p. 78).

Presently, human capital and assets are measured by different financial and economic indicators based on currency as a unifying economic measure. Money communicates only the constraint of present economic resource scarcity, not future scarcity, with no social and environmental constraints. So, from the triple-bottom-line perspective (e.g., Blackburn, 2007), current economic systems refer only to one constraint (economic resource scarcity), and only to the present, not the future, leaving the other to the realm of law (legislation and government administration). For example, sustainability, as indicated by this book, is a subject that is incorporated into the literature of human capital and intellectual capital. Clearly lacking in this discussion are the natural resources, mainly energy, as a production factor and as entropy (Kümmel, 2011). As a result of this omission, Kümmel (2013) asserts that present economic analysis is overvaluing the cost of labor and underestimating the cost of energy. If his hypothesis is validated, this will support not only the need to include energy in this discussion but also our own assertion earlier, that the assumption that education of all should count as an asset could be wrong. Assuming continuous economic growth without including the constraints on substitution among production factors, resulting from including energy (e.g., Ayres, Van den Bergh, Lindenberger, & Warr, 2013) and environment (e.g., Foxon & Steinberger, 2013), is not sustainable. This would suggest that energy conversion processes and energy entropy production both need to be taken into consideration when discussing economic growth (Kümmel, 2011, p. 177), and intellectual and human capital (e.g., Collins et al., 2010; Osranek & Zink, 2014; Zeleny, 1997). The weakness of the present economic system calls for new markets (Dror, 2011; Russ, 2011) that will be based on information regarding not only present economic scarcities but also future states, opportunities, and threats in the economic, social, and environmental spheres.

Some early work has already been done. For example, a number of indicators based on Shannon information theory were recently developed, using "entropy" (a measure of disorder) as the rudimentary building block (see discussion in Fernández, Maldonado, & Gershenson, 2014; Haken, 2006; Leydesdorff, 2006). Hassan and Holt (2003) used entropy to measure software development complexity. Leydesdorff (2006) used second-order interaction between subsystems to induce order into the system level, measured by entropy, to gauge the knowledge base of regional economies. Kan and Gero (2008) use entropy as an indicator for individual designer opportunistic contributions to a team and as a measure for idea development by a team of designers (using the linkography technique; Goldschmidt, 1990). Di Prodi (2012) developed a model of artificial societies using entropy as an internal variety regulator. Menant (2011) developed a meaning generator system linking a system to constraints in its environment. Sims (2003) proposed to use entropy as an explanation for rational inattention. His model was recently extended by Caplin and Dean (2013) to include behavioral implications and by Pavan (2014) to include coordination.

Finally, let me postulate how entropy can play a different role in the three distinct labor markets we identified earlier. The role of management (*skilled* market—see Figure I.2, B at time T_2) can be formulated as a complexity reduction function between the chosen environment (strategy, measured as entropy) for the actors that deliver the value (see additional discussion on employer learning in Habermalz, 2010), when creating the value for customers. Effective and efficient management reduces the entropy (e.g., by using feedback or implementing information systems), so the employees have to deliver the product/service dealing with minimal noise/complexity/entropy (see additional discussion on leadership and coordination in Bolton, Brunnermeier, & Veldkamp, 2013). If the amount and scope of complexity (entropy) the employees are dealing with is minimal and shrinking (think fast food or retail service occupations), then we are in the realm of *labor* (see Figure I.2, A at time T_2). If the amount and scope of complexity (entropy) the employees are dealing with is above the minimum threshold and varies, and they have some control over the scope, then we are in the realm of the *skilled* market (B). Regardless, for *skilled* and *labor* actors, the goal of the organization is to minimize the internal entropy (see Figure I.2, A and B at time T_2) they are dealing with. When the actors have significant control over the scope of complexity (entropy), and when they also have an active role in the choice of timing to explore and experiment (temporarily while searching and increasing entropy) and optimize the entropy, then we are in the realm of *talent* (see Figure I.2, C at time T_2) (see additional discussion in Handscombe & Patterson, 2004).

Human capital then will be defined as the scope and amount of controlled negative entropy an entity possesses at any point in time, within a context (goals and constraints; economic, social, environmental), that can create (presently and potentially in the future) value for an exchange.

Scope and amount of entropy is used here in terms of Renyi's spectrum of entropies (1961). Control entropy is used here in terms developed by McGregor and Bollt (2012) to incorporate complexities and constraints into systems (Bollt, Skufca, & McGregor, 2009; McGregor & Bollt, 2012). When appropriate, invariance entropy might be considered as well (Colonius, 2012; Colonius, Kawan, & Nair, 2013; Kawan, 2009).

A further development of the complete econometric model is beyond the scope of this chapter and will be attempted in future papers.

References

Acemoglu, D., & Autor, D. (2011). Skills, tasks and technologies: Implications for employment and earnings. *Handbook of Labor Economics, 4*, 1043–1171.

Acemoglu, D., & Autor, D. (2012). What does human capital do? A review of Goldin and Katz's "The race between education and technology." *Journal of Economic Literature, 50*(2), 426–463.

Alessandri, T. M., Ford, D. N., Lander, D. M., Leggio, K. B., & Taylor, M. (2004). Managing risk and uncertainty in complex capital projects. *Quarterly Review of Economics and Finance, 44*(5), 751–767.

Anonymous (2014, January 18). The onrushing wave: The future of jobs. *Economist, 240*(8870), 24–28.

Arora, A., & Gambardella, A. (1994). The changing technology of technological change: General and abstract knowledge and the division of innovative labour. *Research Policy, 23*(5), 523–532.

Arthur, W. B. (1989). Competing technologies, increasing returns, and lock-in by historical events. *Economic Journal, 99*(394), 116–131.

Asher, C. C., Mahoney, J. M., & Mahoney, J. T. (2005). Towards a property rights foundation for a stakeholder theory of the firm. *Journal of Management and Governance, 9*(1), 5–32.

Autor, D. (2010). *The Polarization of Job Opportunities in the U.S. Labor Market*. The Hamilton Project and The Center for American Progress, April, 1–40.

Autor, D., & Dorn, D. (2013). The growth of low-skill service jobs and the polarization in the United States. *American Economic Review, 103*(5), 1553–1597.

Ayres, R. U., Van den Bergh, J. C., Lindenberger, D., & Warr, B. (2013). The underestimated contribution of energy to economic growth. *Structural Change and Economic Dynamics, 27*, 79–88.

Banks, J., & Humphreys, S. (2008). The labour of user co-creators: Emergent social network markets? *Convergence: International Journal of Research into New Media Technologies, 14*(4), 401–418.

Barney, J., & Felin, T. (2013). What are microfoundations? *Academy of Management Perspectives, 27*(2), 138–155.

Baron, A. (2007). *Human Capital Management: Achieving Added Value through People*. London: Kogan Page Publishers.

Bates, T. W., Kahle, K. M., & Stulz, R. M. (2009). Why do US firms hold so much more cash than they used to? *Journal of Finance, 64*(5), 1985–2021.

Bator, F. M. (1958). The anatomy of market failure. *Quarterly Journal of Economics, 72*(3), 351–379.

Baumol, W. J. (2010). *The Microtheory of Innovative Entrepreneurship*. Princeton, NJ: Princeton University Press.

Becker, G. S. (1962). Investment in human capital: A theoretical analysis. *Journal of Political Economy, 70*(5), 9–49.

Becker, G. S. (2009). *Human Capital: A Theoretical and Empirical Analysis, with Special Reference to Education*. Chicago, IL: University of Chicago Press.

Berk, J. B., Stanton, R., & Zechner, J. (2010). Human capital, bankruptcy, and capital structure. *Journal of Finance, 65*(3), 891–926.

Bertrand, M., & Mullainathan, S. (2001). Are CEOs rewarded for luck? The ones without principals are. *Quarterly Journal of Economics, 116*(3), 901–932.

Bidwell, M. J. (2013). What happened to long-term employment? The role of worker power and environmental turbulence in explaining declines in worker tenure. *Organization Science, 24*(4), 1061–1082.

Bivens, J., Fieldhouse, A., & Shierholz, H. (2013). From free-fall to stagnation: Five years after the start of the Great Recession, extraordinary policy measures are still needed, but are not forthcoming. Washington, DC: Economic Policy Institute. Briefing Paper 355. Available at http://s3.epi.org/files/2013/bp355-five-years-after-start-of-great-recession.pdf

Bivona, E. (2014). Outlining the impact of intellectual capital accumulation and depletion processes on the performance of an insurance firm: A dynamic resource-based perspective. *Management Control*, Special issue on intellectual capital and management control (Forthcoming).

Blackburn, W. (2007). *The Sustainability Handbook: The Complete Management Guide to Achieving Social, Economic and Environmental Responsibility.* Washington, DC: Environmental Law Institute.

BLS (2013). Labor force projections to 2022: The labor force participation rate continues to fall (December). Available at http://www.bls.gov/opub/mlr/2013/article/labor-force-projections-to-2022-the-labor-force-participation-rate-continues-to-fall.htm

Blyler, M., & Coff, R. W. (2003). Dynamic capabilities, social capital, and rent appropriation: Ties that split pies. *Strategic Management Journal, 24*(7), 677–686.

Bollt, E. M., Skufca, J. D., & McGregor, S. J. (2009). Control entropy: A complexity measure for nonstationary signals. *Mathematical Biosciences and Engineering, 6*(1), 1–25.

Bolton, P., Brunnermeier, M. K., & Veldkamp, L. (2013). Leadership, coordination and corporate culture. *Review of Economic Studies, 80*(2), 512–537.

Bosker, M., Brakman, S., Garretsen, H., & Schramm, M. (2012). Relaxing Hukou: Increased labor mobility and China's economic geography. *Journal of Urban Economics, 72*(2/3), 252–266.

Bowman, C., & Swart, J. (2007). Whose human capital? The challenge of value capture when capital is embedded. *Journal of Management Studies, 44*(4), 488–505.

Brynjolfsson, E., & McAfee, A. (2014). *The Second Machine Age: Work, Progress, and Prosperity in a Time of Brilliant Technologies.* New York, NY: W. W. Norton & Company.

Cainarca, G. C., & Sgobbi, F. (2012). The return to education and skills in Italy. *International Journal of Manpower, 33*(2), 187–205.

Canon, M. E., & Marifian, E. (2013). Job polarization leaves middle-skilled workers out in the cold. *Regional Economist* (January). Available at http://www.stlouisfed.org/publications/pub_assets/pdf/re/2013/a/employment.pdf

Caplin, A., & Dean, M. (2013). *Behavioral Implications of Rational Inattention with Shannon Entropy* (No. w19318). National Bureau of Economic Research.

Cappelli, P., & Keller, J. (2013). Classifying work in the new economy. *Academy of Management Review, 38*(4), 575–596.

Carpenter, M. A., Sanders, W. G., & Gregersen, H. B. (2001). Bundling human capital with organizational context: The impact of international assignment experience on multinational firm performance and CEO pay. *Academy of Management Journal, 44*(3), 493–511.

Cattani, G., Dunbar, R. L., & Shapira, Z. (2013). Value creation and knowledge loss: The case of Cremonese stringed instruments. *Organization Science, 24*(3), 813–830.

CBO (2014). The effects of a minimum-wage increase on employment and family income. Available at http://cbo.gov/sites/default/files/cbofiles/attachments/44995-MinimumWage.pdf

Chen, H. M., & Lin, K. J. (2004). The role of human capital cost in accounting. *Journal of Intellectual Capital, 5*(1), 116–130.

Chevalier-Roignant, B., & Trigeorgis, L. (2011). *Competitive Strategy*. Boston, MA: The MIT Press.

Chipulu, M., Neoh, J. G., Ojiako, U., & Williams, T. (2013). A multidimensional analysis of project manager competences. *IEEE Transactions on Engineering Management, 60*, 506–517.

Coff, R., & Kryscynski, D. (2011). Invited editorial: Drilling for micro-foundations of human capital-based competitive advantages. *Journal of Management, 37*(5), 1429–1443.

Cohen, L. E., & Broschak, J. P. (2013). Whose jobs are these? The impact of the proportion of female managers on the number of new management jobs filled by women versus men. *Administrative Science Quarterly, 58*(4), 509–541.

Collins, S. L., Carpenter, S. R., Swinton, S. M., Orenstein, D. E., Childers, D. L., Gragson, T. L., . . . , Whitmer, A. C. (2010). An integrated conceptual framework for long-term social-ecological research. *Frontiers in Ecology and Environment, 9*(6), 351–357.

Colonius, F. (2012). Minimal bit rates and entropy for exponential stabilization. *SIAM Journal on Control and Optimization, 50*(5), 2988–3010.

Colonius, F., Kawan, C., & Nair, G. (2013). A note on topological feedback entropy and invariance entropy. *Systems and Control Letters, 62*(5), 377–381.

Cornelissen, F., de Jong, T., & Kessels, J. (2012). Knitted patterns or contagious hotspots? Linking views on knowledge and organizational networked learning. *Learning Organization, 19*(6), 469–481.

Corrado, C., & Hulten, C. (2010). How do you measure a "technological revolution"? *American Economic Review, 100*(2), 99–104.

Corrado, C., Hulten, C., & Sichel, D. (2009). Intangible capital and US economic growth. *Review of Income and Wealth, 55*(3), 661–685.

Currid-Halkett, E., & Ravid, G. (2012). "Stars" and the connectivity of cultural industry world cities: An empirical social network analysis of human capital mobility and its implications for economic development. *Environment and Planning—Part A, 44*(11), 2646.

Davies, P., & Gregersen, N. H. (Eds.) (2010). *Information and the Nature of Reality* (Vol. 3). Cambridge, UK: Cambridge University Press.

De Santis, F., & Giuliani, M. (2013). A look on the other side: Investigating intellectual liabilities. *Journal of Intellectual Capital, 14*(2), 212–226.

Di Prodi, P. (2012). Artificial societies and information theory: Modelling of sub system formation based on Luhmann's autopoietic theory. Doctoral dissertation, University of Glasgow. Available at http://theses.gla.ac.uk/2869/1/2012DiProdiPhD.pdf

Dror, Y. (2011). Global leadership development: A fateful humanity resources management challenge. Presented at the 1st Israeli Global Human Resource Management Conference (GHRM), November 23–25, ORT Braude College, Israel.

Eaton, J., & Rosen, H. S. (1980). Taxation, human capital, and uncertainty. *American Economic Review, 70*(4), 705–715.

Eiling, E. (2013). Industry-specific human capital, idiosyncratic risk, and the cross-section of expected stock returns. *Journal of Finance, 68*(1), 43–84.

Ertug, G., & Castellucci, F. (2013). Getting what you need: How reputation and status affect team performance, hiring, and salaries in the NBA. *Academy of Management Journal, 56*(2), 407–431.

Fama, E. F. (1977). Risk-adjusted discount rates and capital budgeting under uncertainty. *Journal of Financial Economics, 5*(1), 3–24.

Farnsworth, K. D., Nelson, J., & Gershenson, C. (2013). Living is information processing: From molecules to global systems. *Acta Biotheoretica, 61*(2), 203–222.

Fernández, N., Maldonado, C., & Gershenson, C. (2014). Information measures of complexity, emergence, self-organization, homeostasis, and autopoiesis. In M. Prokopenko (Ed.), *Guided Self-Organization: Inception* (pp. 19–51). Berlin: Springer. Available at http://arxiv.org/abs/1304.1842.

Filatotchev, I., Liu, X., Lu, J., & Wright, M. (2011). Knowledge spillovers through human mobility across national borders: Evidence from Zhongguancun Science Park in China. *Research Policy, 40*(3), 453–462.

Fisher, I. (1906). *The Nature of Capital and Income*. New York, NY: A. M. Kelly.

Fleck, S., Glaser, J., & Sprague, S. (2011). The compensation-productivity gap: A visual essay. *Monthly Labor Review, 134*, 57–69. Available at http://www.bls.gov/opub/mlr/2011/01/art3full.pdf

Foxon, T. J., & Steinberger, J. K. (2013). Energy, efficiency and economic growth: A coevolutionary perspective and implications for a low carbon transition. Sustainability Research Institute, WP 49, September. Available at http://www.cccep.ac.uk/Publications/Working-papers/Papers/140-149/WP146-Energy-efficiency-and-economic-growth.pdf

Frey, C. B., & Osborne, M. A. (2013). The future of employment: How susceptible are jobs to computerisation? Retrieved January 25, 2014. Available at http://www.futuretech.ox.ac.uk/sites/futuretech.ox.ac.uk/files/The_Future_of_Employment_OMS_Working_Paper_1.pdf

Fulmer, I. S., & Ployhart, R. E. (2014). "Our most important asset": A multidisciplinary/multilevel review of human capital valuation for research and practice. *Journal of Management, 40*(1), 161–192.

Garcia-Parra, M., Simo, P., Sallan, J. M., & Mundet, J. (2009). Intangible liabilities: Beyond models of intellectual assets. *Management Decision, 47*(5), 819–830.

Gavious, I., & Russ, M. (2009). The valuation implications of human capital in transactions on and outside the exchange. *Advances in Accounting, 25*(2), 165–173.

Gershenson, C. (2012). The world as evolving information. In A. Minai, D. Braha, & Y. Bar-Yam (Eds.), *Unifying Themes in Complex Systems* (Vol. VII, pp. 100–115). Berlin: Springer. Available at http://arxiv.org/abs/0704.0304.

Gherardi, S. (2000). Practice-based theorizing on learning and knowing in organizations. *Organization, 7*(2), 211–223.

Gill, I., Koettl, J., & Packard, T. (2013). Full employment: A distant dream for Europe. *IZA Journal of European Labor Studies, 2*(1), 1–34.

Goldin, C. D., & Katz, L. F. (2009). *The Race between Education and Technology.* Boston, MA: Harvard University Press.

Goldschmidt, G. (1990). Linkography: Assessing design productivity. In R. Trappl (Ed.), *Cyberbetics and System '90* (pp. 291–298). Singapore: World Scientific.

Grant, R. M. (1991). The resource-based theory of competitive advantage: Implications for strategy formulation. *California Management Review, 33*, 114–135.

Grant, R. M. (1996). Toward a knowledge-based theory of the firm. *Strategic Management Journal, 17*, 109–122.

Habermalz, S. (2010). Rational inattention and employer learning. IZA Discussion Papers Series, No. 5311. Available at http://www.econstor.eu/bitstream/10419/51921/1/668651571.pdf

Haken, H. (2006). *Information and Self-organization: A Macroscopic Approach to Complex Systems* (3rd Edition). Berlin: Springer.

Handscombe, R. D., & Patterson, E. A. (2004). *The Entropy Vector: Connecting Science and Business.* Sheffield, UK: World Scientific.

Hanka, G. (1998). Debt and the terms of employment. *Journal of Financial Economics, 48*, 245–282.

Hartog, J., Ophem, H. V., & Bajdechi, S. M. (2007). Simulating the risk of investment in human capital. *Education Economics, 15*(3), 259–275.

Harvey, M. G., & Lusch, R. F. (1999). Balancing the intellectual capital books: Intangible liabilities. *European Management Journal, 17*(1), 85–92.

Haskel, J., Lawrence, R. Z., Leamer, E. E., & Slaughter, M. J. (2012). Globalization and U.S. wages: Modifying classic theory to explain recent facts. *Journal of Economic Perspectives, 26*(2), 119–140.

Hassan, A. E., & Holt, R. C. (2003). The chaos of software development. In *Software Evolution, 2003. Proceedings: Sixth International Workshop on Principles of Software Evolution* (pp. 84–94), September. IEEE. Available at http://research.cs.queensu.ca/~ahmed/home/pubs/iwpse2003.pdf

Hayton, J. C. (2003). Strategic human capital management in SMEs: An empirical study of entrepreneurial performance. *Human Resource Management, 42*(4), 375–391.

Hazy, J. K. (2012). The unifying function of leadership: Shaping identity, ethics and the local rules of interaction. *International Journal of Society Systems Science, 4*(3), 222–241.

Howell, D. (2010). Undercounting the underemployed: How official indicators have missed millions of underutilized workers. Schwartz Center for Economic Policy Analysis, Policy note.

Itami, H., & Numagami, T. (1992). Dynamic interaction between strategy and technology. *Strategic Management Journal, 13*(S2), 119–135.

Jaaskelainen, A. (2011). How to measure and manage the risk of losing key employees? *International Journal of Learning and Intellectual Capital, 8*(1), 63–75.

Jacoby, H. G., & Skoufias, E. (1997). Risk, financial markets, and human capital in a developing country. *Review of Economic Studies, 64*(3), 311–335.

Jalava, J. (2006). Trust as a decision, the problems and functions of trust in Luhmannian systems theory. Doctoral dissertation, Research reports, Helsinki: University of Helsinki.

Jarvis, D. S. (2011). Theorising risk and uncertainty in international relations: The contributions of Frank Knight. *International Relations, 25*(3), 296–312.

Jelavic, M., Tan, L., & Nya, C. (2011). Socio-technical knowledge management and epistemological paradigms: Theoretical connections at the individual and organisational level. *Interdisciplinary Journal of Information, Knowledge and Management, 6*, 1–16.

Kan, J. W., & Gero, J. S. (2008). Acquiring information from linkography in protocol studies of designing. *Design Studies, 29*(4), 315–337.

Katz, D., & Kahn, R. L. (1978). *The Social Psychology of Organizations.* New York, NY: Wiley.

Katz, L. F., & Margo, R. A. (2013). *Technical Change and the Relative Demand for Skilled Labor: The United States in Historical Perspective* (No. w18752). National Bureau of Economic Research.

Kaul, A. (2013). Entrepreneurial action, unique assets, and appropriation risk: Firms as a means of appropriating profit from capability creation. *Organization Science, 24*(6), 1765–1781.

Kawan, C. (2009). Invariance entropy of control systems. Doctoral thesis, Institut fur Mathematik, Universitat Augsburg.

Kim, S. H., & Taylor, D. (2012). The value of human capital expenditure: Tracing its relevance, reliability and diminishing marginal return. In 2013 Financial Markets & Corporate Governance Conference, December. Available at http://papers.ssrn.com/sol3/papers.cfm?abstract_id=2190715

Kistruck, G. M., Sutter, C. J., Lount, R. B., & Smith, B. R. (2013). Mitigating principal-agent problems in base-of-the-pyramid markets: An identity spillover perspective. *Academy of Management Journal, 56*(3), 659–682.

Knight, F. H. (1921). *Risk, Uncertainty and Profit.* Boston, MA: Houghton Mifflin.

Kolev, A., & Saget, C. (2010). Are middle-paid jobs in OECD countries disappearing? An overview. Geneva: International Labor Organization (April). ILO Working Paper 96.

Koskinen, K. U. (2013). *Knowledge Production in Organizations.* Switzerland: Springer International Publishing.

Kroeker, K. L. (2011). Weighing Watson's impact. *Communications of the ACM, 54*(7), 13–15.

Krueger, A. B., Cramer, J., & Cho, D. (2014). Are the long-term unemployed on the margins of the labor market? Presented at the Brooking Panel on Economic Activity, March 20–21. Available at http://www.brookings.edu/~/media/projects/bpea/spring%202014/2014a_krueger.pdf

Kuhn, T. S. (1962). *The Structure of Scientific Revolutions* (1st Edition). Chicago, IL: University of Chicago Press.

Kümmel, R. (2011). *The Second Law of Economics: Energy, Entropy, and the Origins of Wealth*. Berlin: Springer.

Kümmel, R. (2013). Why energy's economic weight is much larger than its cost share. *Environmental Innovation and Societal Transitions, 9*, 33–37.

Kurzweil, R. (2005). *The Singularity Is Near: When Humans Transcend Biology*. New York, NY: Viking Books.

Laliberte, P. (2012). Editorial. Social justice and growth: The role of the minimum wage. *International Journal of Labour Research, 4*(1), 7–10. Available at http://www.ilo.org/wcmsp5/groups/public/@ed_dialogue/@actrav/documents/publication/wcms_183568.pdf

Lambrecht, B. M., & Pawlina, G. (2013). A theory of net debt and transferable human capital. *Review of Finance, 17*(1), 321–368.

Langlois, R. N., & Cosgel, M. M. (1993). Frank Knight on risk, uncertainty, and the firm: A new interpretation. *Economic Inquiry, 31*(3), 456–465.

Leoni, R., & Gritti, P. (2013). High performance work practices and educational mismatch: Creation and destruction of competencies. Available at http://www.aiel.it/bacheca/LUISS/papers/leoni_gritti.pdf

Lepak, D. P., Smith, K. G., & Taylor, M. S. (2007). Value creation and value capture: A multilevel perspective. *Academy of Management Review, 32*(1), 180–194.

Lepak, D. P., & Snell, S. A. (1999). The human resource architecture: Toward a theory of human capital allocation and development. *Academy of Management Review, 24*, 31–48.

Lev, B. (2001). *Intangibles: Management, Measurement, and Reporting*. Washington, DC: Brookings Institution Press.

Lev, B., & Schwartz, A. (1971). On the use of the economic concept of human capital in financial statements. *Accounting Review, 46*(1), 103–112.

Levhari, D., & Weiss, Y. (1974). The effect of risk on the investment in human capital. *American Economic Review, 64*(6), 950–963.

Levy, F., & Murnane, R. J. (2012). *The New Division of Labor: How Computers Are Creating the Next Job Market*. Princeton, NJ: Princeton University Press.

Lewin, P., & Baetjer, H. (2011). The capital-based view of the firm. *Review of Austrian Economics, 24*(4), 335–354.

Leydesdorff, L. (2006). *The Knowledge-Based Economy: Modeled, Measured, Simulated*. Boca Raton, FL: Universal Publishers.

Lin, C. Y. Y., & Edvinsson, L. (2010). What national intellectual capital indices can tell about the global economic crisis of 2007–2009? *Electronic Journal of Knowledge Management, 8*(2), 252–266.

Luhmann, N. (1997). *Die Gesellschaft der Gesellschaft*. Frankfurt am Main: Suhrkamp.

Macey, J. R. (1989). Externalities, firm-specific capital investments, and the legal treatment of fundamental corporate changes. *Duke Law Journal, 1989*, 173–201.

Machin, S., Salvanes, K. G., & Pelkonen, P. (2012). Education and mobility. *Journal of European Economic Association, 10*(2), 417–450.

Mäenpää, I., & Voutilainen, R. (2012). Insurances for human capital risk management in SMEs. *VINE, 42*(1), 52–66.

Magalhães, R. (2004). *Organizational Knowledge and Technology: An Action-Oriented Perspective on Organization and Information Systems*. Northampton, MA: Edward Elgar Publishing.

Mahroum, S. (2000). Highly skilled globetrotters: Mapping the international migration of human capital. *R&D Management, 30*(1), 23–32.

Maier, M., Pfeiffer, F., & Pohlmeier, W. (2004). Returns to education and individual heterogeneity. Mannheim. ZEW Discussion Paper 04-32. Available at ftp://ftp.zew.de/pub/zew-docs/dp/dp0434.pdf

Martin, G. P., Gomez-Mejia, L. R., & Wiseman, R. M. (2013). Executive stock options as mixed gambles: Revisiting the behavioral agency model. *Academy of Management Journal, 56*(2), 451–472.

Marzo, G. (2013). Improving internal consistency in IC research and practice: IC and the theory of the firm. *Journal of Intellectual Capital, 15*(1), 38–64.

Maturana, H., & Varela, F. J. (1980). *Autopoiesis and Cognition: The Realization of the Living*. Boston Studies in the Philosophy of Science (Vol. 42). Dordrecht: Reidel Publishing Company.

McGinn, K. L., & Milkman, K. L. (2013). Looking up and looking out: Career mobility effects of demographic similarity among professionals. *Organization Science, 24*, 1041–1060.

McGregor, S. J., & Bollt, E. (2012). Control entropy: What is it and what does it tell us? *Clinical Kinesiology* (Online edition), *66*(1). Available at http://people.clarkson.edu/~ebollt/Papers/McGregor%26Bollt_66_1_7-12.pdf

Menant, C. (2011). Computation on information, meaning and representations: An evolutionary approach. In G. Dodig Crnkovic & M. Burgin (Eds.), *Information and Computation* (chapter 10). World Scientific Series in Information Studies (Vol. 2). Singapore: World Scientific.

Miller, E. M. (1977). Risk, uncertainty, and divergence of opinion. *Journal of Finance, 32*(4), 1151–1168.

Nakamura, L. (2001). What is the U.S. gross investment in intangibles? (At least) one trillion dollars a year! Federal Reserve Bank of Philadelphia Working Paper No. 01-15.

Nonaka, I., Umemoto, K., & Senoo, D. (1996). From information processing to knowledge creation: A paradigm shift in business management. *Technology in Society, 18*(2), 203–218.

Nyberg, A. J., Moliterno, T. P., Hale, D., & Lepak, D. P. (2014). Resource-based perspectives on unit-level human capital: A review and integration. *Journal of Management, 40*(1), 316–346.

Oakes, J., Rogers, J., Blasi, G., & Lipton, M. (2008). Grassroots organizing, social movements, and the right to high-quality education. *Stanford Journal of Civil Rights and Civil Liberties, 4*(2), 339–371.

Oettl, A., & Agrawal, A. (2008). International labor mobility and knowledge flow externalities. *Journal of International Business Studies, 39*(8), 1242–1260.

Osranek, R., & Zink, K. J. (2014). Corporate human capital and social sustainability of human resources. In I. Ehnert, W. Harry, & K. J. Zink (Eds.), *Sustainability and Human Resource Management* (pp. 105–126). Berlin: Springer.

Ostaszewski, K. (2003). Is life insurance a human capital derivatives business? *Journal of Insurance Issues, 26*(1), 1–14.
Ouchi, W. G. (1980). Markets, bureaucracies, and clans. *Administrative Science Quarterly, 25*(1), 129–141.
Partridge, M. D., Rickman, D. S., Olfert, M. R., & Ali, K. (2012). Dwindling US internal migration: Evidence of spatial equilibrium or structural shifts in local labor markets? *Regional Science and Urban Economics, 42*(1), 375–388.
Pavan, A. (2014). Attention, coordination, and bounded recall. Available at http://faculty.wcas.northwestern.edu/~apa522/attention-1-10-14.pdf
Philippon, T., & Reshef, A. (2012). Wages and human capital in the US finance industry: 1909–2006. *Quarterly Journal of Economics, 127*(4), 1551–1609.
Ployhart, R. E., Nyberg, A. J., Reilly, G., & Maltarich, M. A. (2013). Human capital is dead; long live human capital resources! *Journal of Management, 40*, 371–398.
Pratt, R. (2011). A structural model of human capital and leverage. Available at http://www.vanderbiltfmrc.org/wp-content/uploads/2012/01/Pratt_JMP.pdf
Quintini, G. (2011). *Over-Qualified or Under-Skilled. A Review of Existing Literature.* Paris: Organisation for Economic Co-Operation and Development.
Reich, R. B. (2013). The future of learning. *New England Journal of Public Policy, 24*(1), 14.
Reilly, G., Nyberg, A., Maltarich, M., & Weller, I. (2012). Human capital flows: Using context-emergent turnover (CET) theory to explore the process by which turnover, hiring, and job demands affect patient satisfaction. *Academy of Management Journal.* http://amj.aom.org/content/early/2013/04/25/amj.2012.0132.short
Renyi, A. (1961). On measures of entropy and information. In *Proceedings of the Fourth Berkeley Symposium on Mathematical Statistics and Probability, 1* (pp. 547–561). Berkeley, CA: University of California Press.
Romer, P. M. (1989). *Human Capital and Growth: Theory and Evidence* (No. w3173). National Bureau of Economic Research.
Rosen, S. (1981). The economics of superstars. *American Economic Review, 71*(5), 845–858.
Rotman, D. (2013). How technology is destroying jobs. *Technology Review, 116*(4), 28–35.
Russ, M. (2010). *Knowledge Management Strategies for Business Development.* Hershey, PA: Business Science Reference (an imprint of IGI Global).
Russ, M. (2011). Markets of new kind. Leonardo, International Network, International Center Foreign Relations, Member of the UN Global Compact, No. 17, December 30, 2011. Available at http://cecorex.org/17international_leonardo_ing.htm
Russ, M., Fineman, R., & Jones, J. K. (2010). Conceptual theory: What do you know? In M. Russ (Ed.), *Knowledge Management Strategies for Business Development* (pp. 1–22). Hershey, PA: Business Science Reference.
Sachdev, N. (2007). An examination of the wage productivity gap. Department of Economics, Stanford University. Available at http://economics.stanford.edu/files/Theses/Theses_2007/Sachdev2007.pdf

Sánchez, J. M., & Yurdagul, E. (2013). Why are corporations holding so much cash? Federal Reserve Bank of St. Louis, January. Available at http://www.stlouisfed.org/publications/pub_assets/pdf/re/2013/a/cash.pdf

Sapienza, H. J., & Gupta, A. K. (1994). Impact of agency risks and task uncertainty on venture capitalist-CEO interaction. *Academy of Management Journal, 37*(6), 1618–1632.

Sattinger, M., & Hartog, J. (2013). Nash bargaining and the wage consequences of educational mismatches. *Labour Economics, 23*, 50–56.

Schmidhuber, J. (2007). New millennium AI and the convergence of history. In W. Duch & J. Mandziuk (Eds.), *Challenges to Computational Intelligence* (pp. 15–36). Studies in Computational Intelligence (Vol. 63). Berlin: Springer.

Schneider, M., & Somers, M. (2006). Organizations as complex adaptive systems: Implications of complexity theory for leadership research. *Leadership Quarterly, 17*(4), 351–365.

Schultz, T. W. (1961). Investment in human capital. *American Economic Review, 51*(1), 1–17.

Seidl, D. (2004). Luhmann's theory of autopoietic social systems. Munich Business Research Paper (2004-2). Available at http://www.zfog.bwl.uni-muenchen.de/files/mitarbeiter/paper2004_2.pdf

Serenko, A., & Bontis, N. (2013). Investigating the current state and impact of the intellectual capital academic discipline. *Journal of Intellectual Capital, 14*(4), 476–500.

Siemens, G. (2005). Connectivism: A learning theory for the digital age. *International Journal of Instructional Technology and Distance Learning, 2*(1), 3–10.

Sims, C. A. (2003). Implications of rational inattention. *Journal of Monetary Economics, 50*, 665–690.

Smith, A. (1776). *An Inquiry into the Nature and Causes of the Wealth of Nations.* E. Cannon (Ed., 1904). Based on the 1798 fifth edition. London: Methuen & Co.

Snell, S. A., & Dean, J. W. (1992). Integrated manufacturing and human resource management: A human capital perspective. *Academy of Management Journal, 35*(3), 467–504.

Srivastava, R. K., Shervani, T. A., & Fahey, L. (1998). Market-based assets and shareholder value: A framework for analysis. *Journal of Marketing, 62*(1), 2–18.

Ståhle, S., & Ståhle, P. (2012). Towards measures of national intellectual capital: An analysis of the CHS model. *Journal of Intellectual Capital, 13*, 164–177.

Stiglitz, J. (1999). Knowledge as a global public good. In I. Kaul, I. Grunberg, & M. Stern (Eds.), *Global Public Goods: International Cooperation in the 21st Century* (pp. 308–325). New York, NY: Oxford University Press.

Stiglitz, J. E. (2002). Information and the change in the paradigm in economics. *American Economic Review, 92*(3), 460–501.

Tang, S. (2005). Knowledge as a production factor: Toward a unified theory of economic growth. Unpublished. Available at http://yataisuo.cass.cn/UploadFile/2005102203439560.pdf

Ulrich, D., & Ulrich, D. (1997). *Human Resource Champions* (pp. 163–170). Boston, MA: Harvard Business School Press.

Van Marrewijk, M., & Timmers, J. (2003). Human capital management: New possibilities in people management. *Journal of Business Ethics, 44*(2–3), 171–184.

Vines, R., & Hall, W. (2011). Exploring the foundations of organizational knowledge. Available at http://papers.ssrn.com/sol3/papers.cfm?abstract_id=1978316

Walker, R. H., Johnson, L. W., & Leonard, S. (2006). Re-thinking the conceptualization of customer value and service quality within the service-profit chain. *Managing Service Quality, 16*(1), 23–36.

Weiss, A. (1995). Human capital vs. signaling explanations of wages. *Journal of Economic Perspectives, 9*(4), 133–154.

Wright, P. M., McMahan, G. C., & McWilliams, A. (1994). Human resources and sustained competitive advantage: A resource-based perspective. *International Journal of Human Resource Management, 5*(2), 301–326.

Yadev, M. S., & Berry, L. L. (1996). Capture and communicate value in the pricing of services. *Sloan Management Review, 37*, 41–50.

Yamin, A. E. (1996). Defining questions: Situating issues of power in the formulation of a right to health under international law. *Human Rights Quarterly, 18*(2), 398–438.

Zeleny, M. (1997). Autopoiesis and self-sustainability in economic systems. *Human Systems Management, 16*(4), 251–262.

Zuse, K. (1982). The computing universe. *International Journal of Theoretical Physics, 21*(6–7), 589–600.

PART I

Management

CHAPTER 1

Team Composition and Project-Based Organizations: New Perspectives for Human Resource Management

Francesca Vicentini and Paolo Boccardelli

Introduction

Over the past few decades, the increasing significance of "projectification" (Lundin & Steinthórsson, 2003) has generated considerable interest in project-based organizations (PBOs), in terms of both academic contributions and general attention. Literature development has been accompanied by the promotion of "projects as means through which to organize workflows across multiple industries" (Maoret, Massa, & Jones, 2011, p. 428). Drawing from different management subfields, including project management, strategic management, innovation, organizational theory, and social networks, scholars have proposed different approaches to the study of PBOs, resulting in the proliferation of multiple perspectives. Maoret et al. (2001) attributed this proliferation to two main theoretical views. The first view considers PBOs as either temporary, that is, formed to accomplish a specific purpose (DeFillippi & Arthur, 1998), or more stable (Whitley, 2006). The second stream of literature focuses on the concept of latent organizations (Scott & Einstein, 2001; Starkey, Barnatt, & Tempest, 2000). This literature includes variations on themes, such as project ecologies (Grabher, 2004), project networks (Jones, 1996; Manning & Sydow, 2007; Soda, Usai, & Zaheer, 2004; Sydow & Staber, 2002), and social networks (Ferriani, Cattani, & Baden-Fuller, 2009; Uzzi & Spiro, 2005), which focus on the enduring relationships among team members over the duration of the project. Despite the relevance, these contributions on PBOs are mainly focused on the study of the macrostructure at the organizational level, but they do not address the human capital involved in the projects and the different levels of analysis involved.

In PBOs, work is often delegated to smaller units, such as teams (i.e., project teams) and crews, because of their ability to integrate individuals with different competences and expertise, resulting in higher-quality decisions and solutions (Harrison & Klein, 2007; Hinsz, Tindale, & Vollrath, 1997, Sundstorm, 1990). Numerous scholars have stated that the shift toward project-based structures has both positive and negative implications for management, employee relations, and employment contracts. For example, Hovmark and Nordqvist (1996) demonstrated that engineers who work in project settings perceive some positive changes in terms of increased commitment, dynamism, communication, and group autonomy. On the contrary, Packendorff (2002) argued that projects rarely consider the previous experiences of individuals. To investigate the effect produced by the human capital forming the project teams (team members), we analyze how successful project teams should be composed, specifically which individual team member characteristics determine a successful outcome. Furthermore, to fill the gap in the analyses of project-based organizations, we consider how project team characteristics may affect the project-level value created for the consumers (project value for consumers).

Team composition looks at the characteristics of individual team members (Levine & Moreland, 1990; Stewart, 2006). One line of research examines aggregated characteristics to assess whether the inclusion of individuals with desirable dispositions and abilities improves team performance. A similar area of research analyzes how heterogeneity of individual characteristics relates to team outcomes. Bantel and Jackson (1989) support the idea that heterogeneity is more desirable than homogeneity (e.g., Stewart, 2006). Theoretical arguments supporting heterogeneity focus on the creativity associated with diverse viewpoints and skill sets; thus, heterogeneity of team members is usually advocated for teams engaged in creative tasks but not for teams engaged in routine tasks (Guzzo & Dickson, 1996; Jackson, May, & Whitney, 1995). To contribute to heterogeneity studies, we investigate whether the individual diversity of team members may explain the key attributes of a project team and the resulting project value created for the consumers. In particular, we investigate the role of specific individual diversity features on the reputation of the project team and the implications on the value to consumers. Accordingly, we address the following research question: *To what extent, within project-based settings, does individual diversity affect the team's characteristics and what are the implications on the project value created for the consumers?* We address this question in an attempt to answer Engwall and Jerbrant's (2003) call for more empirical studies that analyze PBOs, and human capital PBOs stand out as being a highly relevant organizational context for advanced human capital research for several reasons. First, project settings are common work environments for many employees in today's workplaces (Bredin, 2008). Second, PBOs have certain characteristics that emphasize the importance of human capital, providing challenges for existing models and integrating different theoretical perspectives. Third, PBOs can contribute to the investigation of the effects of project value creation for the final consumers, because projects are open systems that interact with the external environment.

In this chapter, we introduce a multilevel framework (individual and project) that outlines the characteristics of team members selected by project managers to form successful project teams. In the following sections, we first define key theoretical constructs and then develop our research hypotheses for the Italian television drama series industry. We conclude by discussing the broader implications of our multilevel framework and promising framework extensions. This chapter contributes primarily to human capital research and practice because it combines heterogeneity studies and management practices in the specific context of project-based organizations.

Theory and Hypotheses

Core Concepts: Project-Based Organizations and Human Capital

Project-based organizing is becoming increasingly popular in not only traditionally project-oriented construction activities (Bresnen, 1990; Bresnen, Goussevskaia, & Swan, 2004) but also filmmaking and media (DeFillippi & Arthur, 1998; Sydow, Lindkvist, & DeFillippi 2004; Vicentini, 2013), complex products and systems (Hobday, 1998), software development (Grabher, 2004; Ibert, 2004), engineering design (Cacciatori, 2004), and biotechnology (Ebers & Powell, 2007). Pursuant to their pervasive adoption, project-based organizations (PBOs) have been studied in various academic discussions. Project management literature, largely based on normative paradigms, has provided models and practice standards, identifying and disseminating best practices (Packendorff, 1995). By contrast, research on organizations and teams has applied and combined different theories and perspectives (Engwall & Svensson, 2004; Ferriani, Corrado, & Boschetti 2005; Ferriani et al., 2009; Lundin & Söderholm, 1995; Lundin & Steinthórsson, 2003; Maoret et al., 2011; Powell, 2001; Vicentini, 2013; Whitley, 2006), producing some controversial results. A project-based organization is defined as an organizational form in which the project is the primary unit for production arrangement, innovation, and competition, whereas the project can be defined as "any activity with a defined set of resources, goals, and time limit" (Hobday, 2000, p. 872). Investigating the resources within the project, Prencipe and Tell (2001) define project teams as a collection of team members, assembled for a specific purpose, which disbands once the purpose is accomplished. In PBOs, human capital primarily works in temporary project arrangements. Accordingly, we analyze the human capital (HC) construct in terms of human resource management (HRM).

HRM is defined "as the area of management in which the relationships between people and their organizational context are studied" (Brewster & Larsen, 2000, p. 4). In this chapter, the term human capital is used to denote the management of team members involved in the project. The choice of this construct reflects a wish to move away from traditional definitions of HC to provide a more holistic approach to the management of human capital—team members—enrolled within projects. Adopting this approach is particularly relevant for a study of project-based organizations, because they are horizontal, flexible, and decentralized organizational forms (Whitley, 2006). Although the effect of project-based organizing on HRM is acknowledged in several studies, research that focuses specifically on the study of HC in project-based organizations is scarce, as recently reviewed by Bakker (2010). This is because of the lack of consensus on a coherent definition of HRM, which makes it difficult to measure, particularly in a complex project-based context in which there might be confusion on participants' roles, project tasks, and goals. To overcome this concern, we approach the study of team members as human resources involved in the project, adopting a team composition perspective.

Team Composition and Individual Diversity

It is necessary to study the team composition because the team members are the key resources for the project, and the results connected to the project depend on the team members' characteristics. Team composition can be regarded as a contextual factor, a consequence, or a causal factor (Levine & Moreland, 1990, p. 593). We consider team composition as a causal factor. Most of the studies that have adopted this causal view reflect the pragmatic desire to create successful groups by selecting people who can work together. For example, Tziner and Eden (1985) investigated the effects of soldiers' abilities on the team performance of tank crews, demonstrating that the higher the ability levels of each member, the better the group performance. Accordingly, team composition is defined here as the configuration of the team members' characteristics (Bell, 2007; Guzzo & Dickson, 1996). Prior literature considers team composition to include two stages: a selection process and a reciprocal evaluation process (Perretti & Negro, 2006). The former refers to the way in which an organization or a team manager invites potential members to be part of a new or existing team, whereas the latter relates to the vetting of a candidate for the team (Ilgen, Hollenbeck, & Jundt, 2005). In both cases, team performance plays a pivotal role, as suggested by Barrick, Stewart, Neubert, and Mount (1998) and Cattel (1948). The reason for this strong link emanates from the team composition's effect on the amount of knowledge, skills, and characteristics team members must apply to the task for which they have combined (Hackman, 1987). In this chapter, we investigate individual diversity as the team member characteristic that is critical to project team member selection in project-based settings. Specifically, we focus our research on experiential task diversity and experiential role diversity as the individual diversity attributes.

The main goal of the present study is to delineate and test a multilevel model of team composition in project-based organizations. The hypothesized model of relationships, which is depicted in Figure 1.1, incorporates analysis at individual and project team levels.

At the individual level, we look at the experiential task diversity and the experiential role diversity. At the project team level, we investigate the

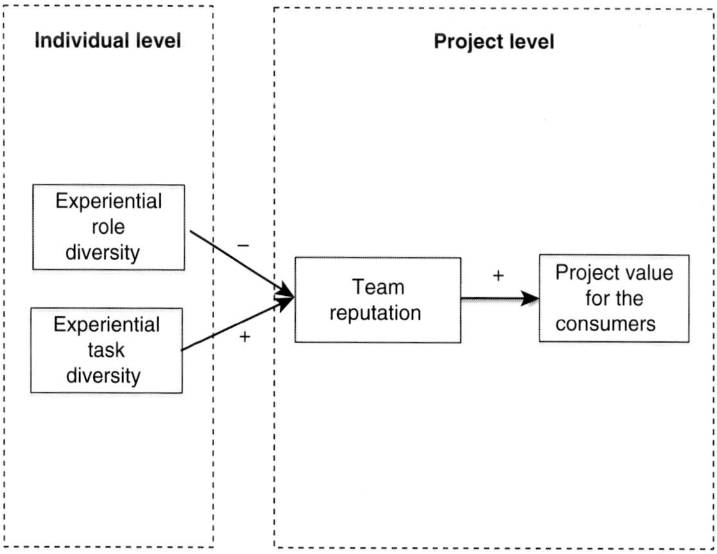

Figure 1.1 Theoretical framework

project team reputation and the project value created for the consumers. The former is defined as the opinion about a team formed by another party, including external stakeholders, such as customers, coworkers, and supervisors (Tyran & Gibson, 2008), whereas the latter is the value of the specific qualities of the final project outcome, as perceived by customers in relation to their needs (Bowman & Ambrosini, 2000).

Experiential Task Diversity, Experiential Role Diversity, and Project Team Reputation

Prior literature conceptualizes experience characteristics as indicators of human capital accumulation at the individual level (e.g., Carpenter, Sanders, & Gregersen 2001; Reagans, Argote & Brooks, 2005) and as proxies for the stock of tacit knowledge at the team level (Berman, Down, & Hill, 2002). Accordingly, individual experiences and experiential diversity are analyzed as potentially unique advantages that may produce higher levels of team performance over time (Bunderson & Sutcliffe, 2002; Carpenter et al., 2001). At the project team level, there is a strong linkage between team member characteristics and the team's mission. Prior literature suggests that task definitions are the *raison d'être* for projects (Bakker, 2010; Lundin & Söderholm 1995). However, project tasks are finite; the tasks finish once they are accomplished. One of the most significant consequences of finite tasks is that the accumulated knowledge can be dispersed as soon as the project team is dissolved and team members assigned to different tasks (Grabher, 2004). However, rejecting the idea supported by Packendorff (2002), whereby projects scarcely take into account the previous experiences of the team members, individuals actually accumulate the experiences in their personal repository, and they may make use of them whenever requested in their future careers and tasks. Two different dimensions characterize the experiences: the depth and the breadth of the experiences. Whereas the former involves the accumulation along a sequence of similar tasks and it positively affects professional specialization, the latter results from the accumulation of knowledge and experiences from diverse tasks. We define this last type of experience, *experiential task diversity*, as the stock of past experiences that each team member accumulates in performing different tasks. There is a trade-off between task specialization and task diversification. Whereas specialization allows team members to complete more repetitions of a specific task within a given time and to gain an in-depth knowledge of the problem domain, diversification allows team members to gain a broader knowledge and improve their abilities to evaluate and use knowledge for other projects (Boh, Slaughter, & Espinosa, 2007). Because team members work in a variety of projects, we support the idea that team members with experience in a diverse set of tasks are more likely to be selected because they can improve task accomplishment. Furthermore, experiencing different tasks allows team members to enhance their latent skills (i.e., talent); over time, these latent skills may represent another individual selection characteristic used by project managers to form project teams. At the project team level, enrolling talented team members may enhance the impression of the team's work quality and the project team reputation. Demonstrating a high-level work quality and enhancing team reputation may favor the project team not only to interact with others outside the project (i.e., customers, suppliers, supervisors, or peers) but also to earn repeat business (Tyran & Gibson, 2008, p. 48). Hence, we hypothesize the following:

Hypothesis 1: Experiential task diversity positively affects project team reputation.

Team members may become participants in new project teams by playing different roles. Roles are usually defined as the positions assumed by an individual that reflect specific skills and abilities (Stark, 2007). Roles and positions are connected by the enactment (Baker & Faulkner, 1991): a role is enacted from a position; therefore, it is stable until the positions are changed. Roles cannot be considered stable (Whitley, 2006); they are modifiable over time and through the experiences. As team members gain experience in more roles, they will acquire and extend their role experience. Thus, we define the exposure to a variety of different roles in the past as *experiential role diversity*, which is the stock of experiences that each team member accumulates from playing different roles. Accordingly, we support the idea that accumulating a high level of experiential role diversity may increase the team member's job market opportunities, enhancing the likelihood of being engaged in future projects. However, at the project team level, selecting team members who have high levels of experiential role diversity may yield negative effects on the team's work quality because of the lack of role specialization. Consequently, the team's work quality and team reputation may be reduced because external entities may evaluate the lack of role specialization negatively.

Hence, we hypothesize the following:

Hypothesis 2: Experiential role diversity negatively affects the project team reputation.

Project Team Reputation and the Project Value for the Consumers

Defining performance is difficult at every level of investigation (organizational, team, and individual) because it cannot be viewed as a simple unidimensional construct (Ancona & Caldwell, 1992). Team literature defines team performance as the "extent to which a team accomplishes its goals or mission" (Devine & Philips, 2001), underscoring that team members must interact interdependently to produce successful outcomes. At the project team level, some motivational problems do not allow the complete application of this team performance definition. First, project teams deliver a final outcome that the project-based organization may sell directly to the reference market (i.e., movie production companies) or through the support of intermediaries (i.e., construction companies). Second, the construct of team performance does not consider the project value created for the customers. Realizing project value for consumers is the prerequisite for each project-based organization and provides the opportunity to capture and retain the consumer's business. Consequently, we use the definition of value proposed by Bowman and Ambrosini (2000 p. 5); project value is "the value referred to the specific qualities of the final project outcome, perceived by customers in relation to their needs." Within project-based settings, there is a strong relationship between project value and project team reputation, which may capture the future expectations for project value creation.

Additionally, because the market is highly competitive and consumers are effective product selectors, the project team reputation may play a pivotal role in the consumer's selection. More specifically, we support the idea that consumers are more likely to assign a high project value when the team reputation is high. Therefore, we hypothesize the following:

> *Hypothesis 3*: Project team reputation positively affects the project value for the consumers.

Methods

The empirical setting investigated is the Italian television (TV) drama series industry. The TV drama series can be conceptualized as temporary projects within large production companies (PBOs), which last from several days to several months and have highly customized and project-specific future results (Sydow & Staber, 2002). Specifically, a TV series is considered to be a previously defined sequence of episodes (generally 25–26 episodes) ranging in duration from 25 minutes to one hour.

Our sample consists of 1,740 team members and 248 episodes produced by the most famous Italian TV drama serial production companies and broadcast on the Italian television channels over 1996–2010. The episodes were selected from completed TV drama series productions. We were thus able to collect the most complete data about the team members involved in each episode, avoiding missing data and sample significance concerns.

To collect information about the episodes, we used the IMDb archival database, considered the most powerful and authoritative database of the world's movie and television productions. For each episode, a well-defined set of resources and team members with diverse experiential characteristics were required to form the project team and were managed together over the task's duration. Specifically, team members may represent a variety of artistic and technical service providers, from the crew to the actors. We excluded the camera, wardrobe, and miscellaneous crew members who produce TV drama series because they are not temporary production company workers and thus rarely change from episode to episode. Additionally, for each actor, we collected data on the number of awards garnered prior to joining the focal project team. In this context, actors' past experiences are particularly relevant because the actors are selected based on their past roles and previous accomplishments.

Analysis

We adopted a cross-level model to describe the relationship among our variables: individual diversity, project team reputation, and the project value for the consumers. In doing this, we ran two separate levels of analysis that we aligned accordingly. First, at the individual level we ran a linear regression model with a robust estimator to account for heteroskedasticity between project team reputation and individual diversity (experiential role diversity and experiential task diversity). We then generated a predicted value of project team reputation to account for individual diversity. To compute our model at the project team level, we needed to collapse across our observations to generate a single record for any episode. At the project team level, we adopted an unbalanced pooled time series model with all variables at the project level, including the predicted value of project team reputation. We chose to use a time series model because our sample contains observations that have a natural ordering in time, with the audience share becoming a set of related variables (Gensh & Shaman, 1980). The use of unbalanced pooled time series methods suggests, however, that the error term shows correlation over time (autocorrelation) and cross-sectional units (heteroskedasticity). We fitted the panel-data linear models using feasible generalized least squares (FGLS) with an autoregressive component of lag 1 and cross-sectional correlation and heteroskedasticity across panels.

Measures

Our research conceptualizes data at two levels of analysis: at the individual level (experiential task diversity and experiential role diversity) and at project team level (project team reputation and the project value for the consumers). To reconcile the two levels of analysis, we adopted the configural team properties, which "emerge from individual team members' experiences, attitudes, perceptions, values, cognitions, or behaviors" (Klein & Kozlowski, 2000, p. 217). The configural team property captures the array, pattern, or variability of individual characteristics within a team.

Variables at the Individual Level

The experiential role diversity is calculated as the number of times that a team member performed a role prior to the focal episode. This procedure implies that team members may have performed different roles not only in terms of different TV drama series productions (such as a TV movie) but also in terms of other media products (such as movies); thus, we differentiate between them. We categorized the experiential role diversity of each team member in the following groups: TV miniseries, TV movies, and TV drama series (the focal project). We normalized it by dividing by the standard deviation to define the level of experiential role diversity.

In TV series productions, actors' tasks can be classified along two main dimensions: the specific character played (e.g., police officer, assassin, doctor, father, girlfriend) and the genre in which the series is classified (e.g., romance, drama, crime, sci-fi). To analyze the specialization or breadth of experience for each team member in the focal team, we calculated the number of different genres in which he/she had performed, not including the current genre. To define the level of experiential task diversity, we normalized by dividing by the standard deviation.

To estimate the role of experiential diversity on project team reputation, we analyzed the effect of individual attributes on the reputation of the entire team. To estimate this indicator, we collected information on the previous awards garnered by the team members. Awards play a pivotal role because they represent an evaluation of the artistic quality demonstrated by each individual and of his/her reputation. Therefore, populating project teams with award-winning team members is indicative of the project team reputation and quality. Specifically, to operationalize the project team reputation, we first totaled the number of awards that each team member previously received and then we normalized by dividing by the standard deviation to define the reputation level.

In addition to the team member characteristics for which we have hypothesized effects, a number of factors may reasonably affect project team reputation. Thus, we account for some controls. First, we control for *veterans*. Within PBOs, teams are formed and continuously reassembled; therefore, the project team may be composed of both veterans (members who have previously worked together) and novice candidates (members who are new to the project team). Controlling for this variable is important because it may affect the ability of the individuals to interact and thus influence the project team reputation. We calculated this variable by summing the number of TV drama series episodes that each of the first seven actors/actresses has participated in and dividing by the total number of episodes in the focal TV drama series. *Total number of episodes*: This variable is the number of TV series episodes that each team member has performed in.

Variables at the Project Level

The project value for the consumers is our dependent variable. It expresses the value created in the consumer market by the outcome of the project. To measure this variable, we used the audience share, which is considered the measure of any TV production's performance (Gensh & Shaman, 1980). We collected Italian audience data from Auditel. Auditel is an independent institution that collects these data by monitoring the Italian TV market using a panel of 5,101 families and over 14,000 individuals, separated into various residential areas, and then sells the data to broadcasters. Because of the highly skewed distribution of this indicator, we used the natural logarithm of the number of people who watched each TV drama series episode. This transformation allowed us to reduce the weight of the tails, particularly those resulting from low performance levels.

Our primary independent and explanatory variable is the project team reputation. As previously explained, to run a multilevel analysis, we take the predicted value of the project team reputation as a result of the first-stage analysis that had been performed at the individual level.

We controlled at the project level for the following factors. *Total TV series hours broadcast by the channel in the year*: Not all TV channels have identical potential to reach large audiences. The Italian broadcasting market is characterized by two main leaders: RAI (the state-owned television corporation) and Mediaset (the major private competitor). Each broadcaster has three main channels to provide TV programs. Consequently, there is a significant variation in the number of hours broadcast by each channel and the number of hours of TV series transmitted yearly, which may affect the project team performance. The variable is measured by counting the number of hours aired by the broadcasters. These data have been gathered from GECA Italy, an Independent Italian company that tracks all data relating to the Italian TV industry. *Project team size*: Because project teams may vary considerably in size, we controlled for the number of project team members enlisted in the crew (Reagans & Zuckerman, 2001; Zaheer & Soda, 2009). *Experience of the producer in each TV series production*: Not all Italian TV production companies are specialized in the production of TV series; they can also produce movies, TV movies, and other TV formats (e.g., sitcom). This lack of specialization may affect the audience share. The variable is measured using the average number of TV series produced by the production companies prior to the focal project. *Total number of TV series episodes*: This variable is the total number of episodes that have been screened for each series. *Progressive number of TV series episodes*: Because TV drama series progress with the development of the script, we accounted for the number of episodes previously released on TV. Thus, this variable is a progressive number from the first episode to the current one. *TV series awards*: This variable represents the number of awards that each TV series garnered.

Results

The descriptive statistics and correlations at the individual level are provided in Table 1.1 None of the correlation coefficients indicates potential multicollinearity problems.

The results of the regression model at the individual level are presented in Table 1.2.

As hypothesized, experiential task diversity yields a positive and significant ($p < 0.001$) effect on the project team reputation, whereas the experiential role diversity negatively and significantly ($p < 0.001$) affects the project team reputation. As presented in the table, both the presence of veterans and the number of episodes performed by the team members negatively and significantly ($p < 0.001$) affect the project team reputation.

The descriptive statistics and correlations at the project team level are provided in Table 1.3. None of the correlation coefficients indicates potential multi-collinearity problems.

The results of the FGLS model are illustrated in Table 1.4. The control variables are introduced in the first column. The full model, with the effect of project team reputation on the project value for the consumers, is presented in columns 3 and 4.

The average audience captured by each channel in the year is positive and significant ($p < 0.001$). Another relevant factor is the television programming strategy of each TV channel broadcasting the TV series. Our control variable suggests that the number of TV series hours broadcast by the channel is positively and significantly ($p < 0.01$) correlated to the audience share. Conversely, a programming strategy with a greater number of TV movie hours presents a negative and significant ($p < 0.001$) effect on the audience

Table 1.1 Correlations and descriptive statistics at the individual level

Variables	*Mean*	*Standard deviation*	*Min.*	*Max.*	*1*	*2*	*3*	*4*	*5*
1. Team reputation	1.84	3.69	–3.81	20.71	1.00				
2. Experiential role diversity	29.08	35.70	0	168	0.08***	1.00			
3. Experiential task diversity	4.86	4.25	1	16	0.30***	0.80***	1.00		
4. Veterans/novice candidates	0.47	0.30	0	1.91	−0.17***	0.05*	0.01	1.00	
5. Number of episodes for TV series	62.60	51.02	0	157	−0.31	0.15***	0.01	0.09***	1.00

Notes: $N = 1,740$.
*Coefficients are significant at $p < 0.05$.
***Coefficients are significant at $p < 0.001$.

Table 1.2 Results of the first-stage model: Individual level

Stage I: Team reputation		
Variables	*Model 1*	
	Coeff.	*Std. Err.*
Experiential role diversity	−0.04***	(0.00)
Experiential task diversity	0.49***	−0.04
Controls		
Veterans	−1.61***	(0.00)
Total number of episodes	−0.19***	(0.00)
Constant	2.37	
Observations	1,740	
R-squared	0.24	
F-statistics	71.04	
Prob. (F-statistics)	***	

Note: ***Coefficients are significant at $p < 0.001$.

share. We can explain these results through the different levels of competition between the TV formats (TV movie and TV series) and other TV products on identical channels. Being a specialized TV series producer is positively and significantly ($p < 0.001$) correlated to the audience share, indicating that the production company strategy and its reputation are important for the TV series' success. Consistent with other studies (Zaheer & Soda, 2009), the project team size, expressed in terms of the number of team members, has a significant and positive effect on the audience share. The total number of TV series episodes seems to have a significant ($p < 0.001$) and negative effect on the audience size, while the number of awards garnered by the TV series has a positive effect on the audience share. According to Hypothesis 3, our model demonstrates that the team reputation positively and significantly ($p < 0.100$) affects the project value for the consumers.

Discussion and Conclusions

This chapter provides an interesting multilevel framework that explores the role of human capital within project-based organizations (PBOs). Whereas prior studies have focused on PBOs in terms of the macrostructure at the organizational level (i.e., Maoret et al., 2011), this study examines PBOs at individual and project team levels, contributing to better defining the human capital construct. By integrating team composition and HRM perspectives, this research advances studies on the importance of human capital within PBOs, which prior literature has scarcely analyzed. More specifically,

Table 1.3 Correlations and descriptive statistics at the project team level

Variables	*Mean*	*Standard deviation*	*Min.*	*Max.*	*1*	*2*	*3*	*4*	*5*	*6*	*7*	*8*	*9*	*10*
1. Project value for consumers	15.73	0.25	15.13	16.20	1.00									
2. Team reputation	1.85	1.57	−0.45	5.31	−0.58***	1.00								
3. TV series awards	0.37	0.37	0	1	0.42***	−0.11*	1.00							
4. Stock of episodes for TV series	200.31	170.79	0	617	0.41***	−0.75***	−0.09	1.00						
5. Total number of episodes for series	136.81	64.65	36	182	0.71***	−0.92***	0.20**	0.66***	1.00					
6. Size of project team	67.86	36.38	0	92	0.76***	−0.83***	0.09	0.62***	0.92***	1.00				
7. Experience of the producer in the TV series production	66.92	26.13	10	119.38	−0.23***	−0.14*	−0.01	0.01	0.01	−0.32***	1.00			
8. Average audience for channel	21.23	9.35	0.226	39.54	−0.00	−0.33***	0.35***	0.17**	0.32***	0.07	0.75***	1.00		
9. Total hours of TV series broadcast by the channel in the year	802.05	632.49	0	2,579	−0.56***	0.82***	0.14*	−0.60***	−0.81***	−0.86***	0.06	0.05	1.00	
10. Total hours of TV movies broadcast by the channel in the year	48, 592.62	112, 690.40	0	454,246.40	−0.53***	0.52***	0.24***	−0.38***	−0.56***	−0.79***	0.43***	0.52***	0.85***	1.00

Notes: $N = 248$.

*Coefficients are significant at $p < 0.05$.

**Coefficients are significant at $p < 0.01$.

***Coefficients are significant at $p < 0.001$.

Table 1.4 Results of the second-stage model: Project team level

Stage II: Project value for consumers				
Variables	*Model 1*		*Model 2*	
	Coeff.	*Std. Err.*	*Coeff.*	*Std. Err.*
Team reputation			0.31*	(−0.02)
Controls				
TV series awards	0.21***	(−0.02)	0.21***	(0.02)
Progressive number of episodes for TV series	−0.00	(0.00)	0	(0.00)
Total number of episodes for TV series	(−0.03)***	(0.00)	−0.03***	(−0.01)
Project team size	0.05***	(−0.01)	0.05***	(0.01)
Experience of the producer in the TV series production	0.00***	(0.00)	0.00***	(0.00)
Average audience for channel in the year	0.08***	(0.01)	0.07***	(0.02)
Total hours of TV series broadcast by the channel in the year	0.00**	(0.00)	0	(0.00)
Total hours of TV movies broadcast by the channel in the year	−0.00***	(0.00)	(−0.00)***	(0.00)
Constant	14.10		14.10	
Observations	248		248	
Wald χ^2	997.62		958.79	
Prob. (χ^2)	***		***	

Notes: *Coefficients are significant at $p < 0.10$.
**Coefficients are significant at $p < 0.01$.
***Coefficients are significant at $p < 0.001$.

we investigated the role of team composition in assembling successful project teams at the individual level, examining the individual diversity in terms of experiential task diversity and experiential role diversity. The findings indicate that the experiential task diversity, defined in terms of the stock of past experiences accumulated by each team member while performing different tasks, yields a positive effect on the team reputation. Gaining knowledge of broader tasks improves actors' abilities to evaluate and use the acquired knowledge for other projects, while also enhancing their latent skills. Our findings show that within project settings, actors' talent plays two main roles. Talent is a selection criterion, used by directors to select the actors to cast, and it enhances the teams' quality reputation. Therefore, to strengthen the team reputation, it is better that project teams select actors with high levels of task diversification.

The second human capital characteristic analyzed is the experiential role diversity, which refers to the stock of past experiences, from playing different roles, which each team member accumulates. Unlike the experiential task diversity results, our findings on the experiential role diversity show that it has a negative effect on the team reputation. Actors must define their own careers playing well-established roles because the stakeholders outside of the projects do not assign a strong reputation to actors with broad role experimentation. The main explanation of this phenomenon is that performing too many roles does not allow actors to define their own identities. As a result, forming project teams with actors who have experimented with too many roles is not completely successful.

It has proved to be innovative to introduce the project value for the consumers as the project team outcome. Prior literature has investigated team outcomes primarily in terms of effectiveness and team performance (i.e., Devine & Philips, 2001; Tyran & Gibson, 2008); the role of project value creation for consumers has never been analyzed. Our findings show that there is a positive relationship between team reputation and project value. Team reputation (high level of talent and actors with broader task knowledge) compels consumers to watch a TV series because they are more likely to give credit to such TV products.

This study suffers from the usual limitations of archival research. First, the data do not provide insights concerning the balancing effects provided by experiential role diversity and experiential task diversity. Therefore, future research should include several variables to address these effects. Second, to provide a complete framework of PBOs, future research should also include data at the organizational level (TV drama series budget). Third, our research has investigated the project value based on the two main Italian broadcasters' audience share, but it would be interesting to include data regarding the pay TV channels to understand whether the effects on the project value would remain positive.

References

Ancona, D. G., & Caldwell, D. F. (1992). Demography and design: Predictors of new product team performance *Organization Science, 3*, 321–341.

Baker, W. E., & Faulkner, R. R. (1991). Role as resource in the Hollywood film industry. *American Journal of Sociology, 97*, 279–309.

Bakker, R. M. (2010). Taking stock of temporary organizational forms: A systematic review and research agenda. *International Journal of Management Reviews, 12*, 466–486.

Bantel, K. A., & Jackson, S. E. (1989). Top management and innovations in banking: Does the composition of the top team make a difference? *Strategic Management Journal, 10*, 107–124.

Barrick, M. R., Stewart, G. L., Neubert, M. J., & Mount, M. K. (1998). Relating member ability and personality to work team processes and team effectiveness. *Journal of Applied Psychology, 83*, 377–391.

Bell, S. T. (2007). Deep-level composition variables as predictors of team performance: A meta-analysis. *Journal of Applied Psychology, 92*, 595–615.

Berman, S. L., Down, J., and Hill, C.W.L. (2002) Tacit knowledge as a source of competitive advantage in the National Basketball Association. *Academy of Management Journal, 45*, 13–31

Boh, W. F., Slaughter, S. A. & Espinosa J. A. (2007). Learning from experience in software development: A multilevel analysis. *Management Science, 53*, 1315–1331.

Bowman, C., & Ambrosini, V. (2000). Value creation versus value capture: Towards a coherent definition of value in strategy. *British Journal of Management 11*, 1–15.

Bredin, K. (Ed.) (2008). *Human Resource Management in Project-Based Organizations—Challenges, Changes, and Capabilities.* Sweden: Linköping. Linköping Studies in Arts and Science, Linköping University.

Bresnen, M. (1990). Project-based learning and the role of learning boundaries. *Organization Studies, 36*, 27–41.

Bresnen, M., Goussevskaia, A., & Swan, J. (2004). Embedding new management knowledge in project-based organization. *Organization Studies, 25*, 1535–1555.

Brewster, C., & Larsen, H. H. (2000). *Human Resource Management in Northern Europe: Trends, Dilemmas and Strategy.* Oxford: Blackwell Publishers Ltd.

Bunderson, J. S., & Sutcliffe, K. M. (2002). Comparing alternative conceptualizations of functional diversity in management teams: Process and performance effects. *Academy of Management Journal, 45*, 875–893.

Cacciatori, E. (2004). "Organizational Memory and Innovation across Projects: Integrated Service Provision in Engineering Design Firms," SPRU, Paper no. 117.

Carpenter, M. A., Sanders, W. G., & Gregersen, H. B. (2001). Bundling human capital with organizational context: The impact of international assignment experience on multinational firm performance and CEO pay. *Academy of Management Journal, 44*, 493–511.

Cattel, R. B. (1948). Concepts and methods in the measurement of group syntality. *Psychological Review, 55*, 48–63.

DeFillippi, R. J., & Arthur, M. B. (1998). Paradox in project-based enterprise: The case of film making. *California Management Review, 40*, 1–15.

Devine, D. J., & Philips, J. L. (2001). Do smarter teams do better? A meta-analysis of cognitive ability and team performance. *Small Group Research, 32*, 507–532.

Ebers, M., & Powell, W. (2007). Biotechnology: Its origins, organization, and outputs. *Research Policy, 36*, 433–437.

Engwall, M., & Jerbrant, A. (2003). The resource allocation syndrome: The prime challenge of multi-project management? *International Journal of Project Management, 21*, 403–409.

Engwall, M., & Svensson, C. (2004). Cheetah teams in product development: The most extreme form of temporary organization? *Scandinavian Journal of Management, 20*, 297–317.

Ferriani, S., Cattani, G., & Baden-Fuller, C. (2009). The relational antecedents of project-entrepreneurship: Network centrality, team composition and project performance. *Research Policy, 38*, 1545–1558.

Ferriani, S., Corrado, R., & Boschetti, C. (2005). Organizational learning under organizational impermanence: Collaborative ties in film project-firms. *Journal of Management and Governance, 9*, 257–285.

Gensh, D., & Shaman, P. (1980). Models of competitive television ratings. *Journal of Marketing Research, 23*, 307–315.

Grabher, G. (2004). Cool projects, boring institutions: Temporary collaboration in social context. *Regional Studies, 36*, 205–214.

Guzzo, R. A., & Dickson, M. W. (1996). Teams in organization: Recent research on performance and effectiveness. *Annual Review of Psychology, 47*, 307–338.

Hackman, J. R. (1987). The design of work teams. In J. Lorsch (Ed.), *Handbook of Organizational Behavior* (pp. 315–342). Englewood Cliffs, NJ: Prentice-Hall.

Harrison, D. A., & Klein, K. J. (2007). What's the difference? Diversity constructs as separations, variety, or disparity in organizations. *Academy of Management Review, 32*, 1199–1228.

Hinsz, V. B., Tindale, R. S., & Vollrath, D. A. (1997). The emerging conceptualization of groups as information processors. *Psychological Bulletin, 121*, 43–64.

Hobday, M. (1998). Product complexity, innovation and industrial organization. *Research Policy, 26*, 689–710.

Hobday, M. (2000). The project-based organization: An ideal form for managing complex products and systems? *Research Policy, 29*, 871–893.

Hovmark, S., & Nordqvist, S. (1996) Project organization: Change in the work atmosphere for engineers. *International Journal of Industrial Ergonomics, 17*, 389–398.

Ibert, O. (2004). Projects and firms as discordant complements: Organisational learning in the Munich software ecology. *Research Policy, 33*, 1529–1546.

Ilgen, D. R., Hollenbeck, J. R., & Jundt, M. D. (2005). Teams in organizations. *Annual Review of Psychology, 56*, 517–543.

Jackson, S. E., May, K. E., & Whitney, K. (1995). Understanding the dynamics of diversity in decision-making teams. In R. A. Guzzo, E. Salas, & associates (Eds.), *Team Effectiveness and Decision Making in Organizations* (pp. 204–261). San Francisco, CA: Jossey-Bass.

Jones, C. (1996). Careers in project networks: The case of the film industry. In M. B. Arthur & D. M. Rousseau (Eds.), *The Boundaryless Career: A New Employment Principle for a New Organizational Era* (pp. 58–75). New York, NY: Oxford University Press.

Klein, J. K., & Kozlowski, S. W. J. (2000). From micro to meso: Critical steps in conceptualizing and conducting multilevel research. *Organizational Research Methods, 3*, 211–236.

Levine, J. M., & Moreland, R. L. (1990). Progress in small group research. *Annual Review of Psychology, 41*, 585–634.

Lundin, R. A., & Söderholm, A. (1995). A theory of the temporary organization. *Scandinavian Journal of Management, 11*, 437–455.

Lundin, R. A., & Steinthórsson, R. S. (2003). Studying organizations as temporary. *Scandinavian Journal of Management, 19*, 233–250.

Manning, S., & Sydow, J. (2007). Transforming creative potential in project networks: How TV movies are produced under network-based control. *Critical Sociology, 33*, 19–42.

Maoret, M., Massa, F., & Jones, C. (2011). Toward a projects as events perspective. In G. Cattani, S. Ferriani, L. Frederiksen, & F. Täube (Eds.), *Project-Based Organizing and Strategic Management* (pp. 427–444). Bingley, UK: Emerald Group Publishing Ltd.

Packendorff, J. (1995). Inquiring into the temporary organization: New directions for project management research. *Scandinavian Journal of Management, 11*, 319–333.

Packendorff, J. (2002). The temporary society and its enemies: Projects from an individual perspective. In K. Sahlin-Andersson & A. Söderholm (Eds.), *Beyond Project Management: New Perspectives on the Temporary-Permanent Dilemma* (pp. 39–58). Malmö; Oslo; Copenhagen: Liber ekonomi; Abstrakt; Copenhagen Business School Press.

Perretti, F., & Negro, G. (2006). Filling empty seats: How status and organizational hierarchies affect exploration versus exploitation in team design. *Academy of Management Journal, 49*, 759–777.

Powell, W. (2001). The twenty-first century firm. In Paul DiMaggio (Ed.), *The Capitalist Firm in the Twenty-First Century: Emerging Patterns in Western Perspective* (pp. 33–699). Princeton, NJ: Princeton University Press.

Prencipe, A., & Tell, F. (2001). Inter-project learning: Processes and outcomes of knowledge codification in project-based firms. *Research Policy, 30*, 1373–1394.

Reagans, R., Argote, L., & Brooks, D. (2005). Individual experience and experience working together: Predicting learning rates from knowing who knows what and knowing how to work together. *Management Science, 51*, 869–881.

Reagans, R., & Zuckerman, E. (2001). Networks, diversity, and productivity: The social capital of corporate R&D teams. *Organization Science, 12*, 502–517.

Scott, S. G., & Einstein, W. O. (2001). Strategic performance appraisal in team-based organizations: One size does not fit all. *Academy of Management Executive, 15*, 107–118.

Soda, G., Usai, A., & Zaheer, A. (2004). Network memory: The influence of past and current network on performance. *Academy of Management Journal, 47*, 893–906.

Stark, R. (2007). *Sociology* (10th Edition). Boston, MA: Thomson Wadsworth.

Starkey, K., Barnatt, C., & Tempest, S. (2000). Beyond networks and hierarchies: Latent organizations in the U.K. television industry. *Organization Science, 11*, 299–305.

Stewart, G. L. (2006). A meta-analytic review of relationships between team design features and team performance. *Journal of Management, 32*, 29–54.

Sundstorm, E. (1990). Work teams: Applications and effectiveness. *American Psychologist, 45*, 120–133.

Sydow, J., Lindkvist, L., & DeFillippi, R. J. D. (2004). Project-based organizations, embeddedness, and repositories of knowledge: Editorial. *Organization Studies, 25*, 1475–1489.

Sydow, J., & Staber, U. (2002). The institutional embeddedness of project networks: The case of content production in German television. *Regional Studies, 36*, 215–227.

Tyran, L., & Gibson, C. B. (2008). Is what you see, what you get? The relationship among surface- and deep-level heterogeneity characteristics, group efficacy, and team reputation. *Group and Organization Management, 33*, 46–76.

Tziner, A. & Eden, D. (1985). Effects of crew composition on crew performance: Does the whole equal the sum of its parts? *Journal of Applied Psychology, 70*, 85–93.

Uzzi, B., & Spiro, J. (2005). Collaboration and creativity: The small world problem. *American Journal of Sociology, 111*, 447–504.

Vicentini, F. (2013). *Does Individual Flexibility Matter in Project-based Organizations?* Saarbrücken: Lambert Academic Publishing.

Whitley, R. (2006). Project-based firms: New organizational form or variations on a theme? *Industrial and Corporate Change, 15*, 77–99.

Zaheer, A., & Soda, G. (2009). Network evolution: The origins of structural holes. *Administrative Science Quarterly, 54*, 1–31.

CHAPTER 2

The Effect of Virtual Work Environments and Social Systems on Human Capital and Assets

Eugene A. Pierce and Sean W. Hansen

Introduction

In recent decades, advances in information technology (IT) have fundamentally altered the outlook of organizations with respect to the identification, development, and deployment of human capital. Specifically, IT is widely credited with enabling new organizational forms and expanding access to talent by reducing the coordination challenges of distance and compressing the time required to communicate information among teams and organizations (Fulk & DeSanctis, 1995; Privman, Hiltz, & Wang, 2013). The combination of IT advances and flexible approaches to organizational design has led to a dramatic increase in distributed work, or *distributed teaming*, environments (Aubert & Kelsey, 2003). The Internet enables project team members in distant locales to work together on common projects efficiently and cost-effectively. As a result, many enterprises today are engaging employees who are not physically present at traditional organizational locations—enabling them to participate in teams that seldom, if ever, meet face to face. Such workers shoulder the same responsibilities and challenges as collocated employees, coupled with the added challenges of managing culture, process, and goal dynamics unique to distributed teams (Chuang, Jackson, & Jiang, 2013).

Like other teams, distributed teams are composed of individuals with complementary skills performing interdependent tasks with a common purpose and mutual accountability for results (Piccoli & Ives, 2003).

Unlike collocated teams, distributed teams work across space and time, employing networks of communication technology (Dubé & Paré, 2001; Hertel, Geister, & Konradt, 2005) to form relationships and complete work. Maynard, Mathieu, Rapp, and Gilson (2012) highlight the fact that, in distributed teaming environments, knowledge workers are simultaneously engaged on multiple teams with most communication occurring virtually (i.e., though computer mediated mechanisms). Kelsey (1999) provides a more detailed definition of distributed teaming:[1]

> a boundaryless network organization form where a temporary team is assembled on an as-needed basis for the duration of a task and staffed by members who are separated by geographic distance and who use computer-mediated communications as their primary form of communication and interpersonal contact.
>
> (p. 104)

Distributed teaming presents organizations with a range of potential benefits for human capital management, including improved access to high-level talent, increased flexibility for knowledge professionals, enhanced ability to serve markets on a global scale, and reduction in travel costs and other expenses associated with traditional meeting arrangements (Bailey, Leonardi, & Barley, 2012; Duarte & Snyder, 2006; Majchrzak, Rice, Malhotra, King, & Ba, 2000). Yet, significant challenges remain. While technology has created new horizons for communication and interaction over time and space, these novel work arrangements demand a set of interpersonal competencies, coordination processes, and leadership skills that are markedly distinct from those required in collocated team environments (Jarvenpaa & Leidner, 1999). To achieve the envisioned human capital benefits of distributed teaming, organizations must bring the right people together at the right time and do so quickly (Daim et al., 2012; Townsend, DeMarie, & Hendrickson, 1998). As distributed work arrangements become increasingly commonplace, it is important to understand the wide variety of factors that influence the effectiveness of a distributed team.

The current study provides a grounded exploration of the factors that drive team effectiveness and the appropriate deployment of human capital within distributed work arrangements. We examine the perceptions, attitudes, and experiences of individuals who have participated in both highly successful and less successful teams to identify both enablers of and impediments to project performance within distributed team environments. Given the significant emphasis on various forms of team trust in the extant distributed teams research literature, we seek to determine the role of technology and enabling process elements in facilitating the generation and maintenance of trust and, in turn, distributed team performance (Jarvenpaa & Leidner, 1999; Kanawattanachai & Yoo, 2002; Sarker, Ahuja, Sarker, & Kirkeby, 2011). Specifically, we are guided by questions of how IT and coordination processes impact a distributed team's ability to

- leverage the human capital of its members to drive collective performance in geographically and temporally distributed settings;
- develop shared values, build social relationships, and develop a positive outlook on a project; and
- monitor team progress and establish clear boundaries of accountability.

To address these questions, we completed a grounded analysis of the insights from US Air Force engineers engaged in distributed team projects focusing on the development or acquisition and customization of information systems for the management of financial, logistical, and human resource functions by the air force. With this focus on the experiences of actual professionals in distributed work environments, we hope to advance research on the dynamics of distributed teams as they occur *in situ*. In developing our analysis, we first provide a brief overview of the research on distributed teams with an emphasis on the role of trust in the management of such groups. We then present the research methodology employed. The methodology is followed by a thorough discussion of our research findings. Finally, we turn to a discussion of the significant implications of the research before offering some concluding thoughts.

Distributed Teams and Distributed Work Dynamics

Distributed Teams

While the term itself has been defined in a wide variety of ways by different authors (Bell & Kozlowski, 2002; Knoll & Jarvenpaa, 1998; Majchrzak et al., 2000), the basic features of a distributed team are geographic and temporal distribution of team members with limited face-to-face communication and interactions mediated by information and communication technologies (ICTs; Poole & Zhang, 2005; A. Powell, Piccoli, & Ives, 2004). In their description, Jarvenpaa and Leidner (1999) note that distributed teams are generally temporary in nature, being rapidly formed (and disbanded) in an effort to address the emergent demands of a changing marketplace. Consistent with this fundamental picture of distributed teams, Henry and Hartzler (1998) offer a more detailed delineation of a team marked by (1) relatively small size (i.e., usually consisting of less than 20 individuals), (2) geographical distribution, (3) working apart more frequently than in the same location,

(4) making decisions based on a stratification of work, and (5) shared accountability for team results.

The emergence of distributed teams over the past two decades has been driven by several factors. Perhaps foremost among these is the tremendous advancement in communications and computing media in the latter half of the twentieth century, including the development of such resources as e-mail, instant messaging, video conferencing, shared data repositories, and other online collaborative systems (Fulk & DeSanctis, 1995; Majchrzak et al., 2000). In addition to these technological enablers, distributed teaming has been encouraged by the development of global markets for goods and services, the expansion of the network organizational form, and the creation of flexible work arrangements in many industries (Poole & Zhang, 2005).

As noted above, distributed teams confront a wide range of both opportunities and challenges. One of the key benefits of distributed work arrangements is that organizations are no longer limited by geography in their pursuit of top-quality personnel (Lipnack & Stamps, 1997). Distributed team arrangements also offer significant cost savings over traditional collocated group efforts, because of reduced travel, less potential for work interruption, and the elimination of unnecessary meetings (Mowshowitz, 1997). Finally, distributed groups enable organizations to explore commercial and other opportunities on a global scale (Kayworth & Leidner, 2001; Lin, Wang, Tsai, & Hsu, 2010).

While there are several apparent advantages to distributed teaming, a range of challenges persist. One of the key lines of questioning in this regard is what is lost when team members are no longer collocated (Cramton, 2001; Hinds & Bailey, 2003). A large body of research reveals that face-to-face communication offers several advantages for group formation, including the social bonding and symbolic commitment of group members (Nardi & Whittaker, 2002), the promotion of cooperative choices (Sally, 1995), and the coordination of group activity (Weick & Roberts, 1993). Indeed, even the mere presence of other individuals (i.e., with no verbal communication) has been shown to have a positive effect of group outcomes, increasing individual attention and feelings of connection (Kiesler & Cummings, 2002). The loss of this social presence combined with the asynchronous nature of their work poses significant communication and coordination challenges for distributed teams' members and managers (DeRue & Ashford, 2010; Montoya-Weiss, Massey, & Song, 2001). These coordination challenges are often exacerbated by the cultural and professional diversity observed in distributed environments (Kayworth & Leidner, 2001; Tannenbaum, Mathieu, Salas, & Cohen, 2012).

Distributed Teams and Human Capital

In the present analysis, we are concerned with the ways in which distributed teaming enables an organization to access and leverage the human capital embodied within its members. While the concept of human capital has been a subject of contention since its emergence in the 1960s, the term has been widely employed to describe the value that individuals provide to organizations and society (Becker, 2009). Specifically, *human capital* may be defined as the knowledge, skills, abilities, and innovativeness that reside in individuals and which contribute to the performance of organizations (Adam & Urquhart, 2009; Flamholtz, 1999; Hsu, 2008; Mårtensson, 2000).[2]

The research on distributed teams has long acknowledged the importance of human capital considerations. As Lipnack and Stamps (2008) note, "Human capital increases when more people work together in more places, meeting new challenges and acquiring new competencies" (p. 84). Distributed teaming enables organizations to access a broader range of human capital by reducing the constraints imposed by geographic and temporal distance (Horwitz, Bravington, & Silvis, 2006; Piccoli & Ives, 2003). At the same time, such teaming arrangements hold the promise of further human capital development by exposing individuals to a more diverse pool of skills and knowledge (Harvey, Novicevic, & Garrison, 2005; Zakaria, Amelinckx, & Wilemon, 2004). However, as we explore in this research, the ability to leverage human capital effectively in distributed environments depends upon the ways in which teams are coordinated and the degree of trust established between members.

Distributed Teams and Trust

Cummings and Bromiley (1996) maintain that a person trusts a group when that person believes that the group (a) makes a good-faith effort to behave in accordance with any commitments both explicit or implicit, (b) is honest in whatever negotiations preceded such commitments, and (c) does not take excessive advantage of another even when the opportunity is available. Researchers have proposed several factors that facilitate the development of team trust, including shared social norms, repeated interactions, and shared experiences (Bradach & Eccles, 1989), as well as the anticipation of future association (W. Powell, 1990). Expectation of future association has been shown to be higher among group members who are collocated than among distributed members (W. Powell, 1990). Collocation, or physical proximity, more generally, is said to reinforce social similarity, shared values, and expectations, and to increase the immediacy of threats from failing to meet commitments (Latané, Liu, Nowak, Bonevento, & Zheng, 1995).

If face-to-face interaction is considered the *sine qua non* for the development of interpersonal trust (Nohria & Eccles, 1992), how can trust be created and maintained in distributed work arrangements? Iacono and Weisband (1997) found that high levels of trust were achieved by distributed teams that remained focused on the work content of their group, moved efficiently between work tasks, and engaged in regular communication. While work focus was important, the researchers also found that groups that achieved significant social penetration (i.e., social understanding between members) early in a project exhibited higher levels of intragroup trust. In addition, Iacono and Weisband (1997) contend that the trust observed within distributed teams tends to take the form of "swift trust" (Meyerson, Weick, & Kramer, 1996), in which team members import expectations of trust from past experiences. Developed to explain behavior in temporary teams such as film crews, theater and architectural groups, and cockpit crews (Meyerson et al., 1996), the theory of swift trust assumes clear role divisions among members who have well-defined specialties. Inconsistent role behavior and "blurring" of roles erode trust.

Jarvenpaa and Leidner (1999) investigated the issue of distributed team trust through the analysis of e-mail archives and interviews with participants in a global distributed collaboration. As with Iacono and Weisband (1997), they found that effective groups tended to exhibit swift trust, and teams marked by significant trust were those in which members maintained a strong task focus and a capacity for managing the ambiguities of their project. Interestingly, many studies of trust in distributed teams are based on *ad hoc* distributed teams in academic contexts (e.g., Jarvenpaa & Leidner, 1999; Kanawattanachai & Yoo, 2002). In contrast, we consider the development of trust and effectiveness in distributed teams as they actually exist in an organizational environment.

Information Technology and Trust

The rapid growth of personal e-mail communication, instant messaging, and online communities has brought attention to the important role of interpersonal trust in online communication (Feng, Lazar, & Preece, 2004; Sarker et al., 2011). Media richness and social presence theories (Daft, Lengel, & Trevino, 1987) suggest challenges to the development of trusting relationships in distributed teams. These theories contend that computer-based communication media may eliminate the communication cues that individuals normally use to convey trust, warmth, attentiveness, and other interpersonal affections (Daft et al., 1987). However, subsequent research has called this assertion into question.

Sproull and Kiesler (1991), reporting increased reliance on the development of supportive interpersonal relationships online, argue that in a networked organization, the relationship between a person and technology is less important than the relationships *between* individuals through technology. Parks and Floyd (1996) found that personal relationships are common in online settings, evolving naturally as a function of time and experience in the online environment, and that online relationships often broaden to include interaction in other channels or settings. Similarly, according to Walther's (1997) social information processing theory, computer-mediated communication does not differ from face-to-face communication in terms of the capability of social information exchange, but rather in terms of a slower rate of transfer.

Olson and Olson (2000) proposed that the keys to designing a trust-engendering online software systems are appropriate background information and attention to trusting and trustworthy behavior. Bos, Olson, Gergle, Olson, and Wright (2002) investigated the emergence of trust in four different communication situations: face-to-face, video, audio, and text chat. Face-to-face, video, and audio combined resulted in significantly higher levels of trust than text chat. Video and audio conferencing groups were nearly as good as face-to-face communication, but both showed some evidence of delayed trust (slower progress toward full cooperation) and fragile trust (vulnerability to opportunistic behavior; Bos et al., 2002).

Finally, it is worth noting that most of the extant literature on computer-mediated communication (CMC) and its impact on interpersonal trust is based on early and relatively simplistic Internet applications, such as e-mail and chat functionality. The findings from this research may warrant reappraisal in the wake of advanced collaborative information environments (Stevens, Papka, & Disz, 2003; Thomas & Bostrom, 2010b) and social networking applications (Dwyer, Hiltz, & Passerini, 2007), which have been broadly grouped under the label of Web 2.0. Such research has been very limited to date, begging the question of whether or not the dynamics of trust in CMC will change as "developers create technological gradients that can bring a power equivalent to the gaze to an online exchange" (Vallor, 2010, p. 166).

Research Design

This research is designed to explore how technology and enabling (or facilitating) processes support the generation and maintenance of trust to drive the performance of distributed teams. As discussed above and illustrated in Figure 2.1, a distributed team consists of people, their network of relationships, and drivers such as management, customers, and suppliers.

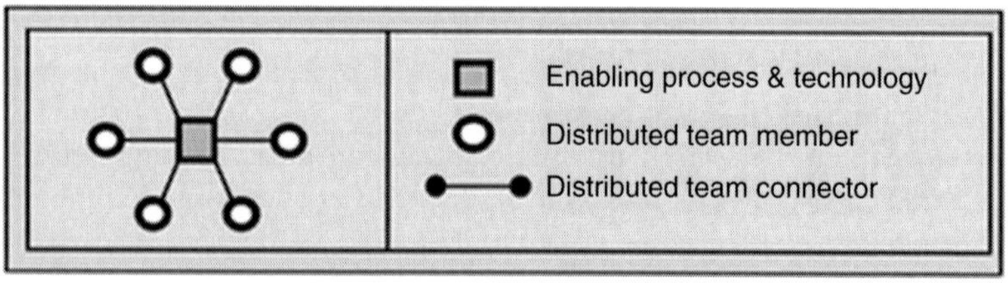

Figure 2.1 Distributed team logical structure—Unit of analysis

We focus in this study on understanding the internal behavior of such a system coping with the dynamic demands of its internal and external environment. Figure 2.1 demonstrates the reliance of geographically distributed team members on enabling processes and technology for vital connectivity. In the following sections we outline the approach adopted to explore these dynamics.

Methodology

The present research employs multiple methods of data collection and analysis to support a grounded exploration of real-world distributed teaming experiences. Specifically, we utilized semi-structured interviews of distributed team participants, as well as a quantitative survey instrument for additional data collection and analysis. Based on our desire to understand the phenomenon of distributed work from the viewpoint of those experiencing it, our interviewing and qualitative data analysis was conducted in line with a grounded theory methodology (GTM; Glaser & Strauss, 1967; Strauss & Corbin, 1990). Semi-structured interviews were employed to capture the perceptions, beliefs, and attitudes of respondents about their experiences of working in geographically distributed teams. We triangulated our research by administering a written survey to assess our subjects' levels of trust, a construct nominated in the literature as a determinant element of team performance.

Data Sample

In line with a GTM approach, we employed a theoretical sampling to identify study participants. Eighteen US Air Force (USAF) engineers participated in the study. They were selected from a pool of 150 such professionals involved in acquiring and developing information systems for managing the financial, logistical, and human resource functions of the USAF. The pool was identified by the director of the USAF's Operational Support Systems

Table 2.1 Summary of interview participants

Respondent	*Gender/age*	*Profession*
Subject 1-A	F/20s	Engineering assistant
Subject 2-B	M/50s	Application engineering
Subject 3-C	M/40s	Engineering manager
Subject 4-D	F/30s	Data engineering
Subject 5-E	M/40s	Information assurance engineering
Subject 6-F	M/60s	Application engineering
Subject 7-G	M/30s	Infrastructure engineering
Subject 8-H	M/50s	Application engineering
Subject 9-I	M/50s	Engineering manager
Subject 10-J	F/30s	Engineering assistant
Subject 11-K	M/50s	Technical engineering
Subject 12-L	M/40s	Application engineering
Subject 13-M	M/50s	Engineering manager
Subject 14-N	M/40s	Technical engineering
Subject 15-O	M/40s	Application process engineering
Subject 16-P	M/40s	Enterprise engineering
Subject 17-Q	M/40s	Application engineering
Subject 18-R	F/50s	Engineering assistant

Wing. Professional systems engineers and junior engineers were interviewed to provide a broad understanding of the issues surrounding distributed team environments and activities. In the interests of theoretical saturation, data collection evolved from general sampling to relational sampling (i.e., seeking to understand relationships) and ended with discriminate sampling (i.e., seeking to differentiate relationships; Strauss & Corbin, 1990).

The project sample represented various age groups, backgrounds, and a variety of different projects based out of Dayton, Ohio; Bedford, Massachusetts; and Montgomery, Alabama. Participants (see Table 2.1) were composed of 14 men and 4 women, ages 25–61.

Data Collection

We gathered data by interviewing people who worked on projects that consisted of members geographically distributed in a variety of organizations. As Mintzberg, Raisinghani, and Theoret (1976) observe, a good way to find out how people do things is to ask them. Engineers and engineering assistants were asked questions regarding their experiences participating in distributed teams. An interview protocol was employed to ensure consistency of questioning across all participants. Specifically, we probed their feelings about the project, relationships with other team members, opinions regarding project structure, and the use of technology to support the team. Team members interviewed had diverse functional expertise and worked from middle to senior managerial levels. In addition to the interview protocol, each respondent was asked to provide an open-ended description of their work within distributed teams and was encouraged to provide personal perspectives with regard to the success of their specific distributed team projects.

The interviews lasted, in most cases, from 60 to 90 minutes, and were conducted face to face at the interviewee's work site. The focus was on the interviewee's own perspective and feelings. In each interview, a successful and a less successful distributed team experience was discussed. As a wrap-up activity the interviewee was asked to describe his or her view with regard to the differences between the two experiences.

Data Analysis

In accordance with GTM, data were analyzed using an iterative approach of constant comparison—going back and forth between the data, the literature, and the theory being developed. The interpretation of the data consisted of an iterative process that began with open-ended coding of each transcript to capture and catalog all themes of potential significance. We refined the coding structure through subsequent iterations of analysis. Coding continued until the researchers deemed that theoretical saturation was achieved—that is, no new themes were being identified and all emergent elements had been categorized. Open coding yielded over 120 thematic codes across all interviews. Through the process of axial coding (Strauss & Corbin, 1990), these codes were reduced to approximately 40 codes. The reduction was a result of unifying codes that were considered to be similar or the same and eliminating those that were irrelevant to the research. During this process, some codes were subsumed into others, and some categorized as "belonging" to more than one of several higher-level categories.

The third iteration of analysis (i.e., selective coding) resulted in identifying degrees of intensity for a number of codes found in the second iteration. For example, some transcripts described significant degrees of trust while others described some trust or very little to no trust. This allowed for a code that represented trust in a successful distributed team to be the same code that would represent trust in a less successful distributed team. The difference is that the code would be assigned a degree of intensity (i.e., "3" or "2" value for teams that experienced significant trust; "1" or "0" value for teams with little to no trust). This selective coding process resulted in 16 codes as shown in Table 2.2.

Table 2.2 Final coding structure

Code label	*Description*
Early trust	Trust that occurs early in a project with no existing relationship; analogous to swift trust in which expectations of trust are imported from past team experiences
Sustained trust	Trust that develops as a result of building relationships
Conflict	Disputes or quarrels between distributed team members
Conflicting priorities	Conflicting views on issues and/or work to be addressed within a project
Challenge	The perceived level of effort of a project task
Motivation	The perceived degree of desire, incentive, or willingness to work
Purpose	The reason for which something exists or is done, made, and/or used
Sponsorship	An organization or person vouches or is responsible for a team project
Team building	The act or activity of building the morale or positive outlook of a team
Leadership (project manager)	The act or instance of leading, guidance, or direction
Accountability	The state of being liable, or answerable to a situation
Goal clarity	An understanding of work to the degree that allows an organization or person to start achieving the work
Role clarity	An understanding of who performs the work to the degree that allows an organization or person to start achieving the work
Communications—e-mail	Communicating through electronic mail
Communications—conf. calls	Communication through conference calls
Communications—face to face	Communicating through face-to-face means

Findings

As noted above, our respondents discussed both successful (high-performing) and less successful (lower-performing) distributed team project experiences. Our analysis revealed nine distinct axes for discrimination of distributed team project success: (1) motivation, (2) purpose, (3) sponsorship, (4) team building, (5) accountability, (6) communications, (7) role/goal clarity, (8) project management, and (9) trust. Participant's perceptions of how each of these factors operates to enhance or inhibit performance are described individually

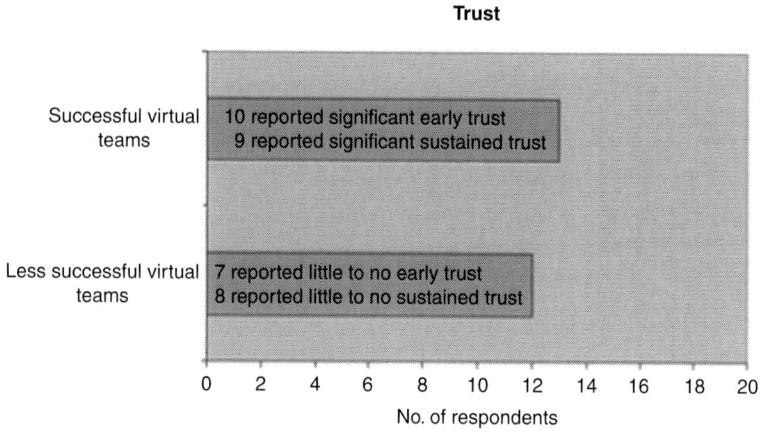

Figure 2.2 Trust: High-performing vs. lower-performing virtual teams

in Figure 2.2 and depicted graphically in a preliminary theoretical model presented in the subsequent section.

Respondents' perception of the nature and influence of trust in distributed teams indicates that trust is a salient point of distinction between high-performing and lower-performing distributed teams. For both project types, respondents highlighted the importance of trust for optimum distributed team performance. Furthermore, in keeping with the literature on small group dynamics, we see evidence of a distinction between the *early* (or "*swift*") *trust,* established at the outset of group interactions, and *sustained trust,* which emerges (or fails to emerge) as interpersonal bonds between team members are nurtured. Specifically, with respect to successful team efforts, respondents described the trust-building process as initiating with swift trust that morphed into sustained trust, recounting purposeful, proactive steps that were taken to build swift trust through supporting management initiatives. Such initiatives are examined in subsequent sections. In contrast, less successful distributed teams reported a deficit of management activities for building overall team structure and alignment for trust.

As documented in Figure 2.2, ten respondents describing successful team performance reported significant early (or "swift") trust and nine respondents reported significant sustaining trust. Seven respondents reporting less successful team performance specifically cited the relative absence of early trust and eight others reported little to no sustained trust as a critical factor. Illustrative statements regarding early and sustained forms of trust in the successful team condition include the following:

Early trust	*Sustained trust*
"Early in the project, we meshed well together and had confidence in each other. The synergy and the cohesiveness was completely there."	*"We have learned to lean on each other and trust each other. There is a camaraderie there . . . you know we're the team."*
"From the start, I had confidence in the developers that were working out at Montgomery, because in the past they always delivered and in fact exceeded expectations."	*"I kind of started being more comfortable and dependent on the folks midway through the project."*

Our findings demonstrate the significance that distributed team members ascribe to the role of management in assuring distributed team performance. In our study, members clearly distinguished between two requisite management capabilities: *social relationship management* and *project team management.*

Social Relationship Management Processes

Among our respondents, activities oriented toward social relationship management include efforts at motivation, establishing a sense of purpose, sponsorship, and team-building efforts.

Motivation

As shown in Figure 2.3, respondents identified motivation as a key factor influencing social relationships in high-performing distributed teams. For successful teams, respondents described how the management process helped cultivate motivation. In most cases, proactive steps were taken to monitor and improve motivation. In contrast, several respondents from less successful distributed teams reported little to no management activities to develop a motivating environment. Exemplary statements from each success category serve to highlight this distinction:

Successful projects	*Unsuccessful projects*
"We were all motivated to have a common laboratory system . . . everybody had a little bit of skin in the game."	*"There weren't enough face-to-face meetings to boost up the excitement, and that was something that should have been happening."*
"[The team members] were very excited. They liked the design challenges in the project."	*"[Several of the team members] just want to peddle in place with no motivation to learn."*

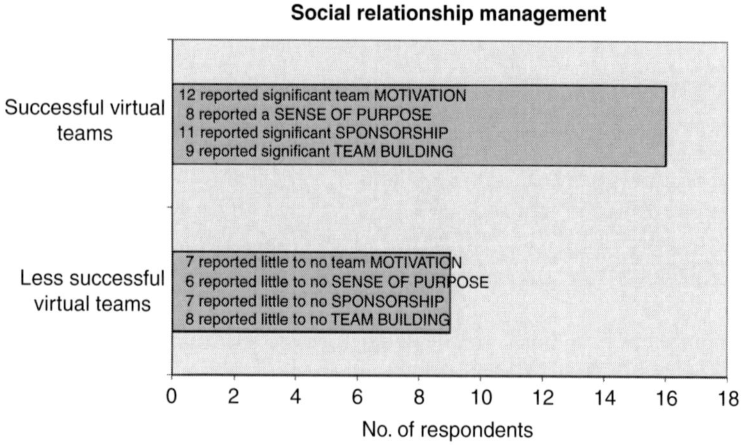

Figure 2.3 Social relationship variables: Successful vs. less successful projects

Sense of Purpose

With respect to successful distributed teams, respondents reported significant sense of purpose in each of their respective projects. Participants discussed the management processes for establishing a sense of purpose that resulted in influencing distributed team social relationships. Respondents noted that managers in these projects actively cultivated a sense of purpose and shared vision among the team members throughout the life of the project. In contrast, for low-performing teams, respondents documented the lack of management activities for establishing a sense of purpose.

Successful projects	*Unsuccessful projects*
"[Team members] had a vested interest in having this capability, so they in many cases volunteered and came to work with us to make it a success."	*"There was no single clear goal with the [client organization] . . . I think there were local goals, rather than a shared goal, and that was killing us."*
"There's a real feeling of mission on this project."	*"You have no confidence that anything you delegate is gonna get completed if you don't have team members with a common objective."*

Sponsorship

For high-performing distributed teams, respondents highlighted significant sponsorship for each of their respective projects, noting that team management explicitly sought and established sponsorship at the outset of the projects. For less successful projects, respondents noted failure to report or the absence of management activity for establishing sponsorship within their project. The following statements exemplify the respondent comments regarding sponsorship in successful and less successful distributed team projects:

Successful projects	*Unsuccessful projects*
"Everybody's rallying around the big challenge, because you get a lot of senior-level support. That says 'This is a great challenge. You've got to do this and make it happen.'"	*"You have to have commitment letters from management that says they're going to support delivering this particular capability. We did not have that."*
"What helped make that a success was that we had tremendous support from the field and senior leadership. They had a vested interest in having this capability."	*"We didn't have a project champion within the Air Force."*

Team Building

In the final factor associated with social relationship management, respondents reported significant team-building activities within high-performing distributed teams. Individuals described management efforts aimed at creating interpersonal cohesiveness and the resulting enhancement to social collaboration among distributed members. Our respondents also delineated the steps taken to monitor and cultivate team building through management initiatives. In contrast, for low-performing distributed teams, respondents did not report management initiatives to establish team cohesiveness and, in several cases, specifically noted their absence.

Successful projects	*Unsuccessful projects*
"We had social activities at close of business, with the objective of getting to know one another better and everybody's personality."	*"There was no socializing—nothing like that . . . There was a mentality of 'You guys are a bunch of idiots' . . . and obviously there is no team."*
"That gave us a lot of opportunity to socialize and learn more about [the team members'] families and what their interests were—hobbies, etc."	*"They didn't talk to one another. They didn't* want *to talk to one another. There was clearly* no *real* team.*"*

Project Team Management Processes

The project team management processes discussed by our respondents included fostering a sense of accountability, establishing explicit norms for

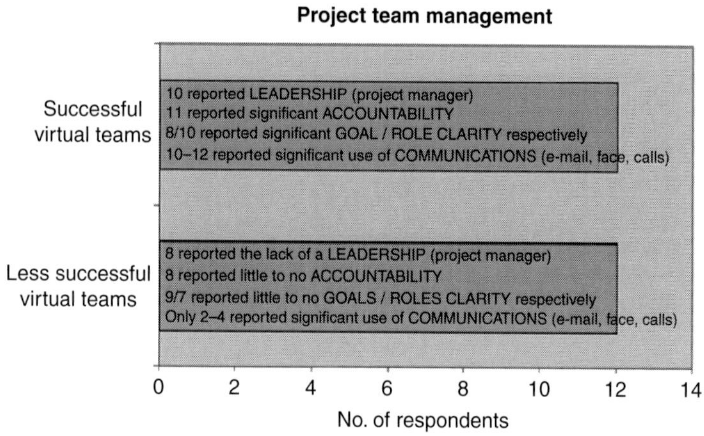

Figure 2.4 Project management variables: Successful vs. less successful projects

communications, maintaining role/goal clarity, and having a formally recognized project manager. Figure 2.4 highlights the prevalence of these factors in respondent perceptions.

Leadership

As shown in Figure 2.4, in describing high-performing projects, ten respondents reported the active presence of a project manager. In contrast, reporting low-performing projects, eight respondents conveyed that their team lacked a clear project manager. Our respondents collectively observed that a project manager is a key determinant of effective project execution. This is supported by the literature in that Thomas and Bostrom (2010a) suggest that team leader strategies are key to enabling a collaborative environment through increasingly improved technology. The following comments illustrate the attitudes regarding the importance of leadership among the respondents:

Successful projects	*Unsuccessful projects*
"On the application and development side, we had a project manager. He was in charge of the overall well-being of the project—the schedule, the delivery of the project."	*"No one was managing it. It's unexecutable! You can execute a standard set of processes across a hundred programs without a project manager."*
"I had confidence in the project task leader to understand the situation and be able to manage the expectations of the sponsors."	*"The challenge we run into is that there is really no project manager . . . The team wanted structure. They were just crying out for some process."*

Accountability

Perceptions regarding accountability in distributed teams reflect a clear contrast between successful and less successful distributed teams. Participants of both types of teams recognized the importance of accountability for optimum project team management. However, in discussing high-performing teams, respondents highlighted managerial efforts aimed at establishing accountability. Conversely, descriptions of low-performing distributed teams reflected the absence or inadequacy of management activities for establishing accountability within the team structure. A few exemplary statements highlight this point:

Successful projects	*Unsuccessful projects*
"I think that's when we matured to the point where people understood their roles. We were expected to deliver."	*"In the commercial world, people deliver. In our project, they did not. It is very hard to terminate a government employee."*
"There was a feeling of responsibility to ensure that deliverables were made."	*"I felt that I couldn't delegate work. You have no confidence that anything you delegate will get done. If you don't have members that deliver, you're screwed."*

Role and Goal Clarity

In discussing both high- and low-performing distributed teams, respondents emphasized the importance of clear roles and goals for optimum project team management. Yet, in an apparent link with accountability, their perceptions of support for these factors in the two conditions suggest a clear point of distinction. The respondents discussing high-performing teams reported strong clarity for both member roles and overall project goals. With respect to successful teams, respondents noted efforts for goal and role development, describing management practices to ensure clarity. In contrast, respondents reported little goal and role clarity for less successful distributed teams, and emphasized their absence as contributing factors to low team performance.

Successful projects	*Unsuccessful projects*
Goals: *"They wanted to put the aircraft owners' feet to the fire to make sure they were going to be compliant by 2009. Basically, they did that by having clear goals and objectives."*	Goals: *"They're all over the place. They're talking about interfaces one moment. They're talking about business rules [the next] . . . We did not see eye to eye on the project goals whatsoever."*
Roles: *"The success factors were the scheduling agendas and the roles were very clearly identified and managed . . . Each of the geographically separated units had its own role."*	Roles: *"As an engineer, the roles were confusing . . . There were parts of the technical team that kind of liked the turmoil and liked the confusion. No one knew what they were doing."*

Communications

Our respondents noted three distinct communication modalities that were used in their distributed team projects—conference calls, e-mail, and face-to-face meetings. In discussing high-performing team experiences, respondents reported the importance of regular and consistent communication among team members regardless of the type of communication employed. In contrast, respondents identified a relative dearth of consistent communication among team members in low-performing distributed teams. Importantly, while the successful teams discussed the specific modalities employed for communication, little discussion of such modalities (either positive or negative) emerged in the reflections regarding low-performing teams. However, clear distinctions between high- and low-performing teams were identified in the discussion of face-to-face communication. For example:

Successful projects	*Unsuccessful projects*
"To create that relationship, you need face-to-face interaction. And so we still were required to go back and forth between ourselves and the customer."	*"There is no communication. I have been a part of the squadron for eighteen months. I have physically seen my squadron leader twice, spoken to him once. Our wing commander, who has been stood up, has visited us three times in eighteen months."*
"On a regular basis—probably every two or three months—we would actually have a face-to-face get-together."	
"I think a big part of the success is we had people there face to face from many different geographical areas."	*"I think it's kind of a mind-set for this project—out of sight, out of mind."*

Common Factors across High-Performing and Low-Performing Distributed Teams

Respondents reported three themes that were approximately equal in degree and magnitude across successful and less successful distributed teams—conflict, differing priorities, and the emergence of challenges. As shown in Figure 2.5, a significant number of respondents reported significant interpersonal conflict, conflicting priorities, and challenges for both high- and low-performing distributed team projects, suggesting that these are inherent characteristics of all distributed teams and operate whether outcomes are positive or not. This finding implies that something other than conflicts and priority clashes are responsible for the degradation of performance in low-performing teams. While participants admitted that conflict and conflicting priorities taxed project team management, they also understood that the

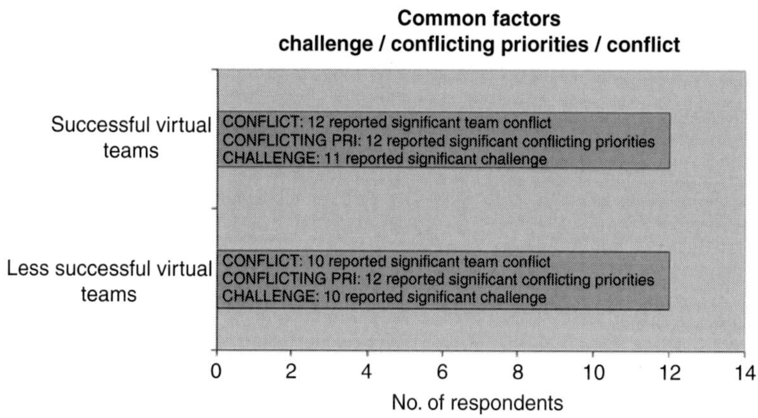

Figure 2.5 Common factors: Less successful vs. successful projects

effective exercise of management practices could overcome these challenges to team achievement. Thus, respondents recognized both the value and the burden of having a challenging team objective.

Discussion

At the outset of this research, we anticipated that both technology and facilitating processes, in and of themselves, have a significant impact on distributed team performance and the leveraging of human capital. Our findings, however, demonstrate that technology and simple project processes are a necessary, but clearly not sufficient, condition for producing high-performing distributed teams. A revised conception of the drivers of distributed team performance based on our respondents' insights highlights a range of distinct activities that influence the development and deployment of human capital resources in distributed team performance. We have grouped these activities into two higher-order classes of managerial processes—social relationship management processes and project management processes. Respondents consistently reported the existence of both types of processes among high-performing distributed teams, as well as their relative absence or inadequate execution in low-performing distributed teams. Team members indicated a need for more advanced processes that provide greater fidelity and integration of project and interpersonal mechanics to better address the diverse needs of actors in distributed teaming conditions.

From the perspective of an ongoing stream of research, the qualitative and quantitative findings from the present study suggest a factor model that is

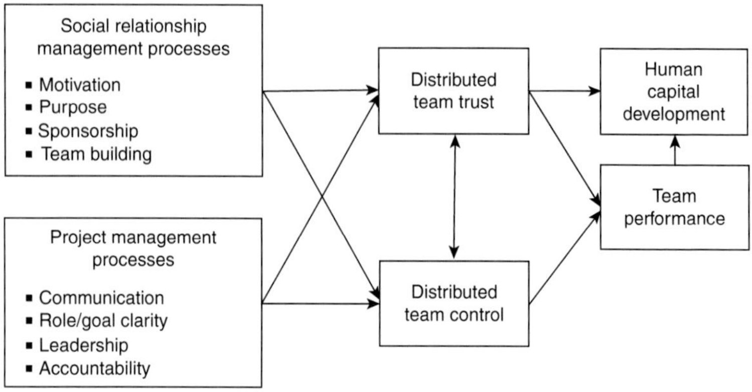

Figure 2.6 Proposed conceptual model

amenable to traditional variance-based research. In this discussion, we introduce this emergent factor model and outline the next steps for research into the drivers of distributed team trust and performance. The new conceptual model, rendered graphically in Figure 2.6, represents the interdependent nature of the key variables and the critical link between distributed team trust and distributed team control. The nature of this balanced relationship is examined in more detail in the remaining discussion.

Team Performance

There seems to be no uniform measure of performance for either collocated or distributed teams (Schweitzer & Duxbury, 2010; Sundstrom, De Meuse, & Futrell, 1990). Sundstrom et al. (1990) define performance broadly as a combination of (a) group-produced outputs (e.g., quantity or quality, speed, customer satisfaction), (b) the consequences a group has for its members, and (c) the enhancement of a team's capability to perform effectively. In this chapter, similarly, we defined distributed team performance broadly as a measure of achievement of an objective for which a distributed team was assembled. This conception might include the ultimate objective or a requirement that leads to, or supports, that objective. Our respondents seemed to generally feel that good process execution facilitated higher trust and control, and consequently better overall distributed team outcomes. Respondents also reported that poor process execution manifested by either too much (or too little) control contributed significantly to less successful outcomes. Returning to the literature, we find precedents for these findings. Dirks (1999) has shown that similar measures of distributed team performance, such as organizational behavior, job satisfaction, and individual job performance, are regulated by trust and control within a team. In later research, Dirks and Ferrin (2001) argued that someone who feels trusted may feel compelled to contribute more ideas and thus achieve higher work performance. As such, a trustor who trusts a team member may be more flexible and provide more information resulting in faster, better, and more economical work performance. Finally, Zolin et al. (2004) argue that trust and control may moderate the effects of social processes (e.g., motivation) on distributed team performance by influencing one's expectations about another's likely behavior, thus increasing or reducing the trustor's motivation and output performance.

Human Capital Development

With respect to the development of human capital resources, we would posit two distinct mechanisms based on the findings in the present study. Specifically, we perceive that the establishment of trust in distributed teams could have both direct and indirect effects on the human capital development of team members. First, as noted above, the establishment of trust within a team encourages individual members to share their ideas and insights more freely with other members (Dirks & Ferrin, 2001). Accordingly, the open exchange of knowledge among diverse participants implies that the human capital development of all members will be enhanced by the creation of trusting atmosphere (Lipnack & Stamps, 2008).

Second, we theorize that team performance also contributes to human capital development. Individuals participating in effective distributed teams gain substantial experience and knowledge, both in the proper execution of distributed collaborations and through the more extensive exchange of knowledge associated with high-performing teams (Harvey et al., 2005). In low-performing teams, the experiences of individuals are less likely to result in novel insights that can be applied in subsequent collaborative undertakings. While our present analysis has primarily focused on the ways in which distributed teams can deploy the human capital of their members, a turn toward evaluating the development of human capital that results in distributed team environments would necessitate a consideration of the extensive literature on human capital valuation (e.g., Bontis & Fitz-Enz, 2002; Namasivayam & Denizci, 2006; Weisbrod, 1961).

Distributed Team Trust

The link between trust and performance articulated by our respondents—and the clear need to include trust in a revised research model based on our findings—similarly has relevant precedence in the research literature. Geographic distance makes it more challenging to create a shared understanding when team members are distributed around the globe and have few opportunities to interact face to face, rely heavily on technology to interact, and have cultural or language barriers (Cramton, 2001). There is continued recognition in the literature of the strategic role trust and control play in geographically distributed teams (Das & Teng, 1998; Iacono & Weisband, 1997; Jarvenpaa & Leidner, 1999). Trust is central to teamwork, leadership, and organizational culture (Fairholm, 1994; Ryan & Oestreich, 1998). A number of characteristics of distributed work could interfere with the development of perceived trustworthiness. When observing geographically distributed teams, Armstrong and Cole (2002) noted that distant team members had a more difficult time reconciling issues. Similarly, Straus and McGrath (1994) observed that distributed teams experienced more conflict than collocated groups because of the challenges they faced in sharing complex information. In addition to spanning geographic distances, these distributed teams are likely to be composed of people from different cultures, engendering cross-cultural exchange challenges (Olson & Olson, 2000).

Distributed Team Control

In addition to the role of trust on distributed team outcomes, our data clearly substantiated team members' appreciation for the role of controls. Das and Teng (1998) suggest that management control is a key source of confidence in partner cooperation. Similarly, our data suggest that management control is a key driver of distributed team performance. Control in teams represents a regulatory process by which the elements of a system are made more predictable through the establishment of standards in the pursuit of some desired objective (Leifer & Mills, 1996). As such, the purpose of control is to fashion activities in accordance with expectations so that the ultimate goals of the organization or team can be obtained.

The Link between Distributed Team Trust and Control

While our study suggests that trust and control need to be reflected in future research predicting distributed team performance, the literature substantiates that the interplay between these factors is anything but clear (Das & Teng, 1998; Morgeson, DeRue, & Karam, 2010). The question is whether or not the deployment of overt control damages trust among team members. As Argyris (1953) observed, the need for a managerial control mechanism may imply that one party does not trust the other. Consequently, the exercise of control may engender a negative cycle, tending toward diminished trust. Following this logic, control may have the potential to undermine the trust level in distributed teams. Indeed, Piccoli and Ives (2003) find that behavioral controls tend to reduce trust in distributed teams by highlighting occurrences of reneging or incongruence by individual team members.

A contrary stance holds that management control mechanisms, if used properly, may support the development of mutual trust (Goold & Campbell, 1987). The basic argument here is that because control mechanisms provide a documented record for those who perform well, trust between the parties will eventually be strengthened. Thus, a documented record and an objective evaluation process may be more conducive for generating trust than an undocumented, subjective evaluation process. Sitkin (1995) suggests that reliance on formal rules and standardized procedures can facilitate the development of trust in organizational settings. Das and Teng (1998) propose that the optimal choice of managerial control mechanisms is determined by team project characteristics (i.e., performance measurability and task configuration). This suggests the need for a fit between project characteristics and the management control mechanisms employed.

Management Processes

As noted above, the present research has highlighted two classes of higher-order managerial processes that may be relevant for distributed team performance. In this study, social relationship management processes constituted processes that facilitate motivation, purpose, sponsorship, and team building in a distributed team. Park, Spitzmuller, and DeShon (2013) suggest that team motivation is particularly critical in a sustainable team model. Project management processes constituted processes that facilitate communication, role clarity, goal clarity, and project leadership. Our findings indicate that the coincident execution of these process mechanisms better predicts and operationalizes team achievement than do technology and enabling process alone. As illustrated in Table 2.3, we find that the literature amply substantiates the relationships our study revealed between these two classes of process and the factors of distributed team trust and control, and by extension team performance and human capital development.

Limitations

As with any research, our study has a number of limitations that must be acknowledged. While our research aims at *theoretical* or *analytical* generalizability (Eisenhart, 2008; Yin, 2003) rather than probabilistic or statistical

Table 2.3 Management processes and distributed team trust

Management processes	*Selected relevant literature*	
	Distributed team trust	*Distributed team control*
Motivation	Griffith and Luck (2003) utilize the notions of motivation and trust in engendering successful cooperation between self-interested agents. Motivations provide a means for representing and reasoning about agents' overall objectives, and trust offers a mechanism for modeling reliability.	Steinfield et al. (1999) report the need for facilitating mechanisms to generate motivation and interaction when team members are temporally distributed. Kirkman et al. (2004) state that intrinsic motivation through team empowerment becomes more critical in distributed teams.
Purpose	Prusak and Cohen (2001) argue that a powerful sense of higher organizational purpose can foster trust and a sense of duty. Lipnack and Stamps (1997) see purpose as the essence of a distributed team, and the best predictor of success.	Hofner-Saphiere (1996) notes that teams typically find that gaining alignment and commitment to their purpose is more challenging for distributed teams
Sponsorship	Cornwell and Maignan (1998) report that the construction of alliances around common sponsorship will help generate trust and commitment between those agents	Sharifi and Pawar (2002) report that commitment and sponsorship of top management is a major element in successful distributed team implementation
Team building	Quick (1992) states that team building helps a group function as a unit—it fosters morale, trust, cohesiveness, communication, and productivity	O'Reilly and Chatman (1996) state that organizational culture developed through team building creates a sense of control, facilitating a higher level of behavioral predictability
Role/goal clarity	Nemiro (2001) suggests that key factors in effective distributed teams have been establishing goal and role clarity, and a sense of trust among distributed team	Das and Teng (1998) suggest that clear goals are important for formal control mechanisms because they specify what is expected of each role or partner
Communications	Thomas and Trevino (1993) report that proactive information exchange is an effective tactic to boost trust among partners	Piccoli et al. (2004) find the impact of controls on member satisfaction in distributed teams is fully mediated by communication effectiveness
Leadership	Martin (1999) defines leadership as a driving force in organizational change, noting the inextricability of leadership and trust	Thite (1999) suggests the importance of leadership as a critical success factor in technical project management
Accountability	Friedman et al. (1999) explore the impact of electronic media on trust and accountability, and whether and how to increase deserved trust and accountability	Das and Teng (1998) suggests structural arrangements, including accountability, rules, and regulations, are the heart of formal control

generalizability, the characteristics of our data set imply certain limits on the generalizability of findings. Interviewees were selected from a single organization (i.e., the Operational Support Systems Wing of the US Air Force), whose members are distributed across three major locations. While the experience base of subjects varied with respect to age, number of experiences, length of project, and type of projects, the respondent pool did not include a significant representation of ethnic minorities or diverse nationalities. Distributed team outcomes were only viewed from the eyes of individual respondents; feedback from multiple perspectives could have lent insight into other phenomena beyond those that emerged in this study. Finally, the research required respondents to recall historical experiences. Some of these were recent while others transpired as long as five years prior to data collection. It is recognized that such data may be compromised by the effects of time on memory. However, while some researchers argue for interviewing based on recent events to ensure accuracy, others prefer historical accounts drawing on the benefits of "hindsight" (Folkman & Moskowitz, 2004).

Conclusion

This study assessed the impact of technology and traditional project processes on trust, human capital deployment, and project performance in distributed teams. The resulting empirical findings reveal that technology is a required, but not sufficient, element to ensure consistent distributed team performance. While distributed teams offer the promise of access to a broader base of human capital, our study underscores the diverse processes necessary to leverage those intellectual resources to enhance the performance of projects and organizations. We find that traditional enabling processes, originally developed for collocated teams, were generally insufficient for supporting distributed team members. Such processes were also significantly deficient in the mechanics required to develop and nurture interpersonal relationships between remote team members. Such process deficiencies reported by respondents resulted in lower levels of project trust and control, and consequently low distributed team performance.

The findings suggest the need for organizations employing distributed teams to place a heavy emphasis on the social needs of distributed team members by providing a consistent motivation for individual contribution, establishing a broader sense of purpose among team members, establishing clear sponsorship for the effort, and enabling members to create a group identity through team-building efforts. In addition, distributed teaming organizations must provide sufficient project management structure by having a formally recognized project manager, fostering a sense of personal accountability, establishing explicit norms for communication, and maintaining clarity around individual roles and shared project goals.

We conclude the study with an indication of plans for subsequent research. This research program includes the articulation of a grounded theoretical model that is amenable to variance-based quantitative research. Our research suggests that there is still little industry awareness that management processes for collocated team projects are not sufficient for consistently successful distributed team projects. We anticipate that additional research will help to clarify the dynamic nature, balance, and interdependence of trust, control, and human capital development in distributed team environments.

Notes

1. Along with others, Kelsey (1999) specifically uses the label of "virtual teams" for these computer-mediated teaming conditions. While the two terms are used interchangeably, in this analysis, we opt for the label of "distributed team." As such teaming environments have become more commonplace, the continued use of the term "virtual team" raises questions regarding the *degree of virtualness* (Martins, Gilson, & Maynard, 2004), which are not relevant for the present analysis.
2. The related concept of *social capital* focuses on the productive knowledge that resides within the networks of relationships among individuals (Coleman, 1988; Nahapiet & Ghoshal, 1998; Subramaniam & Youndt, 2005). While social capital has some applicability to our analysis, the concept has been criticized on the grounds that it is frequently amorphous in application, with an absence of clear demarcation or contextual boundaries (Johnston & Percy-Smith, 2003; Portes, 2000). Accordingly, in the present analysis, we opt for the principle of human capital in discussing the intellectual resources developed and leveraged in distributed team environments.

References

Adam, M. S., & Urquhart, C. (2009). No man is an island: Social and human capital in IT capacity building in the Maldives. *Information and Organization, 19*(1), 1–21.

Argyris, C. (1953). Human problems with budgets. *Harvard Business Review, 31*, 97–110.

Armstrong, D., & Cole, P. (2002). Managing distances and differences in geographically distributed work groups. In P. Hinds & S. Kiesler (Eds.), *Distributed Work* (pp. 167–186). Cambridge, MA: The MIT Press.

Aubert, B. A., & Kelsey, B. L. (2003). Further understanding of trust and performance in virtual teams. *Small Group Research, 34*(5), 575.

Bailey, D. E., Leonardi, P. M., & Barley, S. R. (2012). The lure of the virtual. *Organization Science, 23*(5), 1485–1504.

Becker, G. S. (2009). *Human Capital: A Theoretical and Empirical Analysis with Special Reference to Education* (3rd Edition). Chicago, IL: University of Chicago Press.

Bell, B. S., & Kozlowski, S. W. J. (2002). A typlogy of virtual teams: Implications for effective leadership. *Group and Organization Management, 27*(1), 14–49.

Bontis, N., & Fitz-Enz, J. (2002). Intellectual capital ROI: A causal map of human capital antecedents and consequents. *Journal of Intellectual Capital, 3*(3), 223–247.

Bos, N., Olson, J., Gergle, D., Olson, G., & Wright, Z. (2002). "Effects of four computer-mediated communications channels on trust development." Proceedings of the SIGCHI Conference on Human Factors in Computing Systems, Minneapolis, MN.

Bradach, J., & Eccles, R. (1989). Markets versus hierarchies: From ideal types to plural forms. *Annual Review of Sociology, 15*(1), 97–118.

Chuang, C.-H., Jackson, S. E., & Jiang, Y. (2013). Can knowledge-intensive teamwork be managed? Examining the roles of HRM systems, leadership, and tacit knowledge. *Journal of Management*, doi: 10.1177/0149206313478189.

Coleman, J. S. (1988). Social capital in the creation of human capital. *American Journal of Sociology, 94*, S95–S120.

Cornwell, T., & Maignan, I. (1998). An international review of sponsorship research. *Journal of Advertising, 27*(1), 1–21.

Cramton, C. D. (2001). The mutual knowledge problem and its consequences for dispersed collaboration. *Organization Science, 12*(3), 346–371.

Cummings, L., & Bromiley, P. (1996). The organizational trust inventory (OTI): Development and validation. In R. Kramer & T. Tyler (Eds.), *Trust in Organizations: Frontiers of Theory and Research* (pp. 302–329). Thousand Oaks, CA: Sage Publications.

Daft, R., Lengel, R., & Trevino, L. (1987). Message equivocality, media selection, and manager performance: Implications for information systems. *MIS Quarterly, 11*(3), 355–366.

Daim, T. U., Ha, A., Reutiman, S., Hughes, B., Pathak, U., Bynum, W., & Bhatla, A. (2012). Exploring the communication breakdown in global virtual teams. *International Journal of Project Management, 30*(2), 199–212.

Das, T., & Teng, B. (1998). Between trust and control: Developing confidence in partner cooperation in alliances. *Academy of Management Review, 23*(3), 491–512.

DeRue, D. S., & Ashford, S. J. (2010). Who will lead and who will follow? A social process of leadership identity construction in organizations. *Academy of Management Review, 35*(4), 627–647.

Dirks, K. (1999). The effects of interpersonal trust on work group performance. *Journal of Applied Psychology, 84*(3), 445–455.

Dirks, K., & Ferrin, D. (2001). The role of trust in organizational settings. *Organization Science, 12*(4), 450–467.

Duarte, D. L., & Snyder, N. T. (2006). *Mastering Virtual Teams: Strategies, Tools, and Techniques That Succeed* (2nd Edition). San Francisco, CA: Jossey-Bass.

Dubé, L., & Paré, G. (2001). Global virtual teams. *Communications of the ACM, 44*(12), 71–73.

Dwyer, C., Hiltz, S., & Passerini, K. (2007). "Trust and privacy concern within social networking sites: A comparison of Facebook and Myspace." Proceedings of the Americas Conference on Information Systems (AMCIS'07), Keystone, CO.

Eisenhart, M. (2008). Generalization from qualitative inquiry. In K. Ercikan & W.-M. Roth (Eds.), *Generalizing from Educational Research: Beyond Qualitative and Quantitative Polarization* (pp. 51–66). New York, NY: Taylor & Francis.

Fairholm, G. (1994). *Leadership and the Culture of Trust.* Westport, CT: Greenwood Publishing Group.

Feng, J., Lazar, J., & Preece, J. (2004). Empathic and predictable communication influences online interpersonal trust. *Behavior and Information Technology, 23*(2), 97–106.

Flamholtz, E. (1999). *Human Resource Accounting: Advances in Concepts, Methods, and Applications* (3rd Edition). Norwell, MA: Kluwer Academic Publishers.

Folkman, S., & Moskowitz, J. (2004). Coping: Pitfalls and promise. *Annual Review of Psychology, 55*(1), 745–774.

Friedman, B., Thomas, J., Grudin, J., Nass, C., Nissenbaum, H., Schlager, M., & Shneiderman, B. (1999). Trust me, I'm accountable: trust and accountability online. Proceedings of the ACM SIGCHI Conference on Human Factors in Computing Systems. Pittsburgh, PA.

Fulk, J., & DeSanctis, G. (1995). Electronic communication and changing organizational forms. *Organization Science, 6*(4), 337–349.

Glaser, B., & Strauss, A. (1967). *The Discovery of Grounded Theory: Strategies for Qualitative Research.* Chicago, IL: Aldine Publishing Company.

Goold, M., & Campbell, A. (1987). *Strategies and Styles: The Role of the Centre in Managing Diversified Corporations.* Oxford: Blackwell Publishing.

Griffiths, N., & Luck, M. (2003). Coalition formation through motivation and trust. Proceedings of the 2nd International Joint Conference on Autonomous Agents and Multiagent Systems. Melbourne, Australia.

Harvey, M., Novicevic, M. M., & Garrison, G. (2005). Global virtual teams: A human resource capital architecture. *International Journal of Human Resource Management, 16*(9), 1583–1599.

Henry, J., & Hartzler, M. (1998). *Tools for Virtual Teams: A Team Fitness Companion.* Milwaukee, WI: ASQ Quality Press.

Hertel, G., Geister, S., & Konradt, U. (2005). Managing virtual teams: A review of current empirical research. *Human Resource Management Review, 15*(1), 69–95.

Hinds, P. J., & Bailey, D. E. (2003). Out of sight, out of sync: Understanding conflict in distributed teams. *Organization Science, 14*(6), 615–632.

Hofner-Saphiere, D. (1996). Productive behaviors of global business teams. *International Journal of Intercultural Relations, 20*(2), 227–259.

Horwitz, F. M., Bravington, D., & Silvis, U. (2006). The promise of virtual teams: Identifying key factors in effectiveness and failure. *Journal of European Industrial Training, 30*(6), 472–494.

Hsu, I. (2008). Knowledge sharing practices as a facilitating factor for improving organizational performance through human capital: A preliminary test. *Expert Systems with Applications, 35*(3), 1316–1326.

Iacono, C. S., & Weisband, S. (1997, January 7–10). "Developing trust in virtual teams." Paper presented at the Thirtieth Hawaii International Conference on System Sciences, Wailea, HI.

Jarvenpaa, S. L., & Leidner, D. E. (1999). Communication and trust in global virtual teams. *Organization Science, 10*(6), 791–815.

Johnston, G., & Percy-Smith, J. (2003). In search of social capital. *Policy and Politics, 31*(3), 321–334.

Kanawattanachai, P., & Yoo, Y. (2002). Dynamics of trust in virtual teams. *Journal of Strategic Information Systems, 11*(3/4), 187–213.

Kayworth, T. R., & Leidner, D. E. (2001). Leadership effectiveness in global virtual teams. *Journal of Management Information Systems, 18*(3), 7–40.

Kelsey, B. (1999). "Trust as the foundation of cooperation and performance in virtual teams." Proceedings of the Annual Conference of the Administrative Sciences Association of Canada, St. John, NB.

Kiesler, S., & Cummings, J. N. (2002). What do we know about proximity and distance in work groups? A legacy of research. In P. Hinds & S. Kiesler (Eds.), *Distributed Work* (pp. 57–82). Cambridge, MA: The MIT Press.

Kirkman, B., Rosen, B., Tesluk, P., & Gibson, C. (2004). The impact of team empowerment on virtual team performance: The moderating role of face-to-face interaction. *Academy of Management Journal, 47*(2), 175–192.

Knoll, K., & Jarvenpaa, S. L. (1998). Working together in global virtual teams. In M. Igbaria & M. Tan (Eds.), *The Virtual Workspace* (pp. 2–23). Hershey, PA: Idea Group Publishing.

Latané, B., Liu, J., Nowak, A., Bonevento, M., & Zheng, L. (1995). Distance matters: Physical space and social impact. *Personality and Social Psychology Bulletin, 21*(8), 795–805.

Leifer, R., & Mills, P. (1996). An information processing approach for deciding upon control strategies and reducing control loss in emerging organizations. *Journal of Management, 22*(1), 113–137.

Lin, C.-P., Wang, Y.-J., Tsai, Y.-H., & Hsu, Y.-F. (2010). Perceived job effectiveness in coopetition: A survey of virtual teams within business organizations. *Computers in Human Behavior, 26*(6), 1598–1606.

Lipnack, J., & Stamps, J. (1997). *Virtual Teams: Reaching across Space, Time, and Organizations with Technology*. New York, NY: Wiley & Sons, Inc.

Lipnack, J., & Stamps, J. (2008). *Virtual Teams: People Working across Boundaries with Technology*. New York, NY: John Wiley & Sons.

Majchrzak, A., Rice, R., Malhotra, A., King, N., & Ba, S. (2000). Technology adaptation: The case of a computer-supported inter-organizational virtual team. *MIS Quarterly, 24*(4), 569–600.

Mårtensson, M. (2000). A critical review of knowledge management as a management tool. *Journal of Knowledge Management, 4*(3), 204–216.

Martin, M. (1999). Trust leadership. *Journal of Leadership and Organizational Studies, 5*(3), 41–49.

Martins, L. L., Gilson, L. L., & Maynard, M. T. (2004). Virtual teams: What do we know and where do we go from here? *Journal of Management, 30*(6), 805–835.

Maynard, M. T., Mathieu, J. E., Rapp, T. L., & Gilson, L. L. (2012). Something(s) old and something(s) new: Modeling drivers of global virtual team effectiveness. *Journal of Organizational Behavior, 33*(3), 342–365.

Meyerson, D., Weick, K., & Kramer, R. (1996). Swift trust and temporary groups. In R. M. Kramer & T. R. Tyler (Eds.), *Trust in Organizations: Frontiers of Theory and Research* (pp. 166–195). Thousand Oaks, CA: Sage Publications.

Mintzberg, H., Raisinghani, D., & Theoret, A. (1976). The structure of "unstructured" decision processes. *Administrative Science Quarterly, 21*(2), 246–275.

Montoya-Weiss, M. M., Massey, A. P., & Song, M. (2001). Getting it together: Temporal coordination and conflict management in global virtual teams. *Academy of Management Journal, 44*(6), 1251–1262.

Morgeson, F. P., DeRue, D. S., & Karam, E. P. (2010). Leadership in teams: A functional approach to understanding leadership structures and processes. *Journal of Management, 36*(1), 5–39.

Mowshowitz, A. (1997). Virtual organization. *Communications of the ACM, 40*(9), 30–37.

Nahapiet, J., & Ghoshal, S. (1998). Social capital, intellectual capital, and the organizational advantage. *Academy of Management Review, 23*(2), 242–266.

Namasivayam, K., & Denizci, B. (2006). Human capital in service organizations: Identifying value drivers. *Journal of Intellectual Capital, 7*(3), 381–393.

Nardi, B., & Whittaker, S. (2002). The place of face-to-face communication in distributed work. In P. Hinds & S. Kiesler (Eds.), *Distributed Work* (pp. 83–112). Cambridge, MA: The MIT Press.

Nemiro, J. (2001). Connection in creative virtual teams. *Journal of Behavioral and Applied Management, 3*(2), 92–112.

Nohria, N., & Eccles, R. G. (1992). Face-to-face: Making network organizations work. In N. Nohria & R. G. Eccles (Eds.), *Networks and Organizations: Structure, Form, and Action.* Boston, MA: Harvard Business School Press.

O'Reilly, C., & Chatman, J. (1996). Culture as social control: Corporations, cults, and commitment. *Research in Organizational Behavior, 18*, 157–200.

Olson, G., & Olson, J. (2000). Distance matters. *Human-Computer Interaction, 15*(2), 139–178.

Park, G., Spitzmuller, M., & DeShon, R. P. (2013). Advancing our understanding of team motivation: Integrating conceptual approaches and content areas. *Journal of Management, 39*(5), 1339–1379.

Parks, M., & Floyd, K. (1996). Making friends in cyberspace. *Journal of Communication, 46*(1), 80–97.

Piccoli, G., & Ives, B. (2003). Trust and the unintended effects of behavior control in virtual teams. *MIS Quarterly, 27*(3), 365–395.

Piccoli, G., Powell, A., & Ives, B. (2004). Virtual teams: Team control structure, work processes, and team effectiveness. *Information Technology and People, 17*(4), 359–379.

Poole, M. S., & Zhang, H. (2005). Virtual teams. In S. A. Wheelan (Ed.), *Handbook of Group Research and Practice* (pp. 363–384). Thousand Oaks, CA: Sage Publications.

Portes, A. (2000). Social capital: Its origins and applications in modern sociology. In E. L. Lesser (Ed.), *Knowledge and Social Capital: Foundations and Applications* (pp. 43–67). Boston, MA: Butterworth-Heinemann.

Powell, A., Piccoli, G., & Ives, B. (2004). Virtual teams: A review of current literature and directions for future research. *ACM Sigmis Database, 35*(1), 6–36.

Powell, W. (1990). Neither market nor hierarchy: Network forms of organization. *Research in Organizational Behavior, 12*, 295–336.

Privman, R., Hiltz, S. R., & Wang, Y. (2013). In-group (us) versus out-group (them) dynamics and effectiveness in partially distributed teams. *IEEE Transactions on Professional Communication, 56*(1), 33–49.

Prusak, L., & Cohen, D. (2001). How to invest in social capital. *Harvard Business Review, 79*(6), 86–97.

Quick, T. (1992). *Successful Team Building*. New York, NY: Amacom Books.

Ryan, K., & Oestreich, D. (1998). *Driving Fear Out of the Workplace: Creating the High-Trust, High-Performance Organization*. San Francisco, CA: Jossey-Bass.

Sally, D. (1995). Conversation and cooperation in social dilemmas: A meta-analysis of experiements from 1958 to 1992. *Rationality and Society, 7*(1), 58–92.

Sarker, S., Ahuja, M., Sarker, S., & Kirkeby, S. (2011). The role of communication and trust in global virtual teams: A social network perspective. *Journal of Management Information Systems, 28*(1), 273–310.

Schweitzer, L., & Duxbury, L. (2010). Conceptualizing and measuring the virtuality of teams. *Information Systems Journal, 20*(3), 267–295.

Sharifi, S., & Pawar, K. (2002). Virtually co-located product design teams: Sharing teaming experiences after the event? *International Journal of Operations and Production Management, 22*(6), 656–679.

Sitkin, S. (1995). On the positive effects of legalization on trust. *Research on Negotiation in Organizations, 5*, 185–218.

Sproull, L., & Kiesler, S. (1991). Computers, networks and work. *Scientific American, 265*, 116–123.

Steinfield, C., Jang, C., & Pfaff, B. (1999). Supporting virtual team collaboration: The TeamSCOPE system. Proceedings of the International ACM SIGGROUP Conference on Supporting Group Work. Phoenix, AZ.

Stevens, R., Papka, M., & Disz, T. (2003). Prototyping the workspaces of the future. *IEEE Internet Computing, 7*(4), 51–58.

Straus, S., & McGrath, J. (1994). Does the medium matter? The interaction of task type and technology on group performance and member reactions. *Journal of Applied Psychology, 79*(1), 87–97.

Strauss, A., & Corbin, J. (1990). *Basics of Qualitative Research: Grounded Theory Procedures and Techniques*. Newbury Park, CA: Sage Publications.

Subramaniam, M., & Youndt, M. A. (2005). The influence of intellectual capital on the types of innovative capabilities. *Academy of Management Journal, 48*(3), 450–463.

Sundstrom, E., De Meuse, K., & Futrell, D. (1990). Work teams: Applications and effectiveness. *American Psychologist, 45*(2), 120–133.

Tannenbaum, S. I., Mathieu, J. E., Salas, E., & Cohen, D. (2012). Teams are changing: Are research and practice evolving fast enough? *Industrial and Organizational Psychology, 5*(1), 2–24.

Thite, M. (1999). Identifying key characteristics of technical project leadership. *Leadership and Organization Development Journal, 20*(5), 253–261.

Thomas, D. M., & Bostrom, R. P. (2010a). Team leader strategies for enabling collaboration technology adaptation: Team technology knowledge to improve globally distributed systems development work. *European Journal of Information Systems, 19*(2), 223–237.

Thomas, D. M., & Bostrom, R. P. (2010b). Vital signs for virtual teams: An empirically developed trigger model for technology adaptation interventions. *MIS Quarterly, 34*(1), 115–142.

Thomas, J., & Trevino, L. (1993). Information processing in strategic alliance building: A multiple case approach. *Journal of Management Studies, 30*(5), 779–814.

Townsend, A. M., DeMarie, S. M., & Hendrickson, A. R. (1998). Virtual teams: Technology and the workplace of the future. *Academy of Management Executive, 12*(3), 17–29.

Vallor, S. (2010). Social networking technology and the virtues. *Ethics and Information Technology, 12*(2), 157–170.

Walther, J. (1997). Group and interpersonal effects in international computer mediated collaboration. *Human Communication Research, 23*(3), 342–369.

Weick, K. E., & Roberts, K. H. (1993). Collective mind in organizations: Heedful interrelating on flight decks. *Administrative Science Quarterly, 38*(3), 357–381.

Weisbrod, B. A. (1961). The valuation of human capital. *Journal of Political Economy, 69*(5), 425–436.

Yin, R. K. (2003). *Case Study Research: Design and Methods.* Thousand Oaks, CA: Sage Publications.

Zakaria, N., Amelinckx, A., & Wilemon, D. (2004). Working together apart? Building a knowledge-sharing culture for global virtual teams. *Creativity and Innovation Management, 13*(1), 15–29.

Zolin, R., Hinds, P., Fruchter, R., & Levitt, R. (2004). Interpersonal trust in cross-functional, geographically distributed work: A longitudinal study. *Information and Organization, 14*(1), 1–26.

CHAPTER 3

Perspectives on Human Capital Initiatives

Alyssa Danielson

Introduction

The speed of technology, availability of information, and globalization have forced firms to view their human capital as an asset. With human capital being considered an asset, best modes of management must be examined to ensure it is being properly utilized and realizing the greatest value possible. The question then is the following: how does a firm know they are using their human capital properly, or if they are getting the greatest value from this intangible asset? To answer these questions, it poses the need for a firm's human resources (HR) management to be mindful of the impact that it can have on everyday operations.

Over the years, HR has transitioned from administrative support with traditional roles such as recruiting, selection, placement, and retention, to the present where HR has to become a strategic leader, and aid in the development and retention of a firm's most valuable asset, human capital. Therefore, the purpose of this chapter is to offer a clear definition of what constitutes human capital (HC) from an HR management perspective. Most importantly, we will discuss the implications HR management has on a firm's HC and workforce by implementing selective initiatives. To begin the chapter we will briefly discuss the history of the term "capital" in reference to HC as an asset. From there we will discuss what HR management is, and the different attributes of it at the macro, meso, and micro levels. This discussion is important to linking HR management to human capital valuation and management, and the following will explain why. We will utilize and describe theories to support the notion that HR management is a strategic partner in increasing the value of a firm's human capital.

Defining Human Capital as an Asset

To define human capital today, we will first look to the time when scholars began conceptualizing the term capital, and a time many scholars reference today. We go to the late 1700s, where Adam Smith, a pioneer of the political economy, provided the first concepts of capital, which gave rise to the modern notion of human capital (Library of Economics and Liberty, 2008). Smith has been cited in numerous works of many influential economists from Karl Marx to Irving Fisher and Milton Friedman in the twentieth century (Fisher, 1906; Library of Economics and Liberty, 2008). Many human capital theorists utilized concepts from Smith, and from the early 1900s, Fisher, an American economist, shed light on a new concept of human capital as an asset. This concept was elaborated upon in a book Fisher had published, *The Nature of Capital and Income* (Library of Economics and Liberty, 2008).

Fisher's goal was to provide a general foundation of economic structures, and to form a philosophy of economic accounting (Fisher, 1906). He hoped it would supply a link missing between the ideas and usages of fundamental business transactions, as well as the theories of conceptual economics (Fisher, 1906). In this book Fisher emphasized the importance of income and the role it plays in all economic problems: it is why capital exists; it is the income for labor put forth; it creates the inequality between the wealthy and less fortunate (Fisher, 1906).

Fisher brought attention to the various terms that can be used in place of capital. He stated that resources, assets, utility, and desirability could be used interchangeably with the term capital, which can mean capital value or capital goods (Fisher, 1906). Fisher also highlighted the terms of stock, or fund, as a measurement for the quantity of wealth, as well as flow, or stream (Fisher, 1906). Capital is stock while income is the flow (Fisher, 1906). The proposed concept of capital by Fisher was simple—"a quantity, or stock, of wealth at an instant of time" (Fisher, 1906, p. 58).

Applying this concept to organizations today, the stock and flow of assets help determine an organization's value. From the term capital, one is able to utilize it to measure the quantity of capital by defining where the value is, what the income wealth is, and what service produces the income resulting in wealth (Fisher, 1906). With this concept applied to human capital, employees are an organization's stock of wealth, and the services the employees provide bring income to the organization (Erikson & Nerdrum, 2001). This basic concept provides a link Fisher had desired. It allows one to conceptualize the idea in which organizations can place a value on their employees and see them not as an expense, but as an asset.

Fischer's conclusion and concepts of capital were not universally accepted, nor were other theorists, as previously mentioned, Marx, Fischer, or Friedman. There was misalignment about the kinds of capital that could be considered wealth (Fisher, 1906). For this fact, Fisher went to Smith's definition of capital, as well as other capital theories, and melded them into one (Fisher, 1906). Smith's founding concept of capital—wealth that brings income (Library of Economics and Liberty, 2008)—had the source idea of capital being an interest that brings forth an amount of money (Bohm-Bawerk, 1891). Smith's initial theory is so simple, yet it continues to be referenced and proved as a great foundation.

Fischer took a similar approach as Smith's in order to conceptualize capital in a more encompassing way. There were many concepts and theories of capital that Fisher took to compile in a new basic theory of capital that was "all inclusive" (Erikson & Nerdrum, 2001). What Fisher did was something the other capital theorist did not. He accepted everyone's concept, rather than arguing why one was wrong and theirs right, and took out the overlapping ideas to produce a basic framework. Fisher thus cut through many controversies the capital theorist had on the nature of capital goods. He emphasized that all categories of stock would be capital when resulting in wealth, and even clearly included human beings (Erikson & Nerdrum, 2001). Table 3.1 depicts the differentiation of humans depicted as capital, and human capital.

Table 3.1 Dual-perspective differentiation of human capital

Financial	*Economical*
Capital instruments	Capital value
Human capital = owned physical asset	Human capital = knowledge, skills, abilities, and other characteristics
Complete rights	Partial rights
Taxation	No taxation
Tangible asset	Intangible asset
Homogeneous wealth	Heterogeneous wealth
Valued with depreciation	Trust/stock
Purchased	Production brings forth wealth, in debt to (In credit to human capital, difference made up with pay/salary)

Human Capital Theories

Human capital in an organization is still presented to the economy as an expense, which results in business leaders continuing to mismanage wealth-generating activities. Human capital has continually been diminished and improperly managed. A challenge for firms, in the management of human capital, has been due to the inability to define and categorize it within their organization. While theorists have reached the commonality that, from an HR perspective, human capital can be defined as the knowledge, skills, abilities, and other aspects (KSAOs), experience, and education firms possess through their employees, firms continue to manage HC as if this definition does not change their operations. For that reason, we will identify other commonly accepted theories of human capital to begin to understand the challenges firms face in the information age.

Human Capital Theory

Human capital theory (see Figure 3.1) suggests the basic premise that any stock of knowledge or characteristic the worker has, which contributes to his or her productivity, is considered capital (Campbell, Coff, & Kryscynski, 2012). While this definition is broad, it offers its advantages and disadvantages. One advantage it offers is that one can imply the generality that companies choose the amount of human capital investment they will make by evaluating the investment cost and the potential future benefits (Chen & Min, 2004). Also with the generality comes the need for assumption, and so in this theory we assume that human capital must contain both properties of asset specialized skills and nontransferability (Chen & Min, 2004). This means that a firm's human capital has knowledge and skills that would be difficult to transfer to another firm, if the asset were to separate from the firm.

The benefit this theory adds to the concept of human capital, as an asset, is the support it provides when determining what human capital can be.

Figure 3.1 Human capital theory process flow

Human capital theory does not express ways of evaluating human capital, or about how to measure the change an investment can make or has made in the value. This theory is a helpful baseline; there are many variables in human capital that leaders need to know, and have identified in order to manage effectively (Berggren & Bernshteyn, 2007).

In this concept, human capital is an individual's skills, experience, and knowledge that are utilized to generate economic value to a firm (Bontis & Fitz-enz, 2002), as well as the ability to be impacted by individuals who enhance their own human capital value through education and training (Chen & Min, 2004). Fisher's concept of capital states that income is the service of wealth, and thus the result. From this, human capital services are the foundation for the wealth-creating ability of a firm and should therefore be invested in by companies (Abhayawansa & Abeysekera, 2008). We have now given a reason why to invest, but another important question to answer is how to invest. This question will be addressed later in this chapter offering different methods of selection.

One basic principle of human capital theory is firms do not own the human capital that provides the service; individuals do (Bontis & Fitz-enz, 2002). While this theory does see human capital as an asset, it defines human capital from a micro approach and does not encompass the necessary dimensions firms need to articulate appropriately what the value of their human capital is. Thus, this theory inadequately explains how human capital contributes to achieving sustainable competitive advantage in firms, and we look to additional theories that are offered.

Resource-Based View Theory

The resource-based view theory has also been utilized to conceptualize human capital as an asset. This theory suggests a firm's unique internal resources can be configured in such a way for it to be a source of competitive advantage (Dunford, Snell, & Wright, 2001). This theory, depicted in Figure 3.2, proposes that firms can generate great profits by implementing strategies that develop valuable, rare, costly-to-imitate, and non-sustainable resources (Barney, 1991). This theory is derived from firm theory, which represents the perception that a firm is a collection of productive resources, and suggests it can be a significant driver of unit-level performance (Abhayawansa & Abeysekera, 2008; Moliterno & Polyhart, 2011). In this concept, the firm's human capital is to include only particular aspects of employee attributes (Abhayawansa & Abeysekera, 2008). Employee attributes are the resources a firm needs to generate a competitive advantage. Resources can be defined as a necessary constant input that enables a firm to perform a particular task

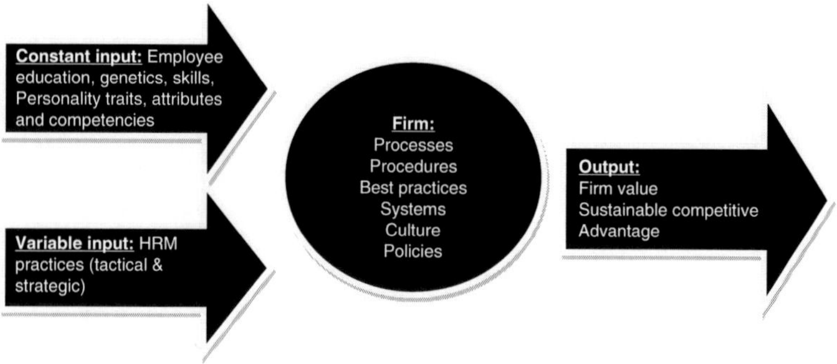

Figure 3.2 Resource-based view theory process flow

(Abhayawansa & Abeysekera, 2008). Resources in this theory are the fixed input and are the core skills of employees that are crucial to a company's competitive advantage, and this can be achieved through internal training and development (Chen & Min, 2004).

One of the more important factors of resource-based view is that a resource does not start as a competitive advantage for a firm. It must be developed to be unique, distinct, immobile, and irreplaceable, and to add value to the firm (Abhayawansa & Abeysekera, 2008). Resources must not only have those attributes; some argue that competitive advantage must come from the alignment of human capital with a firm's systems intentions in order to achieve the capabilities at the organizational level, for example, firm strategy (Dunford et al., 2001). It is the ability or competency of a firm to manage the use of resources that will drive firm competitive advantage (Moliterno & Polyhart, 2011).

This theory allows one to see human capital as an asset, a resource, and a process the firm owns, a process in which human capital resources drive KSAOs (Moliterno & Polyhart, 2011). With resource-based view theory, there is less focus on what human capital resources are, but more on how human capital resources can influence practices related to firm and individual unit performance. This theory also places importance on the firm's competencies, systems, and processes that employees carry out and which may result in a sustainable competitive advantage (Abhayawansa & Abeysekera, 2008). The systems and processes of a firm exist and evolve through strategic management. The strategic management of human capital as an asset is different from other assets. Therefore, a unique and specified approach should be taken to manage in order to leverage and drive firm value. For that, we look to HR management as a strategic partner to align the organizational systems and practices to leverage their value (Abhayawansa & Abeysekera, 2008). The function of HR in a firm should not be limited to the direct effects it has on employee skills and behavior, but HR management should be utilized to provide a strategic impact to a firm and their sustainable competitive advantage (Dunford et al., 2001). The function of HR must be being a strategic partner that employs initiatives to make a firm's human capital value increase and become a source of a sustainable competitive advantage.

The resource-based view provides a fundamental perspective, which suggests human capital is a class of resources, and it can be a proponent in driving individual and firm performance (Moliterno & Polyhart, 2011). This concept may seem simple, but scholars have already taken up this principle and applied it in new ways. It is used in addressing some of the concerns other human capital theories were not able to.

Human Capital Management

Human capital, from an HR perspective, can be defined as the knowledge, skills, abilities, and other aspects (KSAOs) encompassed by a firm or individual. Other aspects can include education, experience, values, and motivation. This definition is commonly accepted, but it was not reached easily. This definition has support by the theories discussed previously in this chapter.

Now, in the twenty-first century, we have reached a point where theories continuously show support to the notion that human capital can add value to a firm, and can be a resource to a competitive advantage. The keyword is "can." Several factors can affect human capital's adding value if it is not appropriately leveraged. For starters, a firm's human capital pool must have both high levels of ability and skill, as well as the willingness to carry out the necessary processes and procedures (Dunford et al., 2001). All firms have access to valuable human capital, but through either the mismanagement of resources and systems, or poor alignment of the strategic impact, its value may not be realized (Dunford et al., 2001).

For decades, scholars have attempted to define human capital, and have done so in numerous ways with several concepts and theories. Each approach sheds a different light on the many dimensions and complexities of human capital. Aside from the theories, human capital has also been conceptualized as the accumulation of personal attributes (i.e., knowledge, abilities, personality, health, etc.) that allow human beings to function (Campbell et al., 2012). In some human capital literature, there are specific indicators, such as entrepreneurial level of education, experience, and self-motivation, that have been suggested to be the ones adding value to a firm (Abhayawansa &

Abeysekera, 2008). Added to this, with the multilevel theory, genetic inheritance and one's attitude about life and business are added dimensions of human capital (Bontis & Fitz-enz, 2002; Moliterno & Polyhart, 2011).

Based on the notion that employees themselves are not the human capital, but the knowledge, skills, and abilities they possess are, employees contain the potential of being converted to human capital by being properly managed (Abhayawansa & Abeysekera, 2008). This entails great challenges, especially since a firm cannot own human capital—the individual owns it. Therefore, the practice of strategic HR management is being utilized. What we have discussed in this chapter, thus far, is not new information, or heavily disputed at that. So why did we go so much in depth? The reason is the importance it has on laying the foundation for the management of the intangible asset human capital. We cannot manage what we cannot see or define. Therefore, we began with the foundation to identify and differentiate human capital as an asset from an HR perspective. We will now begin to identify modes of management that can be employed to leverage human capital to achieve the greatest return.

Human capital has been defined at a micro level and approaches it in terms of the individual differences of KSAOs (Campbell et al., 2012). These KSAOs in turn have a link to an individual-level outcome (Moliterno & Polyhart, 2011). When human capital is defined at a macro level, it is seen as a meso-level resource that can contribute to a firm's sustainable competitive advantage (Moliterno & Polyhart, 2011). The macro unit-level perspective looks at human capital by unit and links it with the collective knowledge, skill, or experience held in the firm (Moliterno & Polyhart, 2011). The macro unit-level approach correlates back to concepts of resource-based view theory, wherein human capital can contribute to a firm's competitive advantage when it meets certain conditions: (1) employees have to add a positive value to the firm, (2) the skills and competencies held by employees must be unique and rare among existing and impending competitors; (3) the human capital stock embodied by the firm's employees must not have the ability to be imitated; and (4) a firm's human capital stock cannot be substituted by another source from another firm (Abhayawansa & Abeysekera, 2008). These conditions affect a firm in what they should consider when identifying and defining human capital.

Other variations of defining human capital in literature have been focused on defining different challenges and dimensions that impact the individual and collective firm human capital (Dunford et al., 2001). Training and development, entrepreneurial skills, equity issues, employee satisfaction, employee relations, employee welfare, and work environment are all attributes that can affect an individual and the firm (Abhayawansa & Abeysekera, 2008).

To begin with, the employee attributes start as experience, which has been described as one's collective skills and knowledge (Dunford et al., 2001). The collective skills and knowledge lead to one's potential of becoming human capital for a firm and adding value (Robinson, 2009). For one to become human capital at a firm, they must become a part of the firm's human capital pool through firm-specific training and development. The result for a firm can be a highly skilled and highly motivated workforce (Dunford et al., 2001). A firm's human capital pool has been identified as the determining factor of organization success or failure (Bontis & Fitz-enz, 2002).

From the varying definitions above, the underlying premise is that when appropriately utilized, human capital will add value to a firm. In order to determine this value, the firm must identify their human capital stock and give it a monetary value. Differences come in when determining a firm's human capital stock, beginning with how to categorize human capital stock or how to categorize levels of stock, along with determining if a firm's stock meets the certain conditions to be considered as a resource for competitive advantage. Each categorization has merit, and meets the same underlying goal. The reason for this is that there are several methods of categorization and definition, which creates several variables for one to measure and value. Without the categorization and variables to measure, a firm is unable to strategically measure and manage their human capital. The difference in each suggested human capital stock categorization is about how the accuracy and validity of the monetary values could be affected, as well as how a firm can utilize their human capital to create benefit.

From these theories, we are able to identify the responsibility of the organization and the responsibility of the employee. A firm has many restrictions, whether it is from federal laws and restrictions or if it is down to their own ethics and responsibility; an organization has many roadblocks that HR management can then provide strategic direction and policy for. A firm's HR management is there to protect not only the organization, but the employees as well. HR management is in place to ensure there are ethical practices put in place that follow the state and federal guidelines. Therefore, many of the practices carried out through HR management impact the value of human capital and the utilization of this asset, and selecting the practices or human capital initiatives is a challenge as well.

Human Resources Management

HR management can be defined as the management process of a firm's workforce activities. Managed activities are comprised of talent acquisition and development, including selection and training, as well as employee relations, performance management, and more specific activities such as succession planning, employee relations, as well as diversity and inclusion. These activities, up until recent years, have been diminished and not included in strategic planning, but as we further ourselves in the information age, it becomes apparent to organizations that great value comes from their employees, thus placing strategic importance on the role human resources management plays.

HR Policy, Practice, and Systems

Within the HR management process, numerous activities affect an organization at different levels. Due to legal and regulatory compliance, HR policies are derived, which are defined as systems of grouped decisions, and established by an organization to support administrative functions and manage a firm's employees (Anca-Ioana, 2013). We suggest there are three parts to the intention of HR policies: (1) lower employment and labor-related litigation, (2) advance performance through employee engagement, and (3) drive employee retention and attraction. Overall, HR policies are there to protect the company and provide "rules" to employees.

What firms must also consider is the strategic impact their policies have on their competitive advantage. For example, if one firm has a vacation policy that after five years of employment you are granted an additional week of vacation time, and a competitor down the street offers employees an additional week of vacation time at three years of employment, an employee may view the organization that offers an additional week of vacation at three years as a nicer place to work. This has the potential to result in an unaccepted offer of employment for a prospective employee, diminished motivation for a current employee, or worse turnover.

This simple example provides a larger meaning in this era of talent shortage and abundant information. It shows how a simple policy from HR can add to or take away from the information available to a firm. While there are HR policies, there are also HR practices, which are the procedures that carry out the policies. It has been suggested that the HR practices and procedures are the detail to particular methods for accomplishing a task, as well as support policies, and specify how policies are to be carried out (Fulmer & Ployhart, 2014). HR practices are used as the tools for building a firm's workforce so it can result in a competitive advantage. With HR practices there are also guidelines and standards, which are tools that, unlike policies, offer suggestive alternatives and preferences for action and behavior but do not indicate necessity. They provide an alternative to policies for issues that organizations want to address but are not a main influencing factor in the operations and employees.

Strategic HR Management

Strategic HR management has been defined by Wright and McMahan (1992) as a guide to the intended human resource initiatives and activities that allow the firm to achieve their strategic goals. From this definition, we can imply it to have four components. First, a firm's "human resources" is the main resource to be strategically leveraged as a source of competitive advantage. Second, the concept of "activities" highlights HR programs, policies, and practices as the means through which the people and firm can be deployed to gain competitive advantage. Third, a firm's "pattern" and "plan" should describe the goal and process of strategy, as well as designed to be aligned, or referred to as "fit" (P. Wright, 1998). Finally, within this definition, the people, practices, and systems have the purpose of achieving goals (P. Wright, 1998).

As research has progressed since this definition, and underlying components uncovered, we would argue that it is a firm's HC, not just a firm's "human resources," that must be leveraged in order to achieve a competitive advantage. While some may not think there is a difference, the change in variance is what truly is being managed. To say a firm's "human resources" are the main source of competitive advantage is saying all their people. When we say a firm's "human capital" is the main source of competitive advantage, that says the people who hold the most important KSAOs to firm performance are the main source of competitive advantage. By differentiating the two, the result would change the who, what, where, when, and why of the HR management practices and systems to be utilized.

Strategic HR management has also been defined as the usage of grouping HR practices, or high-performance work systems, which are utilized in the development of a human capital pool, increased employee motivation, and opportunities contributing to leading an organization's creation ability of sustainable competitive advantage. Another way strategic HR management has been defined is as the collection of practices, policies, and systems that facilitate the strategic objectives of the organizations (Anca-Ioana, 2013).

From these definitions, there are various common themes. The most notable common themes are the combination of policies, practices, and systems of HR management, and the importance of aligning them with business goals and objectives. It has been suggested that by creating horizontal internal alignment among the various HR practices, the practices would act as complements rather than compete with one another (Wrignt & McMahan, 1992). This concept is important as we look to other aspects of strategic HR management.

There are many concepts whereby strategic HR management provides a positive impact on several human capital theories. One concept has been posed suggesting the fields of strategy and strategic human resources to utilize the elements of core competencies, dynamic capabilities, and knowledge as a bridge to unite and apply to a firm's strategic systems and processes (Dunford et al., 2001). Strategic literature has a widely accepted concept of who or what provides a firm with a sustainable competitive advantage, and why. However, there have been minimal proposed techniques to obtain resources for a sustainable competitive advantage. That is where strategic HR management can collaborate and suggest concepts to identify the techniques a firm should use to obtain the necessary HC resources for a competitive advantage (Dunford et al., 2001).

Multilevel Analysis

Identifying which initiatives firm should use to gain a competitive advantage can be derived from the multilevel theory. The multilevel theory focuses on the micro-foundation looking at individual and strategic initiatives. It suggests putting more focus on the explanatory mechanisms, which potentially have been identified in strategic HR literature (Moliterno & Polyhart, 2011). Thus, there is importance to discussing the multi levels from an HR perspective.

Some would explain that HR management's macro- and micro-level concepts have developed in parallel and independently (P. Wright & L. Hisae Nishii, 2007). Thus, by utilizing the process of strategic HR management, we can begin to look at current information to join the independent paths and bridge the divide through multilevel analysis.

The macro level of HR is where internal and external factors influence the functional operations and strategic direction of an organization. For example, a firm must consider legal and regulatory compliance factors, and it must strategically align them with internal operations (Fulmer & Ployhart, 2014). A firm at this level is deriving their strategy to carry out the organizational plan. From the macro level, we go to the meso level. This level acts as a bridge to the micro level. At the meso level, functional units begin to differentiate and define policy of what theoretically should occur based on the macro level (P. Wright & L. Hisae Nishii, 2007). This level often is not differentiated, but we would argue this level is essential to separate in order to manage human capital from a multilevel perspective. The micro level is where the functional unit carries out their policies. It is through practices aligned and derived from the policies and theory that the micro level operates. Table 3.2 depicts the concept of beginning at the macro level and follows through the division of units to the micro level, which are the actual practices carried out by a firm's human capital.

Table 3.2 HR management perspective examples of multilevel activities involving human capital as an asset

Macro strategy	*Meso policy*	*Micro practice*
• National/economic • Workforce • Skill availability • Business competition • Employment and unemployment rate • Industry growth and sustainability • Politics • National economics • Global economics • Environment considerations • Global, federal, state, and local laws and regulations • Physical and social environment • Economic, social, and environmental performance • Business risk • Business opportunity • Renewable and nonrenewable resources • Human rights • Organization strategy • Organization goals	• Firm/operations • Operating system standards • Company values (intended) • Business ethics • Union rights • Financial resources • Social responsibility • Environmental responsibility • Workforce diversity • Employment brand • Human rights • Employee benefits and compensation • Disciplinary policies • Anti-sexual harassment policies • Employee relations • Employee training and development • Industrial hygiene • Legal compliance • Workplace safety • Talent acquisition and development • Employee handbook	• Individual/unit • Company culture (actual) • Work environment • Hiring practices • Job descriptions • Training programs • New hire orientation • Performance reviews • Management programs • Employee handbook interpretation and administration

HR Management Initiatives

So far, we discussed, numerous times and from numerous angles, the ability human capital has to become a source of a sustainable competitive advantage, and ability to increase the asset's value. What we have not addressed is how a firm goes about doing this. This is where we combine what we have learned about HR management from a macro-, meso-, and micro-level perspective, along with the policies, procedures, and systems that are implemented in a firm, and identify which modes of HR initiatives should be utilized under certain circumstances. Some would argue there has been minimal research in determining the amount of value different initiatives add, but what has been found is they do increase the value of a firm's human capital (Fulmer & Ployhart, 2014).

HR management initiatives are an integral part to increasing the value of human capital (Abhayawansa & Abeysekera, 2008; Baudry & Chassagnon, 2010; Bontis & Fitz-enz, 2002; Cheramie, Walsh, & Sturman, 2008; (Fulmer & Ployhart, 2014)). Specifically, human resource initiatives can be defined as the policies, procedures, and process and techniques utilized in managing a firm's human resources and human capital (Fulmer & Ployhart, 2014). HR initiatives occur at different levels of the organization and have different impacts on human capital. From internal influences such as leadership to the individual cognitive influences of the employees, there are numerous factors to consider when employing HR initiatives. Therefore, there is the need to understand the multilevel perspectives of HR management and human capital, and consider them when employing different HR initiatives. From here we will explore different methods and theories one may consider when selecting which HR initiatives to employ in which situations, and to evaluate current impact of HR policies and systems on a firm's operations.

Utility Analysis

The most often used tool for choosing among initiatives, in the past, is utility analysis (Fulmer & Ployhart, 2014). Utility analysis attempts to compute the economic value of HR-related investments or initiatives such as development and training, talent acquisition and selection, or employee satisfaction strategies. Thus, it is the equivalent to the economic contributions approach. This is where HR practices and policies are valued according to how successful they are in recognizing and modifying individual behaviors, which for human capital is looked to for future contributions (Steffy & Maurer, 1998).

While utility analysis is the most often used tool, even this tool is not the answer to aid in choosing among HR initiatives. For one, utility analysis is used to change expected behavioral impact into financial terms (Fulmer & Ployhart, 2014). This is based upon estimation and the change between what is expected with both internal and external factors. A utility analysis approach brings great skepticism to not only this area, but others as well. Other areas of concern that have been outlined include the actual value utility analysis provides to decision-making due to it being an estimation. Along with the fact that there are potential levels of analysis, utility analysis attempts to generalize at the individual (micro) level and misses the meso and macro organizational-economic levels (Fulmer & Ployhart, 2014). Utility analysis has not been all negative though; scholars have largely accepted the research around this concept to demonstrate HR initiatives produce monetary benefits (Fulmer & Ployhart, 2014; Steffy & Maurer, 1998).

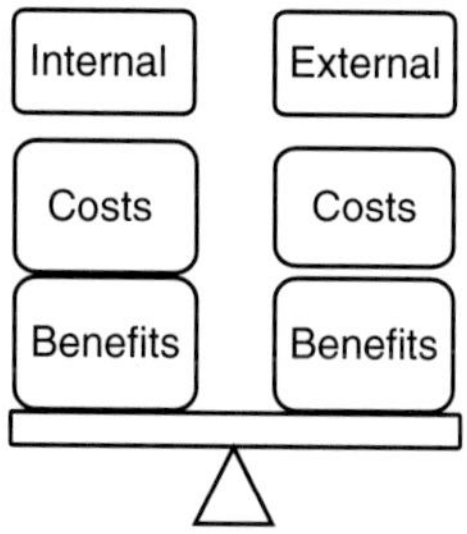

Figure 3.3 Transaction cost economics theory

Transaction Cost Economics Theory

The next theory we discuss is often cited, and is known as the transaction cost economics theory. This theory suggests that organizations want to employ their human talent in the most efficient way, and are faced with choices when doing so (Chen & Min, 2004). Ronald Coase first suggested transaction cost economics theory in 1937 (Williamson, 2010). Coase suggested this theory as a means to fill a gap between an accepted textbook theory of the firm and market organization (Williamson, 2010).

When applying human capital to this theory, it is the initiative of selecting talent, and deciding the mode in which the talent will be obtained. When seeking talent for a job opening, a firm is faced with two options or initiatives, one being to seek new talent externally or the other to seek internally and train/promote existing human talent, depicted in Figure 3.3. With both of these options, a firm will incur a variety of costs: external acquisition of talent incurs hiring costs (transaction costs), while training and promoting existing talent incur training and management as an expense (bureaucratic costs) (Chen & Min, 2004). Between these two options, a firm must choose which talent acquisition option or combination would be most beneficial by comparing all applicable costs and benefits (Chen & Min, 2004).

Coase's approach to the transaction cost economics theory and looking at a firm collectively allows one to consider the organizational dynamics within a firm (Baudry & Chassagnon, 2010). Therefore, Coase created a new perspective for theorists to recognize the dynamic challenges not only in the organizational structure, but also within the transactions of human capital.

Financial Management Approaches

There are also various financial measures that can be employed to aid in the selection of an HR initiative. Financial decision tools seek to review how a particular and known initiative will effect changes in the value of human capital resources (Fulmer & Ployhart, 2014). Some financial measures include measuring the net present value (NPV); a retrospective measure utilized can be the return on investment (ROI), which after the initiative is employed would measure the value change (Fulmer & Ployhart, 2014). While these financial measures are able to put monetary numbers to the change in human capital, they use retrospective data after a formal decision has been made. Therefore, this is still not a good tool in aiding in the selection of HR initiatives.

HR Initiative Selection

Based on our discussion outlined in this chapter, and the minimal tools to measure and aid HR partners and firm leadership in the selection of HR initiatives, we would suggest HR leaders and managers to use the following process, depicted in Figure 3.4. An organization's HR management, leaders,

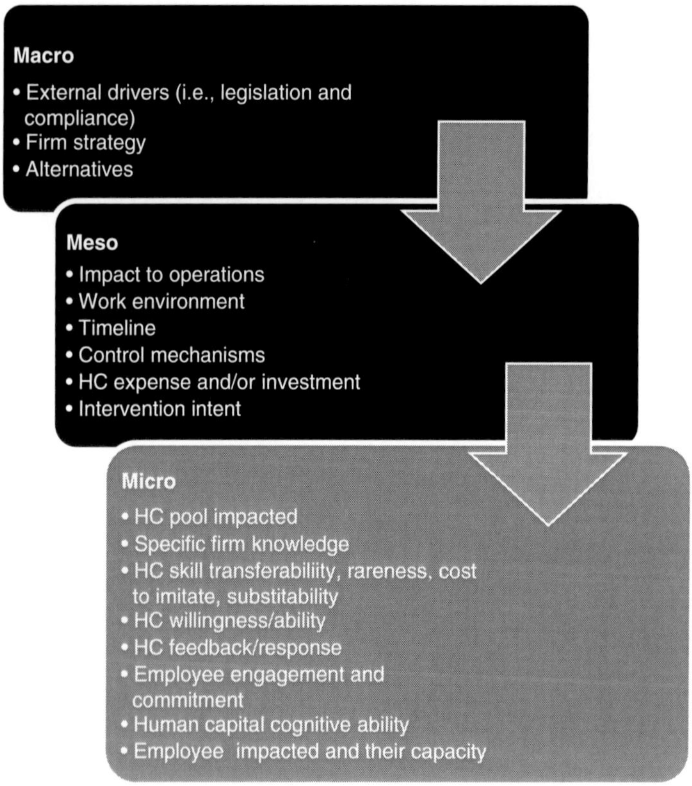

Figure 3.4 HR initiative selection analysis

and mangers can utilize this process when determining which HR initiatives to adjust or employ. The process takes a multilevel approach and begins by analyzing the macro-level factors that are driving the need for such HR initiative. From there we analyze the meso level and ensure alignment with firm strategy. Finally, the micro-level details analyze the findings from the meso-level analysis.

The ultimate goal of this analysis is to collect information for learning to occur. The learning to occur will aid HR management, leaders, and managers in making better HR initiative selections. By following this process for initiative selection, it would set some guidelines. Guidelines would create consistency and add the ability to measure change. Measuring change gives managers continued information for learning and thus continues to make informed decisions.

Essentially, we suggest a three-phase process in determining which HR initiative to employ or adapt to better fit the strategic need of the firm. Throughout this analysis process, one must begin with the end in mind, the end being increasing the value of a firm's HC and increase specialized knowledge of the firm through HR initiatives.

Conclusion

All the theories mentioned in this chapter have been instrumental in human capital literature and determining what is considered human capital, as well as the benefits human capital can provide to a firm from an HR perspective. Firms should not minimize and under-manage human capital. As our world evolves, so do our abilities, which should be reflected within a firm to ensure they are creating sustainable practices and systems. We began this chapter by discussing the history of defining the term capital and the modern notion of human capital.

We determined the definition of human capital is the KSAOs of an individual along with their experience, education, and willingness. Defining human capital was an important step in differentiating human capital as an asset, from a multilevel perspective to manage and leverage. As a part of defining human capital, we explored the human capital theory as well as resource-based view theory, which suggest human capital can be a resource for a sustainable competitive advantage if it is rare, is costly to imitate, has low substitutability, and has low transferability (Abhayawansa & Abeysekera, 2008).

Once we had human capital defined, we began to explore what human capital management meant. We suggest that human capital management is the process of identifying and defining a firm's human capital pool. One cannot manage what one cannot define. Therefore, managers must begin by understanding what their human capital is. From human capital management, we began to discuss HR management, which we defined as the process of a firm's workforce activities. This included talent acquisition and development, training, as well as performance management examples.

Within HR management, there are policies, practices, and systems that carry out workforce activities (Abhayawansa & Abeysekera, 2008). HR policies were defined as grouped decisions established by an organization to support administrative functions, which manage the firm's employees; policies have an intended purpose and are carried out through HR practices and procedures (Fulmer & Ployhart, 2014). Practices and procedures are guidelines for how policies are actually carried out and employed within a firm. The contribution of a firm's HR management policies, practices, and systems to human capital resources can provide a positive impact. One important factor identified was that HR initiatives alone could not form the foundation to a competitive advantage, because HR initiatives can easily be substituted or copied and used by others. Thus, for HR management to help leverage human capital and become a resource of a sustainable competitive advantage, it is argued that a firm's HR systems must be aligned with strategic goals and measured.

For this reason we began to identify how HR management initiatives should be selected; whether it is through utility analysis, or through ROI and NPV, these methods cannot appropriately value human capital. Therefore, it is difficult to manage. Thus, we have suggested an analysis approach. This approach takes a multilevel view and forces one to consider first the macro level, being the economy or job market, down to the micro level, analyzing the firm's employees and their abilities.

While the proposed HR initiative selection analysis does not provide a measure of HC either, it forces one to consider the complexity involved from a multilevel perspective. We are in the information age, surrounded by a global economy, and can no longer get by with only an individual (micro) perspective. We must identify the complexities of the multiple levels and ensure they are in alignment. From there we can begin to identify how to value and leverage human capital. This will result in the increased value of human capital and an opportunity for a sustainable competitive advantage.

References

Abhayawansa, S., & Abeysekera, I. (2008). An explanation of human capital disclosure from the resource-based perspective. *Journal of Human Resource Costing and Accounting, 12*(1), 51–64.

Anca-Ioana, M. (2013). New approaches of the concepts of human resources, human resource management, and strategic human resource managmenet. *Annals of the University of Oradea, Economic Series* (serial online), *22*(1), 1520–1525.

Barney, J. B. (1991). Firm resources and sustained competitive advantage. *Journal of Management, 17*, 99–120.

Baudry, B., & Chassagnon, V. (2010). The close relation between organization theory and Oliver Williamson's transaction cost economics: A theory of the firm perspective. *Journal of Institutional Economics, 6*(4), 477–503.

Berggren, E., & Bernshteyn, R. (2007). Organizational transparency drives company performance. *Journal of Management Development, 26*(5), 411–417.

Bohm-Bawerk, E. (1891). "Library of Economics and Liberty." Retrieved March 6, 2013, from *The Positive Theory of Capital.* Available at http://www.econlib.org/library/BohmBawerk/bbPTC0.html

Bontis, N., & Fitz-enz, J. (2002). Intellectual capital ROI: A causal map of human capital antecedents and consequents. *Journal of Intellectual Capital, 3*(3), 223–247.

Campbell, B., Coff, R., & Kryscynski, D. (2012). Rethinking sustained competitive advantage from human capital. *Academy of Management Review, 37*(3), 376–395.

Chen, H. M., & Min, K. J. (2004). The role of human capital cost in accounting. *Journal of Intellectual Capital, 5*(1), 116–130.

Cheramie, R., Walsh, K., & Sturman, M. (2008). The value of human capital specificity versus transferability. *Journal of Management, 34*(2), 290–316. Retrieved April 15, 2013. Available at http://jom.sagepub.com/content/34/2/290

Dunford, B., Snell, S., & Wright, P. (2001, December). Human resources and the resource based view of the firm. *Journal of Management, 27*(6), 701–721. Retrieved from http://jom.sagepub.com/content/27/6/701

Erikson, T., & Nerdrum, L. (2001). Intellectual capital: A human capital perspective. *Journal of Intellectual Capital, 2*(2), 127–135.

Fisher, I. (1906). *The Nature of Capital and Income.* Norwood, MA: The MacMillan Company.

Fulmer, I. S., & Ployhart, R. E. (2014). "Our most important asset": A multidisciplinary/multilevel review of human capital valuation for research and practice. *Journal of Management, 40*(1), 161–192, doi:10.1177/0149206313511271.

Library of Economics and Liberty (2008). The *Concise Encyclopedia of Economics.* Retrieved March 12, 2013, from page "Adam Smith." Available at http://www.econlib.org/library/Enc/bios/Smith.html

Moliterno, T., & Polyhart, R. (2011). Emergence of the human capital resource: A multilevel model. *Academy of Management Review, 36*(1), 127–150.

Robinson, D. (2009). Human capital measurement: An approach that works. *Strategic HR Review, 8*(6), 5–11, doi:10.1108/14754390910990937.

Steffy, B. D., & Maurer, S. D. (1998). Conceptualizing and measuring the economic effectiveness of human resource activities. *Academy of Management Review, 13*(2), 271–286.

Williamson, O. (2010, June). Transaction cost economics: The natural progression. *American Economic Review, 100*(3), 673–690. Retrieved May 2013. Available at http://www.aeaweb.org/articles.php?doi=10.1257/aer.100.3.673

Wright, P. (1998). Introduction: Strategic HR management research in the 21st century. *Human Resource Management Review, 8*(3), 187–191.

Wright, P., &. Hisae Nishii, L. (2007). "Strategic HRM and organizational behavior: Integrating multiple levels of analysis." Cornell University, School of Industrial and Labor Relations, Center for Advanced Human Resources Studies (CAHRS Working Paper #07-03). Available at http://digitalcommons.ilr.cornell.edu/cahrswp/468

Wright, P., & McMahan, G. (1992). Theoretical perspectives for human resource management. *Journal of Management, 18*, 295–320.

PART II

Valuation and Risk

CHAPTER 4

Models of Human Capital Valuation: A Review with Examples

Franko Milost

Introduction

A company is usually founded by individuals striving to achieve their own or broader goals. Goal achievement related to a company's operations is called business or the business process. There are four basic elements required for a business process, namely means of production, raw materials, services, and human capital (human potential, employees).

Human capital includes the employees' accumulated qualifications and competencies and also their motivation to use these (Becker, 1964; Schultz, 1961).

Several authors consider the importance of human capital (Chadwick & Dabu, 2009; Snell, Youndt, & Wright, 1996; Wright, Dunford, & Snell, 2001). Gamerschlag (2013, p. 327) states:

> Against the background of human capital theories and the resource-based view of the firm, human capital must be regarded as a central factor behind organizations' competitiveness.

However, apart from its role as a means of production and providing of services and products, its value is not disclosed on the assets side of the classical balance sheet.

Are there any solid grounds for such consideration of human capital? Does such consideration of human capital result from underestimating the meaning of this element of the business process? And finally, is not human capital a factor that has a crucial influence on successful business operations?

Such treatment of human capital stems from the belief that employees are not company assets. According to the classical model, an element can be treated as an asset only when

(a) there is a possibility that the presence of this element in a business process is associated with economic benefits, and
(b) the (purchase) value of this asset can be measured reliably.

As mentioned above, all four basic elements are crucial for a company's operations. This further means that their presence in a business process is associated with the achievement of economic benefits. Therefore, the first requirement does need to be elaborated further. This research is more directed at the search of answers associated with the second requirement presented above.

This text pleads for human resource accounting (accounting for people) approach, which "can be defined as the process of identifying, measuring and communicating information about human resources to decision makers" (Flamholtz, 1974, p. 44). An appropriate solution of the human capital valuation issue is essential for establishing this accounting approach.

How to define a relationship between the human resource accounting approach and the intellectual capital (IC) approach?

Intellectual capital seems to be a very popular topic in professional circles. Some questions have agitated both theoreticians and practitioners for more than two decades, and many papers have been published on this topic recently. However, although there are numerous fruitful discussions on the topic, some questions related to the concept of intellectual still remain open. The following may be questioned:

What Are the Elements of Intellectual Capital?

The literature gives various definitions of intellectual capital in light of its elements. Stewart (1997, p. 253), for example, defines it as the sum of human capital and structural capital. Edvinsson and Sullivan (1996, pp. 358–359), and Edvinsson and Malone (1997, p. 11) define it in the same manner. Petrash (1996, p. 366) defines it as the sum of human capital, relational capital, and structural capital. Brooking (1996, p. 13) defines intellectual capital as the sum of human capital, relational capital, structural capital, and intellectual property rights. She defines human capital and relational capital similar to Petrash; however, she defines structural capital not only as the capital embedded in a company's organization, processes, and culture, but also in intellectual property rights (patents, licenses, trademarks, etc.). Chen, Zhu, and Xie (2004, p. 202) define intellectual capital as the sum of human, structural, innovation, and customer capital.

Apparently, there is no single definition of the elements of intellectual capital. In addition, the literature on intellectual capital lacks answers to some other important questions. Therefore, the question is this: Are the elements of intellectual capital the same for all companies? If the answer is negative, it can be questioned what factors influence different elements.

How Should the Value of Each Element Be Defined?

There are several studies on valuating the elements of intellectual capital. It should be emphasized that in all cases the nonmonetary approach of valuation is employed. In accordance with the accounting standards, intangible assets are only those that meet the criteria for their recognition in financial statements and are as such expressed in monetary terms (Jerman, Kavčič, & Kavčič, 2010).

Chen et al. (2004), for example, designed a measurement model and a qualitative index of intellectual capital. Ordóñez de Pablos (2004) defines the value of structural capital as knowledge value embedded in organizational processes, structures, technologies, policies, and culture, etc.

There are also other approaches for valuating intellectual capital. Liebowitz and Suen (2000), for example, discuss some known measurement parameters of intellectual capital and their limitations. Further, Guthrie (2001) presents achievements in the area of measuring and reporting intellectual capital, and suggests some new areas of further investigations. M'Pherson and Pike (2001) present an approach for measuring intellectual capital in hotel organizations and think about the possibilities of enhancing the value in it. Chen (2003) points out that there have been many different schemes presented with regard to measuring intellectual capital in recent years. Rodgers (2003) tries to classify the elements of intellectual capital in order to present them with other items in classic financial statements. Andriessen (2004) tries to establish the reasons for valuating or measuring intellectual capital and to suggest reliable methods.

The above-mentioned trials of valuating intellectual capital could be a good ground for further investigation in this area, although the reliability of such results is not easy to test in practice. However, the designed methods can underestimate the value of an employee or group of employees within a company.

Of course, there are also other opinions. Andriessen (2001, p. 205), for example, states:

> . . . some practitioners have the tendency to treat intangibles the same way we treat tangible assets, by trying to force them into the double-entry bookkeeping system. They forget that the very nature of intangibles contradicts the ground philosophy of this system.

Based on the aforementioned, it is obvious that Andriessen is of the opinion that it makes no sense to valuate some elements of intellectual capital, which further means that it is not reasonable to valuate all intellectual capital. The most important reason for such a conviction seems to lie in the fact that such valuation is very demanding and is a highly professional task to tackle. The question is the following: Should the research be ceased only because the goal cannot be easily reached? However, Dumay and Rooney (2011, p. 352) conclude that it is possible to effectively implement IC practices without using concrete intellectual capital measures.

What Are the Relations among the Elements?

What are the relations among individual elements and how to define them? Some authors are of the opinion that the difference between a company's market and book value equals its intellectual capital value. Pike, Rylander, and Ross (2001) are of the opinion that all the resources of a company combine and interact with each other. They argue that the equation "market value = book value + intellectual capital value" is incorrect because the variables are not separable as required by the equation.

It is obvious that there is no linear relationship between the elements of intellectual capital. A low value of any element of intellectual capital lowers the value of other elements, since it jeopardizes the function of an organization as a unit. However, the authors do not provide any alternative suggestion to explain the nature of the relations among the elements of intellectual capital, and whether these relations are the same in all companies. Moreover, they do not question whether all elements are equally important for a company, and if not, which element is the most important. There have been some trials to answer the above questions, but the reliability of the results is difficult to test in practice. Chen et al. (2004), for example, find a remarkable relationship between the IC elements. Obviously, there are still some questions that lack appropriate answers in the area of relations among the elements of intellectual capital.

There are also other opinions; for example, Andriessen (2001, p. 207) states:

> It is always a combination of intangible assets that makes a company unique and successful. And this is where the classification schemes of IC fail. By separating human capital from structural capital, customer capital from organisational capital, innovation capital from process capital, we lose track of the correlation and synergy between the categories. It is the synergy between intangibles that creates uniqueness and wealth, not the individual assets.

Apparently, Andriessen believes that intellectual capital should be treated as a unit.

However, Dumay (2012, p. 4) suggests that "managers should strive to better understand the possible causal relationships between their people, processes and stakeholders (human, structural and relational capital) rather than adopting someone else's mousetrap." There is also a suggestion of a "dynamic" approach (Meritum, 2002), which assumes that none of the intellectual capital components alone is sufficient for successful performance and that they need to be combined to generate value. Therefore, intellectual capital becomes a phenomenon of interactions, transformations, and complementarities that cannot be understood merely by focusing on resources, but also on processes, rules, activities, and relations (Giuliani, 2013, p. 129). This dynamic approach investigates the relations between intellectual capital components and the relations among intellectual capital and financial performance.

How Does the Value of Intellectual Capital Affect a Company's Book Value?

A company's book value is the value of its shareholders' equity, while the market value of a company equals the number of shares times the price per share. As the market value of a successful company may exceed its book value by several times, there may be a gap between the two.

Professional circles are convinced that the growing gap between book and market value must be bridged. Upton (2001, p. 60) states:

> If accountants put all the assets and liabilities into financial statements, and they measured all those assets and liabilities in the right amounts, the shareholders' equity would equal market capitalization.

The above-mentioned statement confirms the fact that a company's market value may be the result of numerous factors that are not necessarily linked with its successful business operations. Examples of these factors are: monetary policy (interest rate), tax policy (tax on profits), and similar.

The value of intellectual capital does not affect a company's book value. The reason for this lies in the fact that the value of intellectual capital is not disclosed. The above-mentioned methods of valuating intellectual capital are in fact measuring methods. Measuring gives no real values of individual elements of intellectual capital and therefore no real value of the total intellectual capital in a company. Is, therefore, IC accounting just a management fashion (see Fincham & Roslender, 2003)?

What Next?

Based on the above, it is obvious that the existing concept of intellectual capital seems to be related to four open questions or weaknesses. There is no common standpoint among professionals in this field as to what the elements of intellectual capital are, how to valuate them, and what the relationships among them are. Furthermore, since the value of the intellectual capital of a company is not disclosed (which is the fourth weakness), it is logical that it cannot affect the book value of a company. Roslender and Fincham (2001, p. 390) summarize the position: ". . . if we are to be successful in accounting for intellectual capital, we should not expect too much from the models of accounting that are most familiar to us."

The above-mentioned weaknesses of the concept of intellectual capital can be overcome by

(a) replacing the term "intellectual capital" with the term "employees";
(b) valuating the employees in financial terms.

Replacing the term intellectual capital with the term employees is based on the assumption that not only human capital, but also relational capital and structural capital are the result of employees' work. An employee's departure from a company also reduces the value of the other elements of intellectual capital. An employee who leaves a company can "steal" the buyers, suppliers, and business secrets of the company. Additionally, the departure of an employee may jeopardize the organizational structure of a company (its function and further development).

This definition of the concept of employees may eliminate the first and the third weaknesses of the concept of intellectual capital.

Therefore, as discussed above, there are only two remaining weaknesses of the concept of intellectual capital, namely the problem of valuating its elements and the influence of their value on a company's book value. Replacing the term "intellectual capital" with the term "employees" gives an opportunity to eliminate these weaknesses by valuating a company's employees in financial terms.

Why would knowing the value of human capital be important? Is this associated with acquiring expensive yet useless accounting data, or is there more?

Knowing the value of human capital plays an important role in ensuring the following:

(a) Real accounting statements—It is well known that book values do not correspond to market values. In such conditions the accounting statements do not offer accurate information on what is going on in the company and eventually such inappropriate accounting information obstructs quality decision-making about the future.

(b) Appropriate handling of human capital—Knowing the value of goods plays a crucial role in handling them, as well as finding out how successful such handling was. Human capital is no exception to this (Milost, 2007b, p. 229).

Findings on the value of human capital are not new. In fact, its value is well recognized by pre-classical economists, who treat man as an element and source of the national treasure. Over time, this knowledge underwent the process of maturation; nowadays, however, human capital finds its position in financial statements only exceptionally.

Several authors are aware of the complexity of the human capital valuation issue. Kieso and Weygandt (1974, p. 65) state:

> Should accountants value employees for balance sheet and also for income statement purposes? Certainly skilled employees are an important asset, but the problems of determining value and measuring objectively have not yet been solved. Consequently, human resources are not recorded; perhaps when measurement techniques become more sophisticated and accepted, such information will be presented, if only in supplemental form.

Lev and Schwartz (2001, p. 73) establish that systematic research on the measurement and valuation of human resource intangibles is extremely lean.

The results obtained in this area by Stewart (1997), Edvinsson and Malone (1997), and Sveiby (1997) are presented by Theeke (2005, p. 48):

> I think it would be safe to conclude that the failure to adopt is the result of the method's failure to provide an acceptable measurement technique. Together, none of the efforts of this group has resulted in an accepted method for accounting for HR.

Cascio (2000, p. 5) believes that human assets approaches are not sufficient because they are focused only on investments in human capital and ignore outputs produced by these resources.

According to several authors, human capital valuation is substantially more subjective than tangible assets valuation (Guthrie & Murthy, 2009; Mayo, 2005; Roslender, 2009; Roslender & Dyson, 1992; Verma & Dewe, 2008). Theeke questions the feasibility of implementing human capital valuation approach. He argues (2005, p. 50):

> Furthermore, it did not seem (and I still believe it is not) possible for one to value the human resources . . .

As a new direction the author proposes three potential liability approaches, namely

(a) the demand deposit approach,
(b) the lease capitalization approach, and
(c) the contingent liability approach (2005, pp. 50–57).

The idea is further developed in one of his later works (Theeke & Mitchell, 2008) and is also discussed by Giuliani (2013, pp. 127–144).

Human capital valuation is a very complex issue; however, this chapter is not in accordance with the authors who argue that it is impossible to solve. The possibility of solving this problem is shown in this chapter that identifies the most significant nonmonetary and monetary models of human capital valuation. Among nonmonetary models, the Michigan, Flamholtz, and Ogan models are discussed. Among monetary models, the replacement costs model, the opportunity costs model, the discounted wages and salaries model, and the originally designed dynamic model and net value added model are discussed.

Nonmonetary and Monetary Models of Human Capital Valuation

Human capital may be disclosed among the assets on a balance sheet only if it is expressed in value terms. In order to disclose human capital among balance sheet items, one must find a proper method for measuring its value. Several monetary and nonmonetary models are developed for this purpose. Some of the most important models are outlined below. Additionally, the originally designed monetary model of human capital valuation is presented.

Nonmonetary Models of Human Capital Valuation

Nonmonetary models for valuating human capital include organizational and behavioral variables. These variables are not expressed in monetary terms; however, based on changes in their quality one can assume the increased or decreased value of human capital within the company.

Among the nonmonetary models, the Michigan, Flamholtz, and Ogan models are presented here. The first two models are purely nonmonetary, while the third one is combined, since it includes both monetary and nonmonetary methods of valuation.

The Michigan Model

The very first ideas of nonmonetary valuation of employees can be traced to works of researchers from the Institute for Social Research, which operates under the umbrella of the University of Michigan. The researchers of the aforementioned institute designed the model known as the Michigan or Likert model (named after the leading researcher of the institute). The model defines variables that are likely to influence the effectiveness of individuals in an organization and, therefore, the successful operation of a human organization *per se* (Likert, Bowers, & Norman, 1969, pp. 14*ff.*). The Michigan model aims at indirect definition of employee value in an organization. It does not enable determination of their initial value, but rather monitors value changes resulting from changes within the organizational climate. Despite the aforementioned, and though there are numerous open questions to which the authors of the Michigan model find no suitable answers (i.e., the question of various interpretations of such results), Flamholtz (1982, p. 23) is of the opinion that the Michigan model represents the most successful trial of the nonmonetary valuation of employees in an organization.

The Flamholtz Model

Contrary to Likert, Flamholtz designed his nonmonetary model of human capital valuation in terms of the individual. His aim was to explain factors that influence the value of an individual in an organization. This model consists of behavioral and economic variables.

It is based on the assumption that the value of an individual in an organization depends on two interrelated variables, namely

(a) the individual's conditional value, and
(b) the probability of maintaining organizational membership.

The individual's conditional value is determined as the current value of future services that may be rendered by an individual in an organization during his/her expected working life (Flamholtz, 1972a, p. 668). Flamholtz (1972b, pp. 241–266) tests his model in the case of valuating employees in a company registered for services in the area of accounting and business finances.

The Ogan Model

Similar to Flamholtz, Ogan designed a model in which some of the most important variables influencing the value of an individual in an organization are defined. The model aims at valuating human capital especially in those service enterprises where market-determined prices are not in use. Prices of some services, for example, are determined by professional associations such as bar associations, medical associations, etc. This is a combined model since it includes both monetary and nonmonetary measures. The basic idea of the model is to measure the amount of a company's long-term benefit from an employee. The value that an employee has for the company should equal the employee's long-term benefit resulting from his/her employment. This long-term benefit is determined by two factors, namely

(a) the direct benefit of an employee on the account of his employment, and
(b) the certainty of his employment.

The direct benefit of an employee is the sum of all expected benefits resulting from his employment. Employment certainty indicates the level of probability that the employment remains permanent. The value of an employee for the company is obtained by multiplying the values of both factors (Ogan, 1976, p. 311).

Monetary Models of Human Capital Valuation

The value of nonmonetary models should not be underestimated; however, monetary models are of greater importance. So far, a number of monetary models for valuating human capital have been designed, which reflects the importance of this issue. However, there are vast differences in the elaborations of such models.

Among monetary models of human capital valuation, the following are presented: the replacement costs model, the opportunity costs model, the discounted wages and salaries model, the dynamic model, and the net value added model.

The Replacement Costs Model

The replacement costs model was developed by Flamholtz in 1973. This model estimates the cost to replace a firm's existing human capital, for example, cost to the company to recruit, hire, train, and develop employees to their present level of technical proficiency and familiarity with the organization and its operations.

The author acknowledges two concepts of replacement costs: individual and positional. Individual replacement costs are defined as a current sacrifice that is mandatory if one wants to replace an individual of particular capacity with someone (an individual) or something (a machine) of the same capacity. These costs reflect the value of an individual for a company.

However, the value of an individual largely depends on his current and future position in a company (achieved due to his capacity). The author defines positional replacement costs as those resulting from replacing the particular mandatory services of each employee in a particular work position (workplace) in a company (Flamholtz, 1973, p. 11). Thus, this model includes all costs needed for developing the new employee until he (she) attains the level of existing employees.

The usage of this model is limited. The model requires not only a valuation of the amount of costs stemming from replacing an employee with someone or something, but also a valuation of the probability that another employee (or machine) will accomplish the same work. The value of an employee is thus determined on the basis of the value of an individual employee in alternative use. Additionally, valuating the amount of replacement costs of all employees is a rather difficult task.

The Opportunity Costs Model

The opportunity costs model was developed by Hekimian and Jones in 1967. The basis of this model is composed of the opportunity costs of an employee ∂ costs, which reflect the value of an employee shown in case of using his alternative. Opportunity costs are defined as costs of lost benefits in a situation when an employee performs another task and/or as costs resulting from acquisition of the needed employee (Hekimian & Jones, 1967, pp. 108–110). According to this definition, an employee has a certain value only if he/she is an exceptional resource, namely when his/her movement from Department A to Department B causes lack of labor force in Department A. The main weakness of this model is that it does not recognize the possibility of acquiring certain work abilities by employing new people.

The Discounted Wages and Salaries Model

The discounted wages and salaries model was developed by Lev and Schwartz in 1971. According to this model, the value of human capital is defined as the present value of anticipated (future) remuneration of employees corrected for performance ratio. The performance ratio of employees is defined as the ratio between the company's rate of return and the average rate of return in the economy. Positive correction of the present value of anticipated remuneration of employees occurs when a company's rate of return is larger than the average rate of return in the economy, and the contrary, negative correction of the present value of anticipated remuneration of employees occurs when a company's rate of return is lower than the average rate of return in the economy (Lev & Schwartz, 1971). Therefore, the underlying assumption is that the future value of employees' work may be valuated by the amount of their wages and salaries.

The Dynamic Model

The dynamic model (Milost, 2007a, pp. 124–138) is based on the economic concept of value and is intended to valuate

(a) individual employees and
(b) groups of employees (i.e., all employees within a company).

The value of individual employees may be determined directly, while the value of a group of employees may be determined indirectly, as a corrected sum of values of individual employees.

The model is a dynamic one, which means that it enables the establishment of the value of an individual employee or all employees within a company at any moment. It is based on an approach usually used for valuating the majority of tangible fixed assets by recognizing some specific features of employees.

Valuating individual employees
The dynamic model for valuating individual employees is presented in figure 4.1.

Concepts and other items from the model are explained as follows:

The purchase value. The purchase value of an employee is composed of investments in an employee before and directly upon his/her arrival at a company and includes three components, namely

(a) investments in employee training,
(b) investments in employee acquisition, and
(c) employee opportunity costs.

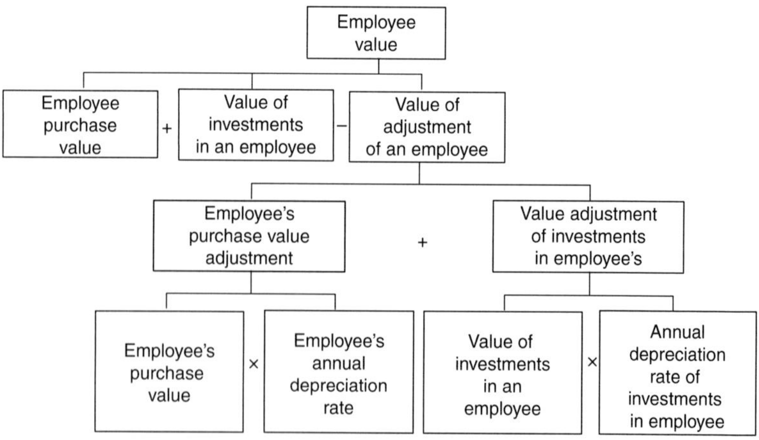

Figure 4.1 The dynamic model for valuating individual employees

Investments in employee training are associated with acquiring his/her work capacity. Investments in employee acquisition include investments in job advertisement and investments in direct employee acquisition. Employee opportunity costs are an individual's investments in his/her own knowledge and development.

Value adjustment. The value adjustment of an employee is a value transferred by an employee, via his cooperation in a business process, to business effects and is presented as follows:

$$\begin{aligned}&\text{Value adjustment of an employee}\\&\quad = \text{employee's purchase value adjustment}\\&\qquad + \text{value adjustments of investments in an employee.}\end{aligned}$$

The employee's purchase value adjustment is obtained by multiplying the employee's purchase value by his annual depreciation rate. The calculation is presented as follows:

$$\begin{aligned}&\text{Employee's purchase value adjustment}\\&\quad = \text{employee's purchase value}\\&\qquad \times \text{employee's annual depreciation rate.}\end{aligned}$$

The annual depreciation rate of an employee is obtained by dividing 1 by his useful life expressed in years. The useful life of an employee, expressed in years, is the period during which the employee shall render services to the company.

The value adjustment of investments in an employee is obtained by multiplying the value of investments in an employee by the annual depreciation rate of these investments. The calculation is presented as follows:

$$\begin{aligned}&\text{Value adjustment of investments in an employee}\\&\quad = \text{value of investments in an employee}\\&\qquad \times \text{annual depreciation rate of investments in an employee}\end{aligned}$$

Investments in employee include

(a) investments in direct assurance of working abilities,
(b) investments in health and well-being, and
(c) investments in loyalty to the company.

Investments in direct assurance of an employee's working abilities are those that are most profoundly relative to the employee's work in a company.

Investments in health and well-being are those that enable regular attendance in the workplace.

Investments in employee loyalty reduce the probability that an employee will quit working for the company due to disability, retirement, or similar reasons.

The remaining item to be defined is the annual depreciation rate of investments in an employee. This rate may be obtained by dividing 1 by the useful life of investments in an employee (expressed in years).

The net carrying amount. The net carrying amount of an employee depends on two factors, namely

(a) the previously determined positive difference between the purchase value of an employee and his/her adjusted value, and
(b) his/her significance to a company, measured by his/her wage and salary.

The salary amount reflects the value of services offered by an individual to a company and also the employee's value to the company.

According to the above, the net carrying amount of the value of an employee must be corrected. The correction factor may be defined as follows:

$$\frac{\text{Annual salary of an employee in a company}}{\text{Average annual salary of an employee in a national economy}}$$

Valuating a group of employees

The value of a group of employees is not a simple sum of the values of individual employees—this value usually differs from such a sum due to synergetic effects.

However, a certain relationship between the sum of values of individual employees and the value of a group of employees exists. This relationship depends on the successful performance of employees in the company compared to the successful performance of employees in an entire economy.

The employees' performance ratio serves as a measure of the successful performance of employees. It is defined as the ratio between the sum of weighted average added value per employee in a company and the entire economy during last three years (numerator) and the sum of the number of years used (denominator). It is calculated as follows:

$$\text{Employees' performance ratio} = \frac{3\dfrac{\text{AA0}}{\text{BB0}}2 + \dfrac{\text{AA1}}{\text{BB1}} + \dfrac{\text{AA2}}{\text{BB2}}}{6}$$

where AAO is the value added per company employee during the last year, BBO is the value added per employee in entire economy during the last year, AA1 is the value added per company employee two years ago, and BB1 is the value added per employee in entire economy two years ago. The remaining two abbreviations in the equation are defined by using the same logic as above.

When the value of a group of employees is to be determined, the aforementioned approach enables recognition of the overall performance of a company for a period longer than a year. The overall performance of a company during the last year is more accentuated than is the performance of previous years.

Net Value Added Model

Model design

A company's business operations have a private and social dimension. The private dimension of a company's business operations relates to achieving economic benefits for the owners, which are reflected in a company's business performance and its pertinent market value growth.

However, a company is not only a means of achieving economic benefits for its owners but also has an important social role. It provides salaries for employees, it pays taxes to the state, and it pays interest to creditors.

The purpose of the net value added model is to calculate the value of a company's employees for their owners. Therefore, the social dimension of business operations is not taken into account. The private dimension of a company's business operations is based on the economic concept of value.

According to the economic concept of value, the value of particular goods depends on the present and future benefits associated with these goods. This also applies to human capital. Therefore, the value of human capital depends on the present value of its expected future services. This economic benefit for owners is related to the concepts of net profit or net return on equity and value added.

Profit is the positive difference between revenue and expenses in an accounting period. Net profit is the profit minus taxes. Net return on equity is the relationship between company's net profit and its capital.

The second measure of economic benefit is value added. A company's business processes are directed toward business results (products and services). There are four basic elements required for a business process, namely means of production, raw materials, services, and employees. However, there is a significant difference between employees and the other three relevant elements: means of production, raw materials, and services, with the value of products and services just being transferred among them. Employees are therefore the only element that adds value to products and services. The amount of value added therefore depends particularly on employee value and investments in them.

Value added could be defined as an increase of market value of products and services resulting from quality growth. This value is thus calculated by reducing the sales value of business results from the purchase value of the resources used. According to the Accounting Standards Steering Committee (ASSC, 1975, p. 4), value added is the most convenient means that can be used to understand the net profit of a company as well as to represent its source. Sufficient value added is a prerequisite for making profit and net profit. Net profit is achieved only when all participants in creating value added are paid off: the state (taxes), employees (salaries), and creditors (interests).

The model is intended to valuate human capital as a whole, that is, all employees within a company. The basis for calculating the value of a company's employees is the part of value added that belongs to owners and is termed as net value added. The model is thus called net value added model (Milost, 2014, pp. 9–13).

Methodology for calculating employee value of a company

The calculation of employees' value consists of two phases. The first phase is aimed at establishing primary (uncorrected) employee value. The basis for calculation is the part of value added that belongs to owners. The second phase of the calculation is aimed at correcting the established employee value. The correction is accomplished by using the business performance ratio based on the ratio between the value of net return on equity in the company and its value in national economy over the last three years. In the following, the phases of employee value calculation are presented:

Establishing primary employee value. To establish primary employee value, the concept of value added (in its wider and narrower sense) should be defined in more details.

Value added, in its wider sense, refers to the total value added in a company. This means that value added is not defined in terms of subjects involved in its creation and distribution.

Value added, in its narrower sense, refers to the part of value added that belongs to owners. It is termed net value added. A part of net value added belongs to owners indirectly (belongs to the company) while another part belongs to them directly. Net value added is thus the part of value added that belongs to

(a) company,
(b) owners, and
(c) supervisory board members and employees.

A part of net value added that belongs to the company is a part of net profit for reserves and undistributed net profit.

A part of net value added that belongs to owners is the part for dividends pertaining to them.

A part of net value added that belongs to supervisory board members and employees does not include the costs allocated to them; it refers to remunerations for supervisory board members and employees, which are derived from net profit. It usually refers to a minor part of net value added.

Net value added is therefore defined as value added reduced by employees', creditors' and state's shares. It includes

(a) labor costs,
(b) interest payable (interest costs), and
(c) profit tax.

The assessment of net value added enables us to calculate primary employee value. Net value added is referred to as net return related to a particular investment. Therefore, it is important to establish the amount of assets needed to achieve net return in the amount of net value added.

The required amount of these assets is calculated by dividing net value added by the interest rate, which reflects owners' expectations, for example, costs of capital, defined as the expected normal return rate belonging to owners.

Correction of primary employee value. The basis for the calculation of primary employee value is the part of value added that belongs to owners. The first phase of calculation is aimed at establishing the primary value of employees while the second phase is aimed at correcting it, using business performance ratio, which is defined as the ratio between net return on equity in the company and in the national economy over the last three years (numerator) and the sum of the number of years used (denominator). The aforementioned ratio of the last year is then multiplied by a factor of 3, the ratio of two years ago by a factor of 2, and the ratio of three years ago by a factor of 1. The sum of the factors (3 + 2 + 1) equals 6. Accordingly, the business performance ratio is calculated as follows:

$$\text{Business performance ratio} = \frac{3\dfrac{\text{REC0}}{\text{REE0}}2 + \dfrac{\text{REC1}}{\text{REE1}} + \dfrac{\text{REC2}}{\text{REE2}}}{6}$$

where REC0 is net return on equity in the company in the last year, REE0 is net return on equity in the national economy in the last year, REC1 is net return on equity in the company two years ago, and REE1 is net return on equity in the national economy two years ago. The remaining two abbreviations are defined using the same logic.

The aforementioned approach enables one to consider company business performance over a longer period of time and not only over the last year. When calculating employees' value, the period selection is a matter of subjective judgment; however, a three-year period seems to be suitable. The business life of a company is rather intensive, and in light of this, a three-year period seems to be sufficiently long. In addition, the overall performance of a company during the last year is accentuated more than the performance of previous years.

Calculation of employee value (example)

The data (in monetary units) including company value added, labor costs, assets value, liabilities, equity and profit, annual interests rate, annual costs of capital, profit tax rate, net returns on equity in the company in last three years, and net returns on equity in the national economy in last three years are presented in table 4.1.

The data needed for calculation of primary employee value are presented in table 4.2.

1. Calculation of primary employee value

$$\text{Primary employee value} = \frac{\text{net value added}}{\text{annual costs of capital}} = \frac{10,000}{0.10}$$

$$= 100{,}000 \text{ monetary units}$$

Table 4.1 The data needed for calculation of employee value

(a) Value added	34,000
(b) Labor costs	20,700
(c) Assets	100,000
(d) Liabilities	40,000
(e) Equity (capital)	60,000
(f) Profit	4,500
(g) Annual interests rate	6%
(h) Annual costs of capital	10%
(i) Profit tax rate	20%
(j) Net return on equity in the company in last year	6%
(k) Net return on equity in the national economy in last year	5%
(l) Net return on equity in the company two years ago	3%
(m) Net return on equity in national economy two years ago	3%
(n) Net return on equity in the company three years ago	2%
(o) Net return on equity in the national economy three years ago	4%

Table 4.2 The data needed for calculation of primary employee value

(a) Value added	34,000
(b) Labor costs	20,700
(c) Interest paid (6% of 40,000)	2,400
(d) Profit tax (20% of 4,500)	900
(e) Net value added	10,000

2. Correction of primary employee value

$$\text{Business performance ratio} = \frac{3\frac{REC0}{REE0}2 + \frac{REC1}{REE1} + \frac{REC2}{REE2} + 3\frac{6}{5} + 2\frac{3}{3} + \frac{2}{4}}{6}$$

$$= \frac{3.60 + 2.00 + 0.50}{6} = 1.017$$

3. Calculation of employee value

Employee value

= primary employee value × business performance ratio

= 100,000 × 1.017 = 101,700 monetary units

The net value added model aims to finding answers to questions associated with human capital valuation, which is a very significant and professionally demanding issue. Currently, this model is in the phase of practical valuation.

Conclusion

Human capital is an economic good and its value should be known. Therefore, it is crucial to know the value of human capital to be able to provide more realistic company financial statements and to manage human resources efficiently. For this purpose an appropriate methodological framework for valuating human capital is needed, that is, estimating the value of a company's human capital.

There are two types of models for human capital valuation: monetary and nonmonetary models. Nonmonetary models are not appropriate for disclosing human capital among the assets on a balance sheet, and most popular monetary models are not appropriate for general use—they can only be used in limited cases.

For this reason, the original model for human capital valuation named net value added model is developed. This could be an important step toward developing a general model for human capital valuation.

References

Andriessen, D. (2001). Weightless wealth: Four modifications to standard IC theory. *Journal of Intellectual Capital, 2*, 204–214.

Andriessen, D. (2004). IC valuation and measurement: Classifying the state of the art. *Journal of Intellectual Capital, 5*, 230–242.

ASSC—Accounting Standards Steering Committee (1975). *The Corporate Report: A Discussion Document*, London.

Becker, G. S. (1964). *Human Capital: A Theoretical and Empirical Analysis with Special Reference to Education*. New York, NY: Columbia University Press.

Brooking, A. (1996). *Intellectual Capital*. London: International Thomson Business Press.

Cascio, W. F. (2000). *Costing Human Resources: The Financial Impact of Behavior in Organizations* (4th Edition). Cincinnati, OH: South-Western College Publishing.

Chadwick, C., & Dabu, A. (2009). Human resources, human resource management, and the competitive advantage of firms: Toward a more comprehensive model of causal linkages. *Organizational Science, 20*, 253–272.

Chen, J. (2003). Valuing intellectual capital using game theory. *Journal of Intellectual Capital, 4*, 191–201.

Chen, J., Zhu, Z., & Xie, H. Y. (2004). Measuring intellectual capital: A new model and empirical study. *Journal of Intellectual Capital, 5*, 195–212.

Dumay, J. (2012). Grand theories as barriers to using IC concepts. *Journal of Intellectual Capital, 13*, 4–15.

Dumay, J., & Rooney, J. (2011). Measuring for managing: An IC practice case study. *Journal of Intellectual Capital, 12*, 344–355.

Edvinsson, L., & Malone, M. S. (1997). *Intellectual Capital: Realizing Your Company's True Value by Finding Its Hidden Brainpower*. New York, NY: Harper Business.

Edvinsson, L., & Sullivan, P. (1996). Developing a model for managing intellectual capital. *European Management Journal, 14*, 356–364.

Fincham, R., & Roslender, R. (2003). Intellectual capital accounting as a management fashion: A review and a critique. *European Accounting Review, 12*, 781–795.

Flamholtz E. G. (1972a). Assessing the validity of a theory of human resource value: A field study. *Journal of Accounting Research, 10*, 241–266.

Flamholtz, E. G. (1972b). Toward a theory of human resource value in formal organisations. *Accounting Review, 47*, 666–678.

Flamholtz, E. G. (1973). Human resource accounting: Measuring positional replacement costs. *Human Resource Management, 12*, 8–16.

Flamholtz, E. G. (1974). Human resource accounting: A review of theory and research. *Journal of Management Studies, 11*, 44–61.

Flamholtz, E. G. (1982). *State-of-the-Art and Future Prospects*. Encino, CA: Dickenson

Gamerschlag, R. (2013). Value relevance of human capital information. *Journal of Intellectual Capital, 14*, 325–345.

Giuliani, M. (2013). Not all sunshine and roses: Discovering intellectual liabilities "in action." *Journal of Intellectual Capital, 14*, 127–144.

Guthrie, J. (2001). The management, measurement and the reporting of intellectual capital. *Journal of Intellectual Capital, 2*, 27–41.

Guthrie, J., & Murthy, V. (2009). Past, present and possible future developments in human capital accounting a tribute to Jan-Erik Grojer. *Journal of Human Resource Costing and Accounting, 13*, 125–142.

Hekimian, J. S. & Jones, C. H. (1967). Put people on your balance sheet. *Harvard Business Review, 43*, 105–113.

Jerman, M., Kavčič, S., & Kavčič, B. (2010). The significance of intangibles: A comparative analysis between Croatia, Slovenia, Czech Republic, Germany and USA. *Economic Research, 23*, 60–69.

Kieso, D. E., & Weygandt, J. J. (1974). *Intermediate Accounting*. New York, NY: Wiley.

Lev, B., & Schwartz, A. (1971). On the use of economic concept of human capital in financial statements. *Accounting Review, 46*, 103–112.

Lev, B., & Schwartz, A. (2001). *Intangibles: Management, Measurement and Reporting*. Washington, DC: Brookings Institution Press.

Liebowitz, J., & Suen, C. Y. (2000). Developing knowledge management metrics for measuring intellectual capital. *Journal of Intellectual Capital, 1*, 54–67.

Likert, R., Bowers, D. G., & Norman, R. M. (1969). How to increase the firm's lead time in recognising and dealing with problems of managing its human organisation. *Michigan Business Review, 22*, 617–632.

Mayo, A. (2005). Helping HR to understand the strategic value chain. *Strategic HR Review, 5*, 32–45.

Meritum (2002). *Proyecto Meritum: Guidelines for Managing and Reporting Intangibles*, Madrid.

Milost, F. (2007a). A dynamic monetary model for evaluating employees. *Journal of Intellectual Capital, 8*, 124–138.

Milost, F. (2007b). *Računovodstvo človeških zmožnosti: Zakaj klasične bilance ne kažejo prave slike o premoženjskem in finančnem stanju podjetij ter o njihovi poslovni uspešnosti?* ("Human resource accounting: Why don't classical financial statements show a true and fair picture of the property, financial position and operating results of a company?"). Koper: Faculty of Management, University of Primorska.

Milost, F. (2014). Net value added monetary model for evaluating human capital. *European Scientific Journal, 10*, 1–16.

M'Pherson, P. K., & Pike, S. (2001). Accounting, empirical measurement and intellectual capital. *Journal of Intellectual Capital, 2*, 246–260.

Ogan, P. (1976). A human resource value model for professional service organisations. *Accounting Review, 14*, 195–217.

Ordóñez de Pablos, P. (2004). Measuring and reporting structural capital—Lessons from European learning firms. *Journal of Intellectual Capital, 5*, 629–647.

Petrash, G. (1996). Dow's journey to a knowledge value management culture. *European Management Journal, 14*, 365–373.

Pike, S., Rylander, A., & Ross, G. (2001). "Intellectual capital management and disclosure." Paper presented at the 4th World Congress on Intellectual Capital. Hamilton, ON: McMaster University.

Rodgers, W. (2003). Measurement and reporting of knowledge-based assets. *Journal of Intellectual Capital, 4*, 181–190.

Roslender, R. (2009). So tell me again . . . just why would you want to account for people? *Journal of Human Resource Costing and Accounting, 13*, 143–153.

Roslender, R., & Dyson, J. R. (1992). Accounting for the worth of employees: A new look at an old problem. *British Accounting Review, 24*, 311–329.

Roslender, R., & Fincham, R. (2001). Thinking critically about intellectual capital. *Acounting, Auditing and Accountability Journal, 14*, 383–398.

Schultz, T. W. (1961). Investment in human capital. *American Economic Review, 51*, 1–17.

Snell, S. A., Youndt, M. A., & Wright, P. M. (1996). Establishing a framework for research in strategic human resource management: Merging resource theory and organizational learning. In (Ferris, G. R. Ed.), *Research in Personnel and Human Resource Management* (pp. 61–90). Greenwich, CT: JAI Press.

Stewart, T. A. (1997). *Intellectual Capital: The New Wealth of Nations*. New York, NY: Doubleday.

Sveiby, K. E. (1997). *The New Organizational Wealth: Managing and Measuring Knowledge-Based Assets*. San Francisco, CA: Berrett-Koehler.

Theeke, H. A. (2005). A human resource accounting transmission: Shifting from failure to a future. *Journal of Human Resource Costing and Accounting, 9*, 40–59.

Theeke, H. A., & Mitchell, J. B. (2008). Financial implications of accounting for human resources using a liability model. *Journal of Human Resource Costing and Accounting, 12*, 124–137.

Upton, W. S. (2001). *Business and Financial Reporting: Challenges from the New Economy*. Norwalk, CT: FASB.

Verma, S., & Dewe, P. (2008). Valuing human resources: Perceptions and practices in UK organizations. *Journal of Human Resource Costing and Accounting, 12*, 102–123.

Wright, P. M., Dunford, B. B., & Snell, S. A. (2001). Human resources and the resource based view of the firm. *Journal of Management, 27*, 701–721.

CHAPTER 5

Investments in Human Capital: Elements of Investments, Their Valuation, a True and Fair View of Financial Statements Compiled by Using the Classical Approach, and the Related Financial Performance Ratios

Franko Milost

Introduction

A company is usually established with the purpose of permanently performing a particular activity. There are four basic elements required for a business process: equipment, materials, services, and human capital (human potential, employees).

In a company, human capital comprises a flow of inputs from which the company generates output. The input includes a range of expenditure and effort devoted to activities while the output partially resides in the employees and partially accumulates in the organizational structure, assets, and products (Wyatt & Frick, 2010). Blundell, Dearden, Meghir, and Sianesi (1999, p. 2) define three main components of human capital—early ability (whether acquired or innate), qualifications and knowledge acquired through formal education, and finally skills, competencies, and expertise acquired through training on the job. Nowadays, the importance of human capital as a factor of production is increasing (Hunter, Webster, & Wyatt, 2010). This is due to the fact that new technologies are now mainly embodied in intangible assets and labor rather than in fixed assets (Kendrick, 1972; Webster, 1999).

Obtaining the elements of a business process is associated with investments. Nevertheless, the investments in human capital are somehow different from investments in other elements, and are crucial for the long-term existence and development of a company and its business performance.

Investing in human capital is a very complex issue, which is discussed from different points of view in various literature. It refers mainly to employee training needs, measuring the value of investments in human capital, and economic benefits associated with those investments.

Employee training needs are, for example, investigated by Gibbons and Waldman (2004) and Au, Altman, and Roussel (2008).

The issues of measuring the value of investments in human capital is, for example, investigated by Cantrell, Benton, Laudal, and Thomas (2008), based on the case of a well-known American corporation. The gap between the economic benefits of company-sponsored education and training and the accounting and disclosure treatment of these costs is investigated by Frederickson, Webster, and Williamson (2010).

Investments in human capital bring economic benefits to individuals, companies, and the economy. These economic benefits are investigated by several authors. Hatch and Dyer (2004), for example, investigate employees' learning as a source of competitive advantage. Walker (2010) investigates the possibility of investments in human capital as an increasingly important source of value creation for industries requiring highly skilled labor. Johanson (1997) investigates profitability of investments in work-oriented rehabilitation. Sakamoto and Kim (2006) investigate employees' screening effects of schooling on productivity in US manufacturing industries. Blundell et al. (1999) investigate returns from education and training on individual earnings, on company performance, and to national economic growth at the macroeconomic level. Almeida and Carneiro (2008) estimate the rate of return to company investments in human capital in the form of formal job training. Focusing on the role of human capital investments as an element of productivity, Haltiwanger, Lane, and Spletzer (1999) investigate the state of the workforce composition and productivity within companies. Syverson (2010) investigates productivity differences in terms of human capital investments. And finally, Hunter et al. (2010) investigate the company's collection of human capital investment data. Several authors provide evidence that these data are not widely collected in a form needed for computing the rates of return. This fact puts the results of a great deal of research in this field under question.

In the following, the elements of investments in human capital and the methods used to valuate these investments are addressed, followed by a presentation of originally created basic and derivative financial performance ratios related to investments in employees along with an originally created system of integrated ratios. The influence that the treatment of investments in employees in classical accounting has on the true and fair view of financial statements is also discussed.

Investments in Human Capital

Elements of Investments in Human Capital

Investments in human capital are composed of numerous elements that can be defined in various ways. Becker (1962) defines four kinds of investments in human capital, namely

(a) investments on the job (which result in an increased productivity of employees by learning new skills and perfecting the old ones while on a job);
(b) schooling (benefits from schooling, as the school is an institution specialized in the production of training);
(c) other knowledge (about the economic system, consumption, production possibilities, etc.); and
(d) productive wage increases (by improving employees' emotional and physical health).

In one of their later works, Becker (1964) and Mincer (1974) define two kinds of investments in human capital, namely investments in general training and investments in company-specific training. The costs and benefits of general training referring to employment opportunities across different companies are borne by the employees while companies and employees share the costs and benefits of company-specific training.

Gibbons and Waldman (2004) propose an additional kind of investments in human capital, which is named as the task-specific investment. The authors suggest that investments in human capital depend on different tasks rather than on different companies. They suggest that much of the accumulated on-the-job training relates to task-specific training, which is closely related to occupation and to industry-specific human capital.

Lazear (2009) suggests skill-weights approach on human capital. Under this approach, there are several skills used on each job, and these skills can be also used in other companies. Each company requires a different combination of skills, and employees do not have incentives to skill up with company-specific skills, so it is obvious that some of the training costs will be borne by the company. As the skill mix becomes more company specific, the employees are not encouraged to bear full training costs. A result of this theory is that finding another occupation with an adequate salary will be easier in more competitive labor markets rather than in the thin ones.

In RG Barry Corporation (Flamholtz, 1974a, p. 74), investments in human capital are defined as the sum of investments in the following: job advertisements, employee acquisition, employee formal and informal training as well as introductory training, the gaining of experience, and employee development.

In one of his recent works, Becker (2006) defines education, training, and health as the most important investments in human capital.

Frederickson et al. (2010) define investments in human capital as recruiting and selecting employees, their education and training, organizing employees within the company, motivating and rewarding employees, and evaluating employee performance.

The aforementioned definitions present a solid ground for further elaboration in this direction; however, they do not encompass all the elements of investments in human capital. Therefore, these investments need to be more broadly defined. They include (Milost, 2007b)

(a) investments in the direct assurance of working abilities,
(b) investments in health and well-being, and
(c) investments in loyalty to the company.

Investments in direct assurance of an employee's working abilities are those that are most profoundly related to the employee's work in a company. They include

- investments in formal training,
- investments in informal training,
- investments in introductory training,
- lower productivity of an employee during the period of his (her) introductory training, and
- lower productivity of an employee prior to his (her) leaving the company (opportunity costs of the company).

The first four elements increase the value of investments in an employee, while the last one decreases it.

Investments in employee's formal training are expenses associated with acquiring the formal knowledge needed for performing certain tasks.

Investments in an employee's informal training are expenses associated with acquiring functional knowledge.

Investments in an introductory training are associated with the period of introductory training. New employees need to be informed about the history of the company, its business policies, and methods of communication within the company, and they also need to be introduced to the employees with whom they will cooperate at work.

Lower productivity of an employee during the period of their introductory training is defined by the difference between the amount of the employee's salary and the value of services offered by this employee to the company. This is a period of investments during which it is expected that the employee will offer services of certain value to the company in the future.

Lower productivity of an employee prior to his leaving the company is defined as negative investments in an employee, namely his opportunity costs. The opportunity costs of the company in this case equal the difference between the amount of the employee's salary during this period and the value of services offered by this employee to the company.

Investments in health and well-being are those that enable regular attendance in the workplace. These investments may have direct (e.g., reducing sick leaves) or indirect (e.g., better achievement as a result of a better physical and mental condition) effects. They include periodic employee medical checkups, cofinancing the lease of recreational buildings, organizing sporting events, etc.

Investments in employee loyalty reduce the probability that an employee will quit working for the company prior to disability, retirement, or similar.

The elements of investments in an employee may differ to a certain extent from company to company. In fact, in some companies or lines of business, some specific knowledge is required, and therefore specific requirements are applied there. However, the aforementioned elements of investments in employees give a solid ground for this particular issue.

Valuating Investments in Human Capital

Accounting assigns values to economic categories. A value becomes a common denominator that enables the disclosure of economic categories that are usually not compared against each other. The value of a particular economic category depends largely on the method of its valuation. This also applies to valuating investments in human capital.

Valuating investments in employees is intended to disclose their value under assets, a process that requires the introduction of some new definitions, namely the purchase value of investments in employees, the value adjustment of investments in employees, and the net carrying amount of investments in employees.

The purchase value of investments in employees equals the value of investments in employees in an accounting period. The value adjustment of investments in employees is the value transferred by employees to business effects in an accounting period, thus their value reduced by depreciation. The net carrying amount of investments in employees is the positive difference between its purchase value and its adjusted value.

Depreciation is usually associated only with fixed assets that gradually, via their usage, transfer their value to business effects (products and services). However, the gradual transfer of value is very characteristic for investments in employees as well; therefore, the terminology in this area should be appropriate.

Investments in human capital could be valued using different concepts. Below, two versions of a depreciation plan for investments in employees are presented. The first one represents a classical accounting approach and the second one human resource accounting approach. The third concept known as combined approach is also presented.

The annual value of investments in employees is 400 monetary units (m.u.) and the useful life of these investments is four years (as acquired knowledge becomes obsolete in four years). Six-year depreciation plans compiled in two ways are presented below: first by using the classical accounting approach and second by using human resource accounting approach.

Classical Accounting Approach

Using the classical accounting approach, investments in employees are disclosed under expenses as they occur. A six-year depreciation plan compiled by using this approach is presented in Table 5.1.

With regard to the table, one can determine that the investments in employees are depreciated using an annual rate of 100 percent, which further means that the useful life of these investments is less than one year.

Table 5.1 Depreciation plan compiled by using classical accounting approach

Year	*Depreciation base*	*Depreciation rate*	*Annual depreciation*	*Cumulative depreciation*	*Net carrying amount*
First	400	4/4	400	400	–
Second	400	4/4	400	800	–
Third	400	4/4	400	1,200	–
Fourth	400	4/4	400	1,600	–
Fifth	400	4/4	400	2,000	–
Sixth	400	4/4	400	2,400	–

Human Resource Accounting Approach

Human resource accounting (accounting for people) approach can be defined as "the process of identifying, measuring and communicating information about human resources to decision makers" (Flamholtz, 1974b, p. 44). This approach is frequently emasculated as a consequence of the power and influence wielded by the accountancy profession, identified as a key agent of capital (more in Roslender & Stevenson, 2009).

Using human resource accounting approach, investments in employees are disclosed under assets in the amount of economic benefits expected from these investments. A six-year depreciation plan compiled by using this approach is presented in Table 5.2

This depreciation plan is compiled under the assumption that no employee leaves the company. If an employee leaves the company, the investment value of that particular employee is annulled.

As is evident in the table, the depreciation base does not change from the fourth year on. The reason for this is very simple. The useful life of investments in employees is four years, which means that investments in employees from the first year are written off at the end of the fourth year. Similarly, at the end of the fifth year, investments in employees from the second year are written off, and so forth.

Furthermore, one can notice the difference between both approaches in the amount corresponding to accumulated depreciation. Using the classical approach, investments in employees are depreciated as they occur; therefore, the fact that the entire value of investments in employees is depreciated within the six-year period under scrutiny should not surprise anyone. On the contrary, when using the human resource accounting approach, investments in employees retain some net carrying amount at the end of the six-year period. In the case presented, the net carrying amount equals 600 monetary units and includes 300 monetary units from the sixth year, 200 monetary units from

Table 5.2 Depreciation plan compiled by using human resource accounting approach

Year	*Depreciation base*	*Depreciation rate*	*Annual depreciation*	*Cumulative depreciation*	*Net carrying amount*
First	400	1/4	100	100	300
Second	800	1/4	200	300	500
Third	1,200	1/4	300	600	600
Fourth	1,600	1/4	400	1,000	600
Fifth	1,600	1/4	400	1,400	600
Sixth	1,600	1/4	400	1,800	600

the fifth year, and 100 monetary units from the fourth year. The amount of investments from the third year, namely 400 monetary units, is already written off at the end of the sixth year. It is obvious that the use of either of the two approaches makes a difference when disclosing the values of investments in employees under expenses during accounting periods. In the case presented, the difference in accumulated depreciation (600 m.u.) is of material significance, as it presents the value of one year and a half of investments in employees. The difference in accumulated depreciation would decrease under the assumption of a shorter period of the useful life of investments in employees and would increase under the assumption of a longer period of the useful life of such investments. Therefore, if the useful life of investments in employees is set to a three-year period, the difference equals the annual amount of investments in employees; however, if the useful life of investments in employees is set to a five-year period, the difference equals the amount of investments in employees made in two years.

The concept for valuating investments in employees via human resource accounting is based on the economic concept of value, according to which the value of particular goods depends on the present and future benefits associated with these goods. Therefore, the value of investments in employees equals the present value of their expected future services. This definition can apply to investments in an individual as well as to investments in a group of people within a company and to investments in all employees.

Valuating investments in employees via classical accounting, however, does not seem to correspond to the economic concept of value. The depreciation plan presented in the tables above shows that classical accounting treats investments in employees as investments whose useful life is less than one year. The value of such investments is written off already as they occur. It means that the value of the expected future services associated with these investments equals zero. However, the aforementioned is contrary to the three principles of classical accounting, namely accrual, substance over form, and prudence. Therefore, the true and fair view of such financial statements may be questioned.

A third concept known as combined approach is proposed by Samudhram, Sanmugam, and Teng Low (2008). The authors build their proposal on a theory that the links between expenditures on human resources and the resulting benefits are likely to differ. They identify four levels of human resource-related expenditure-benefit relationships (Samudhram et al., 2008, p. 659):

(a) low levels of human capital-related expenditures that provide high levels of long-term benefits: these investments in employees are treated as investments;

(b) high levels of human capital-related expenditures that provide high levels of long-term benefits: these investments in employees are treated as investments;
(c) low levels of human capital-related expenditures that provide low levels of long-term benefits: these investments in employees are treated as costs;
(d) high levels of human capital-related expenditures that provide low levels of long-term benefits: these investments in employees are treated as costs.

Level (a) expenditures are those that bring high levels of long-term benefits to the company despite limited human resource-related expenditures. Level (b) expenditures occur when the firm incurs a high level of human capital-related expenditures and also experiences a high level of long-term benefits from such expenditures. Level (c) expenditures occur when the firm incurs limited human capital-related costs for developing its human capital and also reaps limited long-term benefits. Level (d) expenditures occur when the firm experiences heavy human resource-related expenditures that result in limited, if any, benefits.

A True and Fair View of Financial Statements Compiled by Using the Classical Accounting Approach

Do financial statements compiled by using the classical accounting approach express a true and fair view? Francis and Schipper (1999), for example, claim that the financial statements of companies have significantly lost their relevance. Something similar is stated by Chang (1999), Collins, Maydew, and Weiss (1997), Ely and Waymire (1999), Lev and Zarowin (1999), and Roslender (2009). Other authors deal with this issue indirectly. Kanodia, Singh, and Spero (2005), and Milost (2007a), for example, argue that valuating a company's investments is rather imprecise, which casts doubt on the true and fair view of financial statements. Lev (2008) expresses a critical view, above all, on valuation and disclosing of intangibles.

This chapter addresses the above-mentioned issue using an example of different treatments of particular investments in a company. Both the manner of treating investments in tangible fixed assets and that in employees are presented.

It is assumed that a company purchases a machine whose purchase value equals 60 monetary units and whose useful life is five years. The company pays the supplier by the due date, but the payment is not directly associated with expenses as the company depreciates the purchased machine within 60 months—1 monetary unit per month.

However, the situation is rather different if a company sends its employee for education. In such a case, it discloses the relevant expenses at the moment it receives the invoice from the educational institution. It may be questioned if it is not more suitable to raise the value of the employee to the amount written on the invoice and to depreciate this investment during the entire period of usefulness of his acquired knowledge (e.g., within three years). It may be assumed that due to his newly acquired knowledge, the employee will perform his work better.

Obviously, classical accounting treats investments in tangible fixed assets in a different manner than investments in employees. What are the possible reasons? Are there sound professional reasons to justify why all investments are not treated equally? The arguments of the opponents of human resource accounting are presented in the following.

Counterarguments to the proponents of human resource accounting are in most cases the following: employees are not the assets of the company; there are no relevant criteria to valuate employees; giving information on employees is somehow offensive; and human resource accounting would mislead the users of financial statements. An additional sound argument of human resource accounting opponents is that the accounting approach in this area is inappropriate with regard to commonly accepted accounting principles. They especially complain about noncompliance with the principle of prudence.

The classical accounting approach exaggerates in applying the principle of prudence in accounting, leading to a rather high amount of hidden reserves on the balance sheet. Hidden reserves are especially present among assets. The presence of hidden reserves is useful for the long-term existence and development of a company, and therefore the owners are interested in it. Hidden reserves lead to less successful operations, further leading to a lower tax burden in the current period.

Classical accounting does not record investments in employees as higher employee value—it instead discloses the investment amounts under expenses as they occur. They justify it with the principle of prudence in accounting. In other words, classical accounting does not disclose investments in employees under investments because it treats them as investments of high risk. But one may question whether investments in employees are so risky that they need to be treated as high-risk investments.

The classical accounting assumption in this area, namely that investments in employees are of high risk, is totally unjustified and professionally quite disputable. Investments in employees are investments, which generate the highest long-term yields. Furthermore, it is obvious that marketing the business effects of a low share of knowledge in the total costs of products and services is more and more difficult. Knowledge seems to be the only good whose demand will grow, and therefore it is expected to be traded for a price dictated by its high demand. It is expected that companies that do not invest in their employees risk the rapid failure of their economic activity.

The differences between the above-mentioned approaches are presented in the following within the context of two examples. The first example presents the differences graphically, while the second one presents them in terms of value (i.e., in m.u.).

It is assumed that the company has the opening balance sheet as shown in Figure 5.1

The company lacks the necessary equipment and therefore purchases it. The effect of such a business decision on the balance sheet is presented in Figure 5.2

It is obvious from figure 5.2 that the amount of cash decreases due to equipment purchases. However, as the amount of cash decreases, the value of equipment among assets increases.

Figure 5.1 Company's opening balance sheet

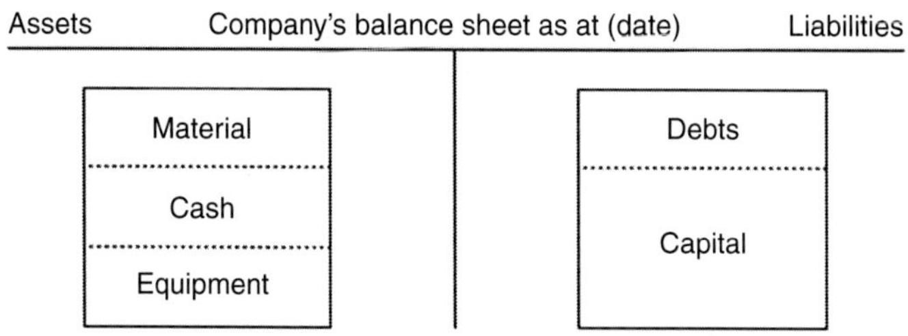

Figure 5.2 Company's balance sheet after purchasing equipment

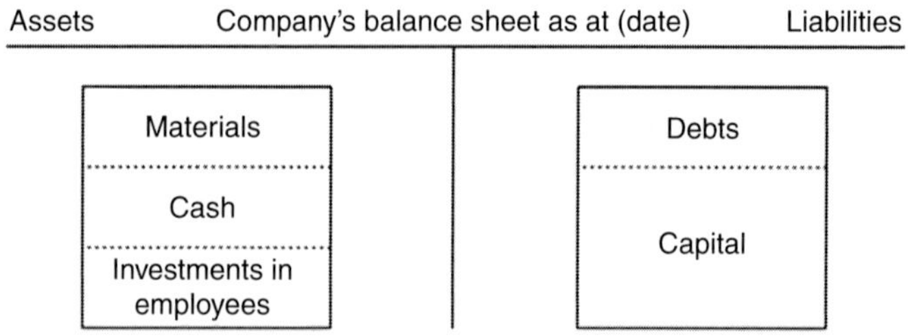

Figure 5.3 Company's balance sheet after making investments in employees

At this point, it is assumed that instead of purchasing equipment, the company invests the same amount in the education and training of its employees. The company's balance sheet after the investment is presented in Figure 5.3

However, investments in employees are not disclosed under assets, which means that they do not increase their value. The effect of investments in employees is presented in Figure 5.4

Investment seems to be the most common method of transforming assets without influencing the value of liabilities. However, investments in employees do not transform assets, because decreasing one asset (e.g., cash when investments in employees are made) does not increase another one (investments in employees are not disclosed under assets). Therefore, in classical accounting, investments in employees ruin the balance of the balance sheet, as there is an assets deficit with regard to liabilities. A ruined balance due to an assets deficit can be reestablished only by decreasing capital (e.g., disclosing a lower increase than in the case of disclosing investments in employees under assets).

In classical accounting, investments in employees can be compared with the irrational spending of money on lottery tickets that will not qualify for

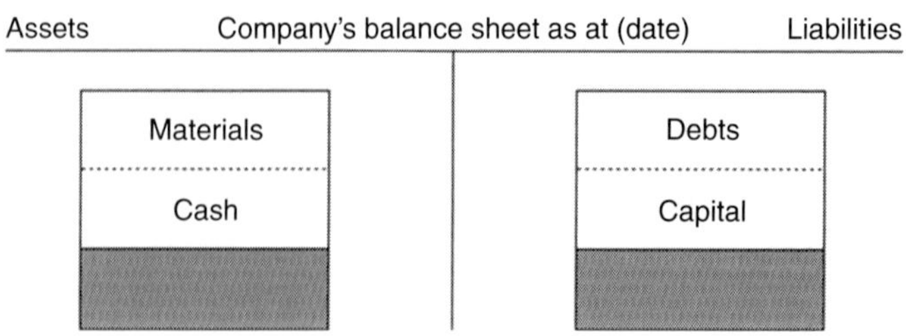

Figure 5.4 Company's closing balance sheet

prizes, since the accounting records do not show any expected benefit from them. Decreasing one asset does not result in increase of another asset or a decrease in liabilities. If investments that are not disclosed under assets result in decreased capital, would their disclosure under assets make capital increase? This question may sound absurd; however, it illustrates the inconsistency of classical accounting with regard to disclosing investments in employees.

The difference between both approaches is presented in the following example using monetary units. It is assumed that the company's revenues equal 1,000 monetary units and its expenses (less depreciation) equal 700 monetary units. In addition, investments in employees equal 100 monetary units and the depreciation of fixed assets 150 monetary units, while the useful life of investments in employees is five years. A portion of an income statement compiled by both classical accounting and human resource accounting is presented in Table 5.3

It is assumed that the company's current assets equal 600 monetary units and its fixed assets 900 monetary units (tangible fixed assets equal 800 m.u. and intangible fixed assets 100 m.u.). The assets side of the balance sheet is presented in Table 5.4

Table 5.3 Income statement compiled by both classical accounting and human resource accounting

Economic category	*Classical accounting*	*Human resource accounting*
1. Revenues	1,000	1,000
2. Expenses	950	870
–Expenses less depreciation	700	700
–Depreciation associated with fixed assets	150	150
–Depreciation associated with investments in employees	100	20
3. Profit	50	130

Table 5.4 Assets side of a balance sheet

Economic category	*Classical accounting*	*Human resource accounting*
1. Current assets	600	600
2. Fixed assets	900	980
–Tangible fixed assets	800	800
–Intangible fixed assets	100	100
–Investments in employees		80
3. Total assets	1,500	1,580

The above examples demonstrate that disclosing investments in employees under assets and depreciating them over their entire useful life enhances business performance. One may ask what kind of company would demonstrate more successful business operations most significantly if human resource accounting is used instead of classical accounting. In other words: Which companies or what operational factors would raise the most doubt with regard to a true and fair view of financial statements compiled by classical accounting?

It can be expected that when using human resource accounting, the biggest differences (compared to classical accounting) would occur in companies where the dynamic of investments in employees changes rapidly (a huge increase or decrease in their value). If investments in employees would increase a great deal, classical accounting would disclose the high costs associated with these investments in the current period. In human resource accounting, increased investments in employees would influence the costs and expenses in the current period to a lesser degree, because these amounts are gradually transferred among costs. However, in the event of a huge decrease in investments in employees, the situation would be the opposite. Classical accounting would disclose rather low costs associated with these investments in the current period, but in human resource accounting the influence of decreased or increased investments in employees on costs and expenses would not be so significant. It is evident from the above that rapid changes in the dynamic of investments in employees are reflected in successful business operations more significantly in classical accounting than in human resource accounting.

Performance Ratios Related to Investments in Employees

Performance Ratios Defined

Performance ratios can be defined in a narrow or broader sense. In a broad sense, they include absolute and relative figures; in a narrow sense, they include only relative figures. An absolute figure can be a particular figure (e.g., price), difference (e.g., operating result), or mean value (e.g., average amount of receivables), while relative figures include participation rate, index, and coefficient. In this article a broad performance ratio definition was applied.

Performance ratios can be subdivided in financial and nonfinancial ratios. Nonfinancial ratios are descriptive, while financial ratios are used when value-expressed amounts are compared. In this chapter financial performance ratios are used.

The Bases of Financial Performance Ratios Related to Investments in Employees

Financial performance ratios are based on (Milost, 2013, p. 514)

(a) asset purchase or cost value, and
(b) value added.

The purchase value of an asset equals the investment value associated with its acquisition. Usually, it is the amount paid to purchase the asset. An asset's cost value equals the amount of the costs needed for its production. Therefore, the concept of cost value should be applied in case of a manufacturer.

Both concepts are related to the economic concept of value, which is, like purchase or cost value, the basis for asset valuation. An important feature of assets is that they are transformed in a business process and the transformation is associated with the achievement of future economic benefits. Therefore, in economic terms, the value of an asset depends on the current value of the future economic benefits or services that can be expected from the asset during its entire useful life. This also applies to investments in employees. The value of investments in employees depends on the present value of their expected future services.

Yet another element of this approach is the value added. Business processes namely generate products and services. Furthermore, there are four basic elements required for a business process: assets, products, services, and human capital (employees). However, there is a significant difference between employees and the other three relevant elements. Assets, products, and services simply transfer their value to business effects. Employees, on the other hand, are the only element adding value to business effects. Therefore, the value added depends largely on the value of investments in employees.

The value added can be defined as the increased market value of business effects as a result of their increased quality. It is determined as the sales value of business effects minus the purchased value of used elements.

The value added reflects a company's concern for its general well-being and usefulness. People get jobs, the state takes its own share via taxes, and investors' and creditors' risk is paid off. Therefore, a company is not only a means to increase capital and thus generate profit but it also plays an important role in the social stratum.

Financial Performance Ratios Related to Investments in Employees

Financial performance ratios related to investments in employees are divided into basic and derivative. In the following, both are presented in detail.

Basic Ratios

Basic ratios are the ground upon which the system of integrated ratios related to investments in employees is built. They include

(a) efficiency of investments in employees,
(b) efficiency of labor costs, and
(c) coefficient of investments in employees.

The efficiency of investments in employees is a ratio of value added to the value of investments in employees:

$$\text{Efficiency of investments in employees} = \frac{\text{value added}}{\text{investments in employees}}$$

The ratio shows the number of monetary units of value added that can be attributed to the monetary units of investments in employees, thus the efficiency of such investments. The optimal value of investments in employees can be determined by observing the value of this ratio over a longer period of time.

Nevertheless, the aforementioned ratio carries powerful information. Value added is a result of employees' work efforts; therefore, it is their output. However, investments in employees are a source of necessary employee resources; therefore, they are the company's input.

In order to make the following discussion simple, let us assume that investments in employees aim only at retaining the working abilities of the employees. In this case the value of investments in employees equals the lost value of employees (the value the employees have added to the business effects) that has to be replaced due to their cooperation in a business process. Knowledge is prone to obsolescence, and a company needs to take care of the health and well-being of its employees as well as their loyalty to the company. According to the assumption that investments in employees equal their lost value replaced, it can be further hypothesized that the value of investments in employees in fact shows the amount of the aforementioned lost value. Furthermore, this means that the ratio showing the efficiency of investments in employees discloses the rate of working abilities' obsolescence or the longevity of such working abilities expressed in years.

When the value of this ratio increases, the management should take it as a sign that the value of investments in employees should be reasonably increased. Their further task is to valuate and determine which element of investments in employees should be increased and to what extent. However, when the value of this ratio decreases, the situation is contrary to the above-mentioned one, although it does not necessarily mean that the value of investments in employees should be decreased. In such a case the management's task is to find out whether the relationship between particular elements of investments in employees is appropriate.

From the point of view of a particular employee, the value of this ratio depends on how demanding the work he/she performs is, namely their value to the company (value of services he/she is providing to the company). However, from the point of view of the company, this value depends on the economic activity and the employee's qualifications.

Labor cost efficiency is a ratio of value added to labor costs:

$$\text{Labor cost efficiency} = \frac{\text{value added}}{\text{labor costs}}$$

The ratio shows the number of monetary units of value added that can be attributed to the monetary units of labor costs.

As already mentioned, the employees are the only element of a business process that can add value, while the other elements only transfer their value to business effects. However, the presence of employees in a business process is associated with labor costs. Furthermore, it should be assumed that these labor costs are lower than the value of the economic benefits or services the employees offer to the company, and thus lower than the value added, as other subjects beside employees are involved in sharing value added.

The labor cost efficiency value is usually greater than 1 and allows an indirect valuation of the overall performance of a company. The greater the labor cost efficiency ratio, the greater the shares of other participants in sharing value added (the state through taxes, lenders through interest, companies through profit reserves and retained net profit, and owners through dividends), which shows greater overall performance. If the value of the ratio is low, the situation is contrary to the above.

The coefficient of investments in employees is a ratio of labor costs to the value of investments in employees:

$$\text{Coefficient of investments in employees} = \frac{\text{labor costs}}{\text{investments in employees}}$$

It is obvious from the above equation that labor costs are an important part of the value of services employees offer to a company; thus they significantly contribute to the value added. However, investments in employees show the value of such investments associated with the achievement of future economic benefits, thus greater future value added.

The greater the ratio, the lower are the investments in employees. Based on the assumption that investments in employees aim at replacing the value the employees have added to the business effects, it can be speculated that a low value of such investments results in a low value added. Conversely, a low value of the ratio is the result of greater investments in employees and consequently higher value added.

Derivative Ratios

Derivative ratios are defined as participation rates. They show a share of a particular characteristic of a phenomenon within the whole and therefore also the relative meaning of it. These ratios are

(a) significance of investments in employees,
(b) significance of investments in knowledge,
(c) significance of investments in health and well-being, and
(d) significance of investments in loyalty to the company.

Significance of investments in employees is a ratio of the value of investments in employees to the value of all investments in a company:

$$\text{Significance of investments in employees} = \frac{\text{investments in employees}}{\text{investments}}$$

The ratio shows the share of investments in employees within the value of all investments in a company, thus the relative meaning of investments in employees. The value of this ratio influences the ratio between the future value added and the retained value in a company, thus the amount of future value added.

The concept of investments in employees is rather broad as they are composed of three elements. The value of this ratio largely depends on the business segment. Higher values of the ratio can be expected especially in companies characterized by a high share of knowledge included in the total costs of products and services.

Significance of investments in knowledge is a ratio of the value of investments in knowledge to the value of investments in employees:

$$\text{Significance of investments in knowledge} = \frac{\text{investments in knowledge}}{\text{investments in employees}}$$

The ratio shows the share of investments in knowledge within the value of investments in employees, thus the relative meaning of investments in knowledge. It depends mainly on the useful life of employee knowledge, thus the rate of knowledge obsolescence (more on this issue can be find in Milost, 2007a, pp. 149–150). Higher values of the ratio can be expected especially in companies characterized by a high share of knowledge included in the total costs of products and services.

Significance of investments in health and well-being is a ratio of the value of investments in health and well-being to the value of investments in employees:

$$\text{Significance of investments in health and wellbeing} = \frac{\text{investments in health and well-being}}{\text{investments in employees}}$$

The ratio shows the share of investments in health and well-being within the value of investments in employees, thus the relative meaning of investments in health and well-being. Its value depends mainly on the business segment and the working conditions. Higher values of the ratio can be expected in companies where working conditions unfavorably influence the health of employees.

Significance of investments in loyalty to the company is a ratio of the value of investments in loyalty to the company to the value of investments in employees:

$$\text{Significance of investments in loyalty to the company} = \frac{\text{investments in loyalty to the company}}{\text{investments in employees}}$$

The ratio shows the share of investments in loyalty to the company within the value of investments in employees, thus the relative meaning of investments in loyalty to the company. Its value depends mainly on the permanency of employment. Higher values of the ratio can be expected especially in companies characterized by less permanent employment, thus greater employee turnover.

A System of Integrated Financial Performance Ratios Related to Investments in Employees

Basic financial performance ratios related to investments in employees as formed above can be integrated in a system. This system of integrated financial performance ratios is based on the efficiency of investments in employees and is composed of a comparison between value added and the value of investments in employees. With integrated financial performance ratios, the efficiency of investments in employees is defined as a multiple of two ratios, namely the labor cost efficiency ratio and the coefficient of investments in employees. Efficiency of labor costs is a ratio of value added to the value of labor costs, while the coefficient of investments in employees is a ratio of labor costs to investments in employees (Milost, 2013, p. 518). The system of integrated ratios related to investments in employees is presented in figure 5.5.

Higher value added compared to labor costs favorably influences labor cost efficiency and therefore the efficiency of investments in employees. Furthermore, it means that the value of both ratios is higher in companies where the share of other entities in the process of creating and sharing the value added is greater.

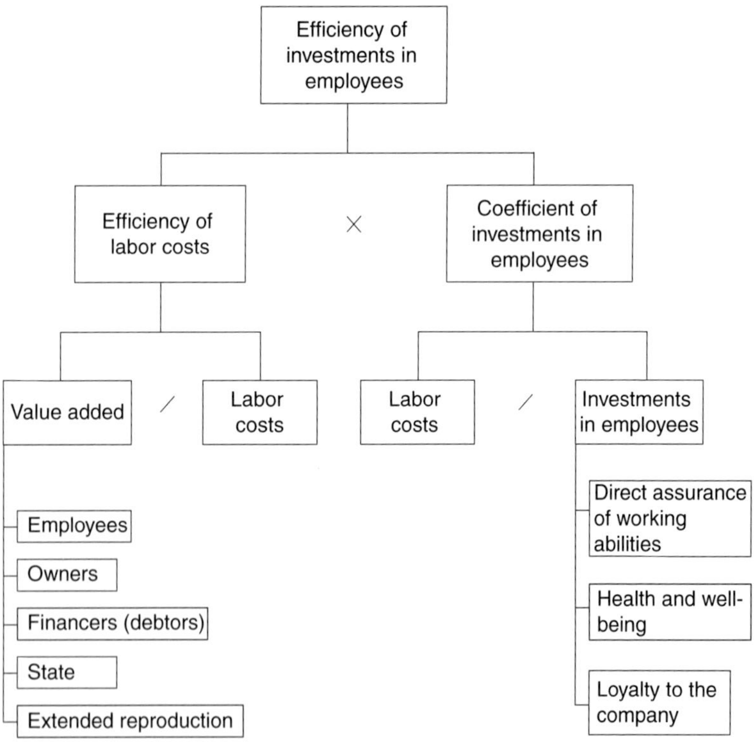

Figure 5.5 System of integrated financial ratios related to investments in employees

The same holds for the coefficient of investments in employees, which is a ratio of labor costs to investments in employees. Higher labor costs at a given value of investments in employees or a lower value of investments in employees at a given labor cost favorably influences the value of this ratio and thus the value of the efficiency of investments in employees.

The comparison of the values of the two aforementioned ratios gives rise to the power of information of basic ratios. It enables the comparison of current and past achievements in this area within the company as well as the comparison of companies in the same business segment and within the economy as a whole.

Conclusion

Apart from other elements of the business process, the value of human capital is not disclosed on the assets side of the classical balance sheet. The same applies to investments in human capital. The classical accounting approach does not transfer the value of investments in human capital among expenses during the entire period of their useful life—rather, it discloses investment amounts among expenses as they occur at the moment of the received invoice from an institution of education or other provider of relevant services. This is justified with the consistent recognition of the principle of prudence in accounting. The key assumption of this approach is that investments in employees are of high risk.

However, this assumption is professionally very disputable. Therefore, do financial statements compiled by using the classical approach provide a true and fair view? Is there any reason to doubt their true and fair view? Nowadays, there are companies whose market value is several times higher than their book value. Such differences are too profound to simply label them as an operating surplus.

If one were in a position of an authorized auditor who, together with his colleagues, would have to evaluate the operations of such a company, what kind of an auditor's opinion would one give? Would one really claim that the financial statements show a true and fair view of the property, financial position, and operating performance of the company?

As the data on investments in employees are not disclosed among assets, it is logical that performance ratios based on the data of classical financial statements lack these data too. Uniquely shaped financial performance ratios related to investments in employees as well as the system of integrated ratios presented in this chapter aim at filling the above-mentioned gap as the value of investments in employees is going to significantly influence the value added of a company in the future.

References

Almeida, R., & Carneiro, P. (2008). "The return to firm investments in human capital." The World Bank, Social Protection & Labour, SP Discussion Paper No. 0822, 1–30.

Au, A. K. M., Altman, Y., & Roussel, J. (2008). Employee training needs and percieved value of training in the Pearl River Delta of China. *Journal of European Industrial Training, 32*, 19–31.

Becker, G. S. (1962). Investment in human capital: A theoretical analysis. *Journal of Political Economy, 70*, 9–49.

Becker, G. S. (1964). *Human Capital: A Theoretical and Empirical Analysis, with Special Reference to Education*. New York: NBER.

Becker, G. S. (2006). *Human Capital: The Concise Encyclopedia of Economics*. Liberty Fund, Inc., Library of Economics and Liberty, 1–6.

Blundell, R., Dearden, L., Meghir, C., & Sianesi, B. (1999). Human capital investment: The returns from education and training to the individual, the firm and the economy. *Fiscal Studies, 20*, 1–23.

Cantrell, S., Benton, J. M., Laudal, T., & Thomas, R. J. (2008). Measuring the value of human capital investments: The SAP case. *Strategy and Leadership, 34*, 43–52.

Chang, J. (1999, January). "The decline in value relevance of earnings and book values." Working Paper, Philadelphia, PA: University of Pennsylvania.

Collins, D., Maydew, E., & Weiss, I. (1997). Changes in the value-relevance of earnings and book values over the past forty years. *Journal of Accounting and Economics, 23*, 39–67.

Ely, K., & Waymire, G. (1999). Accounting standard setting organizations and earnings relevance: Longitudinal evidence from NYSE common stocks, 1927–93. *Journal of Accounting Research, 37*, 293–317.

Flamholtz, E. G. (1974a). *Human Resource Accounting*. Encino, CA: Dickenson.

Flamholtz, E. G. (1974b). Human resource accounting: A review of theory and research. *Journal of Management Studies, 11*, 44–61.

Francis, J., & Schipper, K. (1999). Have financial statements lost their relevance? *Journal of Accounting Research, 37*, 319–352.

Frederickson, J. R., Webster, E., & Williamson, I. O. (2010). Is the current accounting treatment of education and training costs appropriate? *Australian Accounting Review, 20*, 265–273.

Gibbons, R., & Waldman, M. (2004). Task-specific human capital. *American Economic Review, 94*, 203–207.

Haltiwanger, J. C., Lane, J. I., & Spletzer, J. R. (1999). Productivity differences across employers: The roles of employer size, age and human capital. *American Economic Review, 89*, 94–98.

Hatch, N. W., & Dyer, J. H. (2004). Human capital and learning as a source of sustainable competitive advantage. *Strategic Management Journal, 25*, 1155–1178.

Hunter, L., Webster, E., & Wyatt, A. (2010). "Identifying corporate expenditures on intangibles using GAAP." Working Paper No. 07/09, Intellectual Property Research Institute of Australia. Melbourne, VIC: The University of Melbourne.

Johanson, U. (1997). The profitability of investments in work life-oriented rehabilitation. *Personnel Review, 28*, 395–415.

Kanodia, C., Singh, R., & Spero, A. E. (2005). Imprecision in accounting measurement: Can it be value enhancing? *Journal of Accounting Research, 43*, 487–519.

Kendrick, J. (1972). The treatment of intangible resources as capital. *Review of Income and Wealth, 18*, 109–125.

Lazear, E. P. (2009). Firm-specific human capital: A skill-weights approach. *Journal of Political Economy, 117*, 914–940.

Lev, B. (2008). A rejoinder to Douglas Skinner's 'Accounting for intangibles—A critical review of policy recommendations'. *Accounting and Business Research, 38*, 209–213.

Lev, B., & Zarowin, P. (1999). The boundaries of financial reporting and how to extend them. *Journal of Accounting Research, 37*, 353–385.

Milost, F. (2007a). *Računovodstvo človeških zmožnosti: Zakaj klasične bilance ne kažejo prave slike o premoženjskem in finančnem stanju podjetij ter o njihovi poslovni uspešnosti?* ("Human resource accounting: Why don't classical financial statements show a true and fair picture of the property, financial position and operating results of a company?"). Koper: Faculty of Management, University of Primorska.

Milost, F. (2007b). A dynamic monetary model for evaluating employees. *Journal of Intellectual Capital, 8*, 124–138.

Milost, F. (2013). Investments in human capital: Elements of investments, their valuation, and the related financial performance ratios. *Chinese Business Review, 12*, 509–520.

Mincer, J. (1974). *Schooling, Experience and Earnings*. New York, NY: Columbia University Press.

Roslender, R. (2009). So tell me again . . . just why would you want to account for people? *Journal of Human Resource Costing and Accounting, 13*, 143–153.

Roslender, R., & Stevenson, J. (2009). Accounting for people: A real step forward or more a case of wishing and hoping? *Critical Perspectives on Accounting, 20*, 855–869.

Sakamoto, A., & Kim, C. (2006). "Estimating the human capital screening effects of schooling on productivity in US manufacturing industries, 1979–1996." Paper presented at the Population Association of America 2006 annual meeting program, Los Angeles, CA, March 30–April 1.

Samudhram, A., Sanmugam, B., & Teng Low, K. L. (2008). Valuing human resources: An analytical framework. *Journal of Intellectual Capital, 9*, 655–667.

Syverson, A. (2010). "What determines productivity?" NBER Working Paper 15712. Cambridge, MA: National Bureau of Economic Research.

Walker, J. (2010). The use of performance-based remuneration: High versus low-growth firms. *Australian Accounting Review, 20*, 256–264.

Webster, E. (1999). *The Economics of Intangible Investment*. Cheltenham, UK: Edward Elgar Publishing Ltd.

Wyatt, A., & Frick, H. (2010). Accounting for investments in human capital: A review. *Australian Accounting Review, 20*, 199–220.

CHAPTER 6

Intellectual Capital Efficiency and Corporate Performance: Some Empirical Evidence

Domenico Celenza, Marco Lacchini, and Fabrizio Rossi

Introduction

In recent decades, the vision of the company has changed considerably. Recent studies have attributed vital importance to knowledge management (Trequattrini, 2008) and intellectual capital reporting (ICR) as drivers for the creation of firm value (Skandia, 1998). The importance of the interaction between physical assets and intellectual capital could contribute to two basic explanations: not only does the value of the firm depend on tangible and financial capital, but the efficiency of equity markets also depends on the efficiency of the intellectual capital employed.

The study of intellectual capital according to a financial perspective leads inevitably, in the authors' opinion, to the theory of the valuation of a company and the assumption of efficient markets.

At the end of the 1950s, a famous article by Modigliani and Miller (1958) pointed out the irrelevance of financial structure for the purpose of creating value. More specifically, the authors argued that the market value of any firm is independent of its capital structure and is obtained by capitalizing its expected return at the discount rate appropriate to its risk class. The two authors, starting from extremely strong hypotheses, showed that in a perfect market (in the absence of taxes, transaction costs, information asymmetry, and bankruptcy costs, and assuming that all users have the ability to lend and borrow any amount of resources at a risk-free rate), the value of a business depends solely on the nature of the assets regardless of the type of funding sources used to finance them.

Modigliani and Miller's thesis represented the precursor of the capital asset pricing model (Sharpe, 1964), according to which there is a linear relationship between risk and return that is explained by beta, the coefficient of systematic or nondiversifiable risk. In other words, the performance of equity securities depends only on the beta and no other factor.

Instead, Ball and Brown (1968) tried to demonstrate the existence of a relationship between accounting data and equity performance. Fama, Fisher, Jensen, and Roll (1969) studied empirically the degree of informational efficiency of stock markets in the presence of equity splits by demonstrating the efficiency of markets.

Markets tend toward efficiency but are not perfectly efficient. Markets are efficient to the extent that the prices of securities fully reflect available information that may affect their value in one way or another. The price of the stock should be equal to its intrinsic value, which in turn is a function of macroeconomic and microeconomic variables: it cannot be constant, but varies with the variation of intrinsic value.

The efficiency of a market is characterized by the speed with which the stock price incorporates all the information; however, this means that, since the price is equal to the intrinsic value, the stock is in a state of equilibrium. In other words, the price of the securities should be equal to the present value of the future cash flows that investors expect according to the risk profile.

Fama (1970) has identified three different forms of efficiency: weak, semi-strong, and strong. The weak form provides for the use of information limited only to historical prices, in which case operators would not be able to obtain abnormal returns by simply resorting to the observations of the performance that the securities have registered in the past. Moreover, in such a context, even technical analysis would prove to be practically ineffective, since it is based on past observations.

Semi-strong efficiency starts from the assumption that stock prices rebalance immediately when information is published. In this reality, prices reflect both past information as well as all current business information (dividend announcements, annual reports, and all other news incorporated by the media of financial information). In this way it is clear that operators are unable to achieve abnormal returns because the information quickly becomes publicly available and is therefore immediately reflected in stock prices.

In the strong form of efficiency, which is an extreme situation and therefore rarely corresponds to a verifiable hypothesis, stock prices reflect both public and private information.

A market, therefore, is defined as efficient if at any time the stock prices reflect fully, correctly, and promptly all available information.

Shiller (1981), on examining the time series of the Standard & Poor's (S&P) for the period 1971–1979, observed an excessive volatility in prices, in such a way as to challenge the postulates of the efficient market hypothesis. The author concluded, in fact, with the argument that prices move more on the basis of volatility rather than rationality; the gap between market value and fundamental value is too wide and persists for long periods of time. The volatility of the stock market is too high to be justified by the variation in dividends.

Therefore, there has been a change in the prospects of study: from an exclusively financial perspective, there has been a shift to a vision of the company marked also by the interaction between assets and their relational capabilities and the evaluation of human capital (Zanda, Lacchini, & Oricchio, 1993).

In more recent years, in fact, there has been an increasing emphasis on the importance of human capital, intellectual capital in general, and its interaction with physical assets (Grossman & Hart, 1986; Hart, 1995; Hart & Moore, 1990, 1994), to the point of considering the firm as an independent summation of assets (Moore, 1992).

Zingales (2000) highlighted the changes that have taken place within the enterprise as a result of the market's growing demand for innovation, which has increased the importance of human capital. The company is now seen as a network of specific investments that cannot be replicated by the market (Rajan & Zingales, 2001).

The bursting of the speculative bubble at the end of the 1990s once again highlighted the irrationality of markets, emphasizing the interest in the study of intellectual capital for the role that the intellectual capital (IC) could have on equity markets.

The objective of this chapter is to present the results of some empirical evidence on the relationship between IC and financial performance. The discussion will address the topic of human capital in the broader context of intellectual capital. The work is structured in six sections. This first section is devoted to introduction, the second section is devoted to intellectual capital and capital reporting, the third section examines its measurement using the Value Added Intellectual Coefficient (VAIC^{TM}), the fourth section reviews the literature on the relationship between IC and financial performance, the fifth section presents the empirical evidence with particular reference to the Italian scenario, and the last section ends with a summary and conclusions.

Intellectual Capital and Capital Reporting

Intellectual capital (IC) is a set of intangible assets that in the knowledge economy are taking a leading role in creating value for businesses. While there is no generally accepted definition, it may be useful to consult Stewart's definition (1997), according to which IC is the "packaging of useful knowledge" (p. 67).

Intellectual capital is distinguished from financial capital and can be divided into three subcategories: human capital, structural capital, and relational capital (Bontis, 1996).

Sharabati, Jawad, and Bontis (2010) define the three components of intellectual capital. Human capital represents the intangible resources and more particularly the intellectual heritage individuals: learning and education, experience and expertise, innovation and creation. Structural capital is the organization's resources in terms of systems and programs, research and development (R&D), and intellectual property rights. Relational capital, however, is understood as strategic alliances, licensing, commercial agreements, the relational networks that enterprises create with partners, suppliers and customers, and the knowledge that develops within the relational network.

A detailed definition of the three components of intellectual capital is reported in MERITUM (2002, p. 13):

> Human capital is defined as the knowledge that employees take with them when they leave the firm. It includes the knowledge, skills, experiences and abilities of people. Some of this knowledge is unique to the individual, some may be generic. Examples are innovation capacity, creativity, know-how and previous experience, teamwork capacity, employee flexibility, tolerance for ambiguity, motivation, satisfaction, learning capacity, loyalty, formal training and education.
>
> Structural capital is defined as the knowledge that stays within the firm at the end of the working day. It comprises the organizational routines, procedures, systems, cultures, databases, etc. Examples are organizational flexibility, a documentation service, the existence of a knowledge centre, the general use of Information Technologies, organizational learning capacity, etc. Some of them may be legally protected and become Intellectual Property Rights, legally owned by the firm under separate title. Relational capital is defined as all resources linked to the external relationships of the firm, with customers, suppliers or R&D partners. It comprises that part of Human and Structural Capital involved with the company's relations with stakeholders (investors, creditors, customers, suppliers, etc.), plus the perceptions that they hold about the company. Examples of this category are image, customers loyalty, customer satisfaction, links with suppliers, commercial power, negotiating capacity with financial entities, environmental activities, etc.

The interest in the study of intellectual capital increased toward the second half of the 1990s as a result of the irrationality of the stock markets, and many scholars see this driver as a possible explanation for the gap between the market value and book value of listed companies (Edvinsson & Malone, 1997), arguing that IC may provide additional information compared to the traditional financial statement (Bontis & Fitz-enz, 2002; Sharabati et al., 2010).

According to Edvinsson (1997), the market value of a company is influenced not only by physical capital but also by intellectual capital.

In this context, the composition of a company's intellectual capital report is an integral part of company information. The reporting tool is an expression of the surveys, values, and results that are not covered in the company information. The preparation of an intellectual capital report requires the presence of two objectives: an internal and an external objective. The first considers the document as a useful planning tool for the strategic management of knowledge. A few quantitative analyses (Danish Ministry of Science, Technology, and Innovation, 2003) conducted on the subject show how the strategic management of intellectual capital generates new knowledge and, therefore, new value. With regard to the external goals, the intellectual capital report can represent a communication driver for the value of the knowledge, initiatives, and results of management.

Sonnier, Carson, and Carson (2008) investigated a sample of 141 listed companies in the United States operating in traditional sectors of the economy in order to assess the level of intellectual capital disclosure between 2000 and 2004. They noted an increase of intellectual capital disclosure during the period examined, and an increased focus by management in disseminating information about the intangible assets.

The main purpose of companies that have published an intellectual capital report is linked to the need to demonstrate their level of business innovation and flexibility. Although these assets can be "invisible," since they are not directly represented in financial statements, they represent an important economic resource for the enterprise.

Several research and institutional initiatives have been undertaken on the issue of intangible assets and intellectual capital in order to highlight the differential competitive advantage. Hall (1992), for example, argues that the differential and sustainable competitive advantage results from a series of intangible assets ranging from patents to reputation, to know-how.

Ordóñez de Pablos (2004) also recognized that it is knowledge-based resources that provide the firm with a competitive advantage in the changing economy.

The majority of the pilot experiences took place, however, in northwestern Europe.[1] The first company to be interested in the methods of representation and valuation of intangibles was Skandia, a Swedish financial/insurance firm, in 1991, which began producing an intellectual capital report aimed at visualizing elements and parameters related to its intangibles. Skandia was also the first to introduce the figure of chief knowledge officer (CKO).

A few years later, the Danish Ministry of Industry and Trade launched a project entitled "Intellectual Capital Statement," whose result was a report on ten companies that realized an intellectual capital statement. After the success of the initiative, in 1998 and in 2001, a year after the publication of the first report, the experiment was repeated, this time with an initial sample of 19 companies, which reached approximately 100 firms in the last phase.

Another experience was the "Nordika" project implemented by the Nordic Industrial Fund,[2] with the purpose of defining the guidelines for the preparation and publication of new forms of company intellectual capital reports. The result was the *Intellectual Capital—Managing and Reporting* (2001), a document structured in three parts:

- reasons for preparing a financial statement of intangibles,
- the process of implementing a statement for intangibles, and
- cases of companies that have produced an intellectual capital report.

An operational approach was used: a list of indicators that should be part of the intellectual capital statement[3] was provided.

In the Italian economic scenario, companies such as Brembo,[4] Agrileasing Plastal, and IGuzzini have experienced forms of intellectual capital reporting.

In addition, the European Union has recognized the importance of intangibles through industrial policies aimed at promoting innovation and technological diffusion. To this end, the establishment of the High Level Expert Group (HLEG) should be mentioned, an interdisciplinary working group set up by the Directorate General "Enterprises" of the European Commission. This project, which began in 2000, has produced a report that describes the influence of intangibles on management and corporate performance and the resulting implications for companies, financial markets, public institutions, and regulators (Eustace, 2001; RICARDIS, 2006).

The response to these European initiatives was a study conducted in 2001 by the US Brookings Institution, entitled *The Unseen Wealth* (Blair & Wallman, 2001). More recently, there is a detailed study that examines the development of intellectual capital employed in the United States and other countries in the world (Lin & Edvinsson, 2011).

The need to produce additional information with respect to the past is due to the fact that intangibles have changed the dynamics of the world economy. There has been a shift from a conservative approach based on the annual budget (Figure 6.1) prepared by companies to the request for additional

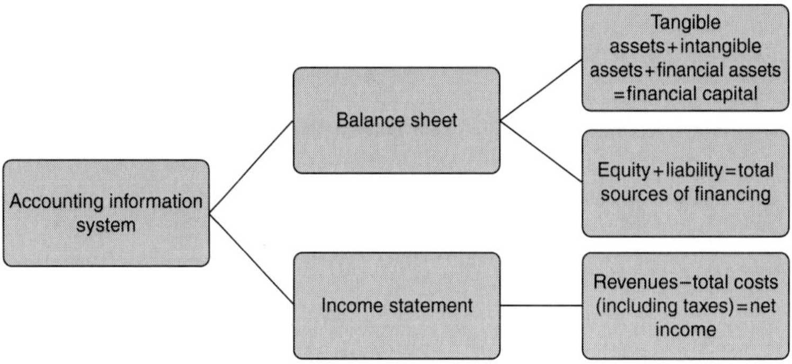

Figure 6.1 Conservative accounting approach

information regarding precisely intellectual and human capital, which are the bases of intangibles.

Although the information flow required comes mainly from accounting information, it is necessary to process and convey optional information of a qualitative nature to the outside, by writing selected reports, which are useful for the representation of certain disclosures on the company system.

The tools of the company information system, together with intellectual capital reporting (ICR), allow for the definition of a new model of stock value (Figure 6.2).

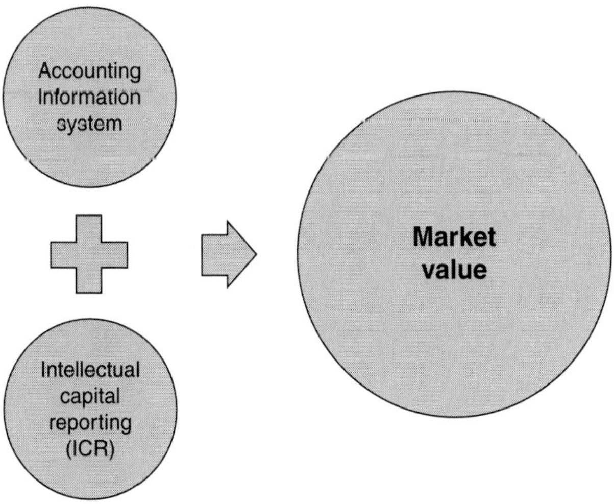

Figure 6.2 New approach to market value

The disclosure is based on ethical and social communication, of a purely qualitative nature. The information on intellectual capital, as inferred by the annual financial statement and by the social statement, is not entirely satisfactory (Rusconi, 1988). The first document represents qualitative-quantitative information, taking a prudent approach to intangibles; the second focuses mainly on one of the dimensions of intellectual capital: relational capital.

In light of this, the composition of an innovative model for the representation of intellectual capital completes the company's information system.

The intellectual capital report can be described as a document capable of integrating the traditional reporting system of the company. Its value is closely linked to the continuity and periodicity of its composition, which allows for comparison of the results obtained over time.

The structure and content of a sustainable model of an intellectual capital report (RICARDIS, 2006) can be characterized by the following key factors:

1. the purpose of the report,
2. the methodological premise,
3. descriptions of methodologies used for reporting intellectual capital,
4. the evaluation process;
5. conclusions: the value of intellectual capital.

The purpose of this model lies in providing a clear and comprehensive representation of intellectual capital: the information is integrated qualitatively and quantitatively compared to the other documents of its information system. The additional information tends to increase the level of knowledge addressed to all stakeholders (Freeman, Rusconi, & Dorigatti, 2007).

The methodological premise defines the implementing procedures of the report; intellectual capital is identified and defined, in light of its components, in qualitative and quantitative terms.

The analysis of the intangible asset, in quantitative terms, can be carried out, starting from the financial statements, by determining the real value of intellectual capital. The use of *ad hoc* evaluation methods allows one to determine the value of human capital (Zanda et al., 1993), structural capital, and relational capital: in this case, evaluation methodologies refer to those mentioned in the previous chapter.

In consideration of the results obtained using the application of the method(s) chosen, it is possible to valorize each dimension of intellectual capital.

An intellectual capital report structured in this way allows defining the distinctive characteristics of company disclosure, more in line with stakeholders' needs (Freeman, 1984). In fact, this report, regardless of the accounting information included in the financial statements and in the social statement, allows pointing out a precise value for each dimension of intellectual capital (Freeman et al., 2007).

Thus, the company information system is integrated, since the obligatory and supplementary communication are accompanied by the support of a model that allows for the valorization of intellectual capital. In addition to the valorization of intellectual capital, it is possible to determine innumerable summary indicators of intellectual capital for the reporting of human capital, structural capital, and relational capital.

In this sense, the report proposed is sustainable: it is motivated by the fact that the needs of corporate stakeholders must be satisfied, starting from clear and comprehensive communication.

Capital reporting could help to reduce information asymmetry. Lev and Sougiannis (1996), for example, noted that by considering the potential gains resulting from the capitalization of expenditure on R&D, relevant information is obtained that affects the flow of future revenues and therefore the value of companies.

Edvinsson (1997) believes that IC may represent a sort of balance between the market value and the financial capital of companies.

Sveiby (1997) presents a measurement model of intangible assets called the intangible asset monitor, assuming that intangibles can be divided into three categories: internal structure, external structure, and human resources skills.

Lev and Sougiannis (1999) investigated the relationship between book-to-market value and subsequent equity returns, as there appears to be a relationship only for intensive R&D companies. They found that if the capital in R&D is considered in the regression, the correlation between book-to-market and R&D is not significant. In other words, the authors try to understand whether completely unexploited intangibles can explain the book-to-market "enigma."

Rylander, Jacobsen, and Roos (2000) instead argue for an integration of intellectual capital within the balance sheet or, alternatively, to draw up an intellectual capital report. The existing asymmetries between firms and the market are multiplying, and many managers believe that their companies are underrated; therefore, it could be useful to take a different approach that takes into account the opportunity to supplement the balance sheet.

Healy and Palepu (2001), after an extensive and critical review of literature, ask themselves how the disclosure will affect the cost of capital.

Whiting and Miller (2008) investigated the relationship between IC disclosure and the "hidden value" of 70 companies in New Zealand and concluded that firms that are reevaluated according to unconsidered value show a positive correlation.

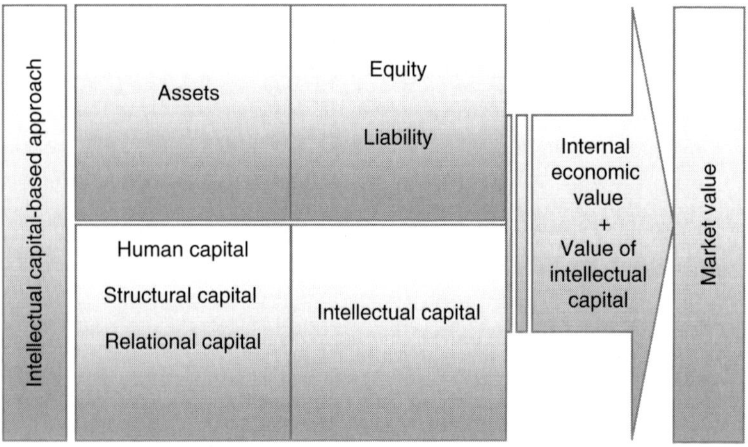

Figure 6.3 Theoretical framework

The use of classical accounting information and ICR creates a new reference model for the determination of market value (Figure 6.3).

The illustrated theoretical model highlights two important aspects: the need for additional information with respect to the classical information flow and the application of a model for the measurement of intellectual capital efficiency. The Value Added Intellectual Coefficient (Pulic, 2000), despite its criticism, is currently a widely used indicator in empirical literature for the measurement of intellectual capital efficiency.

Value Added Intellectual Coefficient as an Indicator of IC (the VAIC™ Method)

The Value Added Intellectual Coefficient is a model proposed by Pulic (2000, 2004) and is based on some key steps calculated as follows:

$$VA = OUT - IN$$

where VA = value added of the company; OUT = total sales revenue; and IN = all of the operating costs excluding personnel costs, depreciation, and amortization.

The VA can be calculated as follows:

$$VA = OP + EC + D + A$$

where OP = operating profit; EC = cost of employees; D = depreciation; and A = amortization.

The next step is to determine the coefficients as follows:

$$\text{VAHC} = \frac{\text{VA}}{\text{HC}}$$

where HC = total personnel costs for the enterprise. VAHC measures the efficiency of human capital.

Structural capital is the second component of the intellectual capital and is calculated as follows:

$$\text{SC} = \text{VA} - \text{HC}$$

From the latter is obtained

$$\text{STVA} = \frac{\text{SC}}{\text{VA}}$$

where SC = structural capital. The value added structural capital coefficient (STVA) shows the contribution of SC in the creation of value and measures the efficiency of structural capital.

Finally, the VACE (value added capital employed coefficient) or VACA is calculated, which measures the ability of the capital employed in creating value for the company and is calculated as follows:

$$\text{VACA} = \frac{\text{VA}}{\text{CA}}$$

where CA = the sum of the physical and financial capital employed.

The VAIC™ is obtained from the sum of the three indicators (VAHC, STVA, and VACA):

$$\text{VAIC} = \text{STVA} + \text{VAHC} + \text{VACA}$$

which measures efficiency in the creation of value.

According to Pulic, the VAIC measures the efficiency of intellectual capital, and the cost of personnel is considered as an investment and not a cost; as he explains, "VAIC measures how much new value has been created per invested monetary unit in each resource. A high coefficient indicates a higher value creation using the company's resource, including its intellectual capital" (p. 65).

In the following analysis, this indicator thus calculated for all linear regression models was used.

A Review of Literature

Several empirical studies demonstrate the impact of intangible assets on both the company's financial performance and stock returns. Aboody and Lev (2000) showed that the impact of generating IC on the current and future operating earnings was very strong. With reference to the chemical industry, for example, they showed that increase in R&D investments doubled the operating profits.

Bornemann, Knapp, Schneider, and Sixl (1999) found that firms that manage their IC more effectively were able to secure a very strong competitive advantage over other companies and to perform better than them.

There is no single definition of IC. Stewart (1997), for example, defined IC as the "packaging of useful knowledge" (p. 67). Instead, Petty and Guthrie (2000) gave IC a much more incisive meaning. They considered it instrumental both in determining the value of the company and in improving the economic performance of a nation. In the literature, there is also a widely accepted idea of the existence of a strong relationship between IC and the market value of firms. For example, Lev and Zarowin (1999), Lev (2001), and Lev and Radhakrishnan (2003) had focused on the gap between the market value and book value of companies, while trying to investigate the invisible values that did not appear in financial statements. More generally, there have been hypotheses about the weight that IC can have on the value of the company and on the need to consider not only the financial variables but also the value of IC.

Edvinsson and Malone (1997), indeed, defined IC as the gap that is observed between a firm's market value and book value.

Marr, Schiuma, and Neely (2004) proposed an organizational approach based on the knowledge assets map and the knowledge assets dashboard. The introduction of the knowledge assets map and knowledge assets dashboard can help firms to identify their key knowledge assets. In particular, the knowledge assets dashboard stresses the important actor/infrastructure relationship and the dynamic nature of these assets.

Pulic (2000) offered an additional measure of the value of IC through the VAIC™, which included both physical capital and human and structural capital.

Firer and Williams (2003) tested the VAIC. However, they failed to find a strong relationship with the company's profitability.

On the contrary, Chen, Cheng, and Hwang (2005) found that IC had a very strong impact on the market value and the performance of firms. In particular, investments in R&D can provide additional information on structural capital and generate a positive effect on firm value and profitability.

Cabrita and Vaz (2005) investigated a sample of 53 Portuguese banks and found that IC is significantly correlated with the organizational performance of the banks and that the interaction between the components of the IC generates greater value.

Tan, Plowman, and Hancock (2007) investigated 150 companies listed on the Singapore stock exchange during the period 2000–2002 and found a positive relationship between the VAIC and financial performance in several sectors, including manufacturing. The results of the manufacturing sector would seem statistically more robust. The authors also divided the sample into three groups according to the values of the VAIC and found that groups of companies with higher VAIC values correspond to results that are positive and statistically more robust than the values recorded by the companies with the lowest VAIC.

Huang and Wang (2008) investigated 37 companies listed on the Taiwan stock market (14 firms belonging to traditional industrial sectors and 23 to the electronics industry) during the period 2001–2003. The two authors used Ohlson's model (1995) by including in the model both the EVA® (Economic Value Added) indicator and intellectual capital in order to capture residual information. The two authors found that by including certain variables as proxies of IC, the explanatory power of the regression model increases. In other words, the intellectual capital proxy, together with the EVA, provides incremental information for the evaluation of companies.

Kamath (2008), however, did not see any relation between IC and the traditional performance measures, such as profitability and market value. Even Ghosh and Mondal (2009), after investigating 80 companies operating in the pharmaceutical and information sector and testing the relationship between IC and company performance, found that market value and productivity were not significantly related to IC. However, they pointed out that IC was a good predictor of productivity.

Puntillo (2009) examined a sample of banks listed on the Italian stock market, but he failed to find a strong relationship between IC, return on investment (ROI), and return on assets (ROA).

Muhammad and Ismail (2009) examined 18 Malaysian financial companies in 2007 and found a positive and statistically significant relationship between the VAIC and ROA.

Carlucci and Schiuma (2010) addressed the issue from another perspective and dwelt on the need to identify performance indicators to be placed in the perspective of an analytical network approach, as the selection of these performance indicators is one of the biggest challenges companies will have to face in order to develop an efficient system of performance measurement.

The authors emphasized the importance of the interaction of the indicators as a guideline for decision-makers.

Clarke, Seng, and Whiting (2010) investigated a sample of Australian-listed companies during the period 2004–2008 and found a direct relationship between IC and the performance (ROA and ROE) of companies.

Ferraro and Veltri (2011) investigated a large sample of companies listed on the Italian stock market through Ohlson's model and found that the variables of the IC did not show a significant relationship with the market value of firms.

Gigante and Previati (2011) investigated the Italian banking sector during the period 2003–2007, using stock returns as the dependent variable. The results obtained indicated a positive but not statistically significant relationship between equity returns, the VAIC, and its components.

Maditinos, Chatzoudes, Tsairidis, and Theriou (2011) investigated the relationship between IC, market value, and financial performance of a sample of 96 Greek-listed companies during the period 2006–2008. The results are not in line with most of the hypotheses made, thus emphasizing the failure of the hypothetical relationship between IC and the market-to-book value (M/BV). However, they identify a statistically significant relationship between the efficiency of human capital and ROE.

Rehman, Rehman, Rehman, and Zahid (2011) investigated 12 Pakistani companies and found a positive and statistically significant relationship between the components of the VAIC and the ROE.

A recent study by Ståhle, Ståhle, and Aho (2011) brings into question the validity of the VAIC in the measurement of the efficiency of intellectual capital. Specifically, the authors investigated, on the one hand, 125 Finnish companies during the period 2006–2008 and did not find any relationship either between the VAIC and market value, or between the VAIC and changes in market value, except for the efficiency of human capital. On the other hand, they investigated the validity of the methodological VAIC and concluded that the model is approximate and therefore is not valid to measure the efficiency of intellectual capital.

Venugopal and Subha (2012) examined 41 firms producing software in India during the period 2000–2010 and found that, although the efficiency of capital employed and the efficiency of structural capital were both significantly and positively related to the financial performance, there was no direct relationship between the VAIC (served as an indicator for measuring IC) and the financial performance. They emphasized, however, that "the model which studied the relationship between components of VAIC and financial performance explained the firm's value better" (Venugopal & Subha, 2012, p. 130).

Celenza and Rossi (2012a), examined a sample of 11 Italian-listed companies during the period 2003–2008 and measured the relationship between the VAIC and M/BV and between the VAIC and the profitability indicators (ROI and ROE) and did not find a significant relationship between the variables.

Celenza and Rossi (2012b) proposed a methodology consisting in the construction of an adjusted multiplier based on a simplified version of the VAIC™. The adjusted multiplier is obtained from the product between the simplified VAIC and the ratio of the ROE of the firm to the ROE of the sector the firm belongs to. The algorithm allows for a better illustration of the efficiency of the intellectual capital in a context of sectoral performances.

Javornik, Tekavcic, and Marc (2012) investigated 12,000 Slovenian companies during the period 1995–2008 and found a positive and statistically significant relationship between VAIC, ROA, and ROE and between the components of the VAIC and financial performance.

Janosevic, Dzenopoljac, and Bontis (2013) investigated 100 Serbian companies in 2010 and found a positive and statistically significant relationship between the ROE and the efficiency of capital employed and between the ROE and the efficiency of human capital.

Celenza and Rossi (2014a) investigated 23 Italian-listed companies belonging to different sectors, during the period 2003–2008, and found no relationship between financial performance and the VAIC. However, they found a positive and statistically significant relationship between the changes in market value and changes in the VAIC and between changes in performance indicators (ROI, ROE, and return on sales (ROS)) and changes in the VAIC, concluding that the VAIC improves the explanation of the regression analysis and assuming its utility as an "additional coefficient" in the analysis of equity performance.

More recently, Celenza and Rossi (2014b) investigated the existence of a relationship between the efficiency of intellectual capital and the financial performance of Italian manufacturing firms in the period 2002–2011. The analysis was divided into three methodological stages. In the first stage the relationships between the M/BV and the VAIC and between the financial indicators (ROI, ROE, ROS) and the VAIC were examined. The results suggest a positive and statistically significant relationship for both the ROI and ROE. In the case of the M/BV, however, there is no relationship with the VAIC. The results obtained in the second stage, by rearranging the sample according to the values of the VAIC, point out a positive and more robust relationship between the variables examined, with the exception of the M/BV. In the last stage of the analysis, the results suggest that the high-VAIC portfolios record a higher average performance compared to low-VAIC portfolios and that intellectual capital could be a discriminating variable in returns.

The Results of the Empirical Evidence

The empirical evidence on the relationship between IC and the performance of listed companies shows conflicting results. Studies conducted on the Asian situation tend to confirm the relationship between financial performance and the VAIC. Table 6.1 shows some study results.

The table shows how the studies concerning Europe do not always confirm this relationship. In Italy, for example, the relationship between IC and financial performance is confirmed in the manufacturing sector (Celenza & Rossi, 2014b). Interesting results emerge instead from Celenza and Rossi (2014a), who tested the relationship between the changes in market value and the changes in the VAIC. The results obtained emphasize the importance of the VAIC as an "additional factor" in the explanation of the variations in market values over time.

New Empirical Evidence from Italy: Methodology and Results

Following the methodology already tested in Celenza and Rossi (2012a), a new analysis is proposed in this context in order to verify the relationship between the VAIC and business performance on a larger sample, both in numbers and in relation to a temporal horizon.

In particular, a sample of 43 Italian-listed companies during the period 2002–2011 was examined, whose data were obtained from Datastream and Mediobanca, and all apply to companies with a high content of intellectual capital.

The hypotheses tested are the following:

H0: there is a positive and statistically significant relationship between the VAIC and its coefficients (STVA, VAHC, VACA);
H1: there is a positive and statistically significant relationship between the market-to-book value (M/BV) and the VAIC;
H1a: there is a positive and statistically significant relationship between the M/BV and the components of VAIC (STVA, VAHC, VACA);
H2: there is a positive and statistically significant relationship between ROI and VAIC;
H2a: there is a positive and statistically significant relationship between the ROI and the components of VAIC (STVA, VAHC, VACA);

Table 6.1 The results of the studies relating to various countries in the world

Authors	*Country/region*	*Model*	*Results*
Firer and Williams (2003)	South Africa	Regression analysis (ROA, M/BV, VAIC)	Negative relationship with Value added human capital (VAHU)
Chen et al. (2005)	Taiwan	Regression analysis (M/BV, ROA, ROE, VAIC)	Positive relationship
Shiu (2006)	Taiwan	Regression analysis (ROA, M/BV, VAIC)	Positive relationship
Appuhami (2007)	Thailand	Regression analysis (capital gains, VAIC)	Positive relationship
Chan (2009)	Hong Kong	Regression analysis (M/BV, ROA, ROE, ATO, VAIC)	Positive relationship
Ting and Lean (2009)	Malaysia	Regression analysis (ROA, VAIC)	Positive relationship
Zéghal and Maaloul (2010)	UK	Regression analysis (ROS, ROA, M/BV, VAIC, VACA)	Positive relationship with VAIN and VACA
Wang (2011)	Taiwan	Regression analysis (M/BV, ROA, ATO, VAIC)	Positive relationship with VAHU
Maditinos et al. (2011)	Greece	Regression analysis (ROE, M/BV, ROA, growth revenues (GR), VAIC elements)	Negative relationship M/BV-VAIC, positive relationship ROE-VAHU
Celenza and Rossi (2012a)	Italy	Regression analysis (ROE, M/BV, ROI, ROS, VAIC elements)	Positive but insignificant relationship (M/BV-VAIC; ROE-VAIC; ROI-VAIC)
Mojtahedi (2013)	Malaysia	Regression analysis (earning per share (EPS), return on capital employed (ROCE), growth of annual sales (GS), VAIC elements)	Positive relationship with VACA, VAHC, STVA
Celenza and Rossi (2014a)	Italy	Two steps of analysis. First step: regression analysis ROE, ROI, ROS, M/BV, and VAIC. Second step: Regression analysis ΔROI, ΔROE, ΔROS, ΔMV, and ΔVAIC	No relationship between financial performance and the VAIC for the first step. Positive and statistically significant relationship for the second step
Celenza and Rossi (2014b)	Italy	Three steps of analysis. First step: regression analysis ROE, ROI, ROS, M/BV, and VAIC. Second step: regression analysis ROI, ROE, ROS, M/BV, and high VAIC. Third step: difference between the returns on portfolios of high and low VAIC	Positive and statistically significant relationship for the first step (ROI-VAHC; ROI-STVA; ROI-VAIC; ROE-VAIC; ROE-STVA). Second step: ROE-VAIC, ROS-VAIC, and ROI-VAIC, positive and statistically significant relationship. Third step: The high-VAIC portfolios seem to outperform the low-VAIC portfolios

H3: there is a positive and statistically significant relationship between ROE and VAIC;
H3a: there is a positive and statistically significant relationship between ROE and the components of VAIC (STVA, VAHC, VACA);
H4: there is a positive and statistically significant relationship between ROS and VAIC;
H4a: there is a positive and statistically significant relationship between ROS and the components of VAIC (STVA, VAHC, VACA);
H5: the VAIC explains part of the changes in market value (MV);
H5a: the components of the VAIC (STVA, VAHC, VACA) explain part of the changes in MV.

The models used to test the listed hypotheses are the following:

$$\text{VAIC}_{\text{it}} = \alpha_0 + \alpha_1\text{STVA}_{\text{it}} + \alpha_2\text{VAHC}_{\text{it}} + \alpha_3\text{VACA}_{\text{it}} + \varepsilon_{\text{it}} \quad \text{(M1)}$$

$$\text{Performance}_{\text{it}} = \alpha_0 + \alpha_1\text{VAIC}_{\text{it}} + \varepsilon_{\text{it}} \quad \text{(M2)}$$

$$\text{Performance}_{\text{it}} = \alpha_0 + \alpha_1\text{STVA}_{\text{it}} + \alpha_2\text{VAHC}_{\text{it}} + \alpha_3\text{VACA}_{\text{it}} + \varepsilon_{\text{it}} \quad \text{(M3)}$$

where Performance is equal alternatively to M/BV, ROI, ROE, ROS, and ΔMV.

Table 6.2 shows the statistical values of the variables used in the regression model.

The M/BV recorded a mean value of 1.78 and a median value of 1.58, both higher than unity.

The average value of ΔMV is 0.52 and the median value is 0.05. The average value of VAIC is equal to 3.24 and the median value is equal to 2.56. The value of the VAIC proves that all listed companies with a high content of

Table 6.2 Descriptive statistics for the selected variables

	VAIC	*M/BV*	*STVA*	*VAHC*	*VACA*	*ROI*	*ROE*	*ROS*	*ΔMV*
Average	3.24	1.78	0.30	2.61	0.49	0.15	0.01	0.07	0.52
SE	0.54	0.17	0.17	0.48	0.23	0.04	0.08	0.05	0.26
Median	2.56	1.58	0.44	1.77	0.24	0.08	0.08	0.09	0.05
SD	3.53	1.12	1.14	3.15	1.48	0.25	0.54	0.32	1.69
Min	−5.15	0.33	−6.54	0.69	−1.56	−0.01	−3.37	−1.28	−0.89
Max	21.27	6.16	1.73	20.23	9.66	1.37	0.73	1.13	8.79
No. of firms	43	43	43	43	43	43	43	43	43

Note: SE = Standard error. SD = Standard deviation.

intellectual capital were included in the sample. Further evidence of the high content of intellectual capital of the 43 companies also results from the mean and median values of VAHC, equal to 2.61 and 1.77, respectively.

Table 6.3 shows the results gathered from the three econometric models used to test the hypotheses.

The results obtained emphasize the positive and statistically significant relationship only between the VAIC and its components, and this was to be expected. However, this demonstrates the usefulness of the VAIC as a tool for measuring the efficiency of intellectual capital. The hypothesis H0 must therefore be accepted.

The other hypotheses must all be rejected. In particular, the relationship between the M/BV and the VAIC is negative and statistically significant, as well as that between the M/BV and the components of the VAIC.

As for the ROI, the relationship with the VAIC and its components is almost always positive but it is not statistically significant. Even between the VAIC and ROE, there is a positive relationship but not statistically significant. The situation is different for the ROS, as there is a positive and statistically significant relationship only with the STVA.

Of particular interest, however, is the relationship between the changes in market value and the VAIC and its components. The relationship is almost always positive but not statistically significant, except with the VACA.

These results could be interpreted in two ways:

(a) equity performance is not at all affected by the efficiency of intellectual capital;
(b) equity performance is affected only by the efficiency of the physical and financial capital employed (VACA).

Human capital does not statistically affect the performance of firms. However, the efficiency of human capital, measured by VAHC, seems to be the most statistically significant variable in the regression with the VAIC. The coefficient is positive and the *t*-value (73.42) is the highest of the three coefficients of the regression (see Table 6.3). This demonstrates that the efficiency of human capital is a key variable in the VAIC model.

Summary and Conclusions

The objective of this work is to measure the efficiency of intellectual capital and to review the empirical evidence on IC. The empirical literature on the relationship between the VAIC and firm performance is vast and discordant. While in most Asian countries there is a positive and statistically significant

Table 6.3 The results of the hypotheses tested

Coefficient	*H0*	*H1*	*H1a*	*H2*	*H2a*	*H3*	*H3a*	*H4*	*H4a*	*H5*	*H5a*
	VAIC	*M/BV*		*ROI*		*ROE*		*ROS*		*ΔMV*	
VAIC		−0.09*		0.00		0.02		0.00		0.00	
(t-value)		(−1.97)		(0.22)		(1.25)		(0.58)		(0.00)	
STVA	0.95***		−0.33**		−0.00		0.02		0.10**		0.07
(t-value)	(25.25)		(−2.27)		(−0.03)		(0.26)		(2.40)		(0.47)
VAHC	0.99***		−0.04		0.00		0.01		−0.01		−0.03
(t-value)	(73.42)		(−0.80)		(0.19)		(0.69)		(−0.69)		(−0.53)
VACA	0.30***		−0.08		0.00		0.08		0.00		0.85***
(t-value)	(10.50)		(−0.71)		(0.00)		(1.40)		(0.21)		(7.18)
Intercept	0.20***	2.08***	2.03***	0.14***	0.14***	−0.08	−0.08	0.03	0.05	0.52	0.16
(t-value)	(3.67)	(9.25)	(9.15)	(2.77)	(2.74)	(−0.78)	(−0.77)	(0.58)	(091)	(1.46)	(0.67)
R^2	0.99	0.09	0.15	0.00	0.00	0.03	0.06	0.00	0.13	0.00	0.57
Adj. R^2	0.99	0.06	0.09	−0.02	−0.07	0.01	−0.01	−0.01	0.06	−0.02	0.54
F-test	2,360***	3.89*	2.38*	0.05	0.01	1.56	0.83	0.34	1.94	0.00	17.48***

Note: *, **, and *** indicate significance at 10 percent, 5 percent, and 1 percent levels, respectively.

relationship between performance and the VAIC, in Europe and especially in Italy this relationship does not seem to exist.

The further empirical testing proposed here, which involved 43 Italian-listed companies belonging to various sectors of the economy during the period 2002–2011, does not seem to validate the relationship between intellectual capital efficiency and financial and equity performance. The main indicators tested (M/BV, ROI, ROS, ROE, and ΔMV) are not affected by the VAIC and more precisely are not affected either by the efficiency of structural capital, or by the efficiency of human capital. Some significant relationships seem to emerge between the changes in market value and VACA and between ROS and STVA.

The results differ from other studies in the literature (Chan, 2009; Chen et al., 2005; Zéghal & Maaloul, 2010) and instead appear to be in line with the work of Celenza and Rossi (2012a, 2014a), Maditinos et al. (2011), and Firer and Williams (2003).

In Italy, just like in other countries, there does not seem to be any relationship between the VAIC and the M/BV and financial performance. There could be various reasons:

(1) the absence of capital reporting would affect the non-acquired information flow resulting from the intellectual capital efficiency;
(2) the VAIC could not be regarded as a valid decision-making tool for measuring intellectual capital efficiency, consistent with the view taken by Ståhle et al. (2011);
(3) the stock market is more interested in the use of physical and financial capital than of intellectual capital.

As regards human capital, instead, there is a different interpretation. The coefficient VAHC, which theoretically should measure the efficiency of human capital in Pulic's model (2004), is highly significant, as mentioned above, in the regression with the VAIC. The coefficient is positive but never significant with regard to ROI and ROE. In this connection it should be verified if VAHC really is a good proxy for human capital and whether, in the Italian context, the incidence of the cost of work affects the significance of the coefficient.

However, it is risky to draw definitive conclusions because of both the sample size and the time period examined. It must be kept in mind that since 2008 there has been a financial and economic crisis of vast proportions, which is still in progress and which has hit many European countries, Italy in particular, and which is putting enterprises to the test. More empirical studies are needed both to measure the efficiency of intellectual capital and to test the relationship between financial performance and the VAIC.

With regard to the relationship between the M/BV and the VAIC, the authors believe that a greater in-depth conceptual analysis is required. The M/BV is known to be an indicator that should measure, indirectly, the degree of efficiency of the stock market, but this does not mean that the difference between the market value and book value should be referable to intellectual capital alone. And if it were, intellectual capital efficiency in Italy could be reasonably lower than that of countries Brazil, Russia, India, China, South Africa (BRICS) with a high gross domestic product (GDP) growth rate.

Moreover, in a closed capitalist context, like the Italian one, it is unlikely that the M/BV will assume a value of 1, in the authors' opinion, at least for two reasons:

(1) the Italian stock market is less efficient than others because in Italy there is a "bank-centric" economic system;
(2) the ownership shares traded on the stock market do not represent the majority of the capital and at times do not reach 50 percent of the total share capital.

In a perfectly competitive environment, a prerequisite of market efficiency, the increase of free float is expected to reduce the traded share prices, and consequently the market value of companies, thus reducing the gap with regard to the book value of the stock.

Notes

1. At the European level, guidelines have been issued to help businesses prepare their intellectual capital statements. The main ones are those of the International Federation of Accountants (IFAC) in 1998, the Danish Agency for Trade and Industry (DATI) in 2000 and 2003, the Nordika project in 2001, and the MEasuRing Intangibles To Understand and improve innovation Management (MERITUM) project in 2002.
2. The Nordic Industrial Fund is a public financial institution shared by Norway, Sweden, and Finland.
3. The Nordika project continued with another project carried out by the Nordic Industrial Fund; the confederations of Nordic countries Danish industry, Confederation of Finnish Industry and Employers, Helge Løvdal, the Confederation of Norwegian Business and Industry, and Confederation of Norwegian Business and Trade and the association of Icelandic information technology (IT) companies. The objectives of the project were

- to develop methods and practices for the measurement and reporting of intangibles through the creation of a network of Nordic companies;
- to increase the awareness of existing methods and practices aimed at them through dialogue and cooperation with companies, institutions, etc.;
- to launch learning initiatives in the field, aimed at the companies included in the sample, made up of small and medium-sized businesses that wished to work with the reporting and management of intangibles.

4. Brembo was founded in 1961 in Paladina (Bergamo) and today is present with 23 subsidiaries or affiliates in 14 countries on four continents. It has production sites in Italy, Spain, Poland, the United Kingdom, Mexico, Brazil, Japan, and China and sells in 70 countries. The distinguishing feature of the company is the vertical integration of the production process, covering all stages of manufacturing. It is currently structured in five business units (Automobiles, Commercial Vehicles, Motorcycles, Racing, After Market) plus the Industrial Division, supported by the central management. The company has almost 4,000 employees. Source: Gruppo Brembo (2005).

References

Aboody, D., & Lev, B. (2000). Information asymmetry, R&D, and insider gains. *Journal of Finance, 55*(6), 2747–2766.

Appuhami, R. (2007). The impact of intellectual capital on investors' capital gains on shares: An empirical investigation of Thai banking, finance & insurance sector. *International Management Review, 3*(2), 14–25.

Ball, R., & Brown, P. (1968). An empirical evaluation of accounting income numbers. *Journal of Accounting Research, 6*(2), 159–178.

Blair, M. M., & Wallman, S. M. H. (2001). *The Unseen Wealth, Report of the Brookings Task Force on Intangibles*. Washington, DC: Brookings Institution Press.

Bontis, N. (1996). There's a price on your head: Managing intellectual capital strategically. *Ivey Business Journal* (formerly *Business Quarterly, Summer, 6*(4), 40–47.

Bontis, N., & Fitz-enz, J. (2002). Intellectual capital ROI: A causal map of human capital antecedents and consequents. *Journal of Intellectual Capital, 3*(3), 223–247.

Bornemann, M., Knapp, A., Schneider, U., & Sixl, K. I. (1999). *Holistic Measurement of Intellectual Capital. International Symposium: Measuring and Reporting Intellectual Capital: Experiences, Issues, and Prospects*, Amsterdam: OECD, June 9–10.

Cabrita, M., & Vaz, J. L. (2005). Intellectual capital and value creation: Evidence from the Portuguese banking industry. *Electronic Journal of Knowledge Management, 4*(1), 11–20.

Carlucci, D., & Schiuma, G. (2010). Determining key performance indicators: An analytical network approach. In A. Gunasekaran & M. Sandhu (Eds.), *Handbook on Business Information Systems* (pp. 515–536). Singapore: World Scientific Publishing Company.

Celenza, D., & Rossi, F. (2012a). The relationship between intellectual capital (IC) and stock market performance: Empirical evidence from Italy. *Journal of Modern Accounting and Auditing, 8*(11), 1729–1741.

Celenza, D., & Rossi, F. (2012b). The human capital valuation in IC paradigm: An empirical proposal. *China-USA Business Review, 11*(11), 1525–1541.

Celenza, D., & Rossi, F. (2014a). Intellectual capital and performance of listed companies: Empirical evidence from Italy. *Measuring Business Excellence, 18*(1), 22–35.

Celenza, D., & Rossi, F. (2014b). "Value Added Intellectual Coefficient (VAIC™) and financial performance: Empirical evidence from the Italian manufacturing sector. In D. Cagáňová & M. Čambál (Eds.), *Proceedings of the 6th European Conference on Intellectual Capital ECIC 2014* (pp. 168–178). Trnava, Slovak Republic: Slovak University of Technology (STU).

Chan, K. H. (2009). Impact of intellectual capital on organisational performance. An empirical study of companies in the Hang Seng Index (Part 2). *Learning Organisation, 16*(1), 22–39.

Chen, M. C., Cheng, S. J., & Hwang, Y. (2005). An empirical investigation of the relationship between intellectual capital and firms' market value and financial performance. *Journal of Intellectual Capital, 6*(2), 159–176.

Clarke, M., Seng, D., & Whiting, R. H. (2010). "Intellectual capital and firm performance in Australia" Working paper series no 12, Department of Accountancy and Business Law, University of Otago, New Zealand. Available at http://otago.ourarchive.ac.nz/bitstream/handle/10523/1585/Working_paper_Clarke-Seng-Whiting-revised.pdf

DMSTI (2003). *Intellectual Capital Statements—The New Guideline.* Copenhagen: Danish Ministry of Science, Technology, and Innovation.

Edvinsson, L. (1997). Developing intellectual capital at Skandia. *Long Range Planning, 30*(3), 366–373.

Edvinsson, L., & Malone, M. S. (1997). *Intellectual Capital: Realizing Your Company's True Value by Finding Its Hidden Brainpower.* New York, NY: Harper Business.

Eustace, C. (2001). *The Intangible Economy—Impact and Policy Issues.* Report of the High Level Expert Group on the Intangible Economy. Luxembourg Office: European Commission. Available at http://bookshop.europa.eu/en/intangible-assets-and-industrial-competitiveness-hleg-report-pbNB3100772/downloads/NB-31-00-772-EN-C/NB3100772ENC_001.pdf;pgid=y8dIS7GUWMdSR0EAlMEUUsWb0000Qv43608S;sid=BUIqVTE5IMUqcmBA3HK08lMcp4FWBTbqA5E=?FileName=NB3100772ENC_001.pdf&SKU=NB3100772ENC_PDF&CatalogueNumber=NB-31-00-772-EN-C

Fama, E., Fisher, L., Jensen, M., & Roll, R. (1969). The adjustment of stock prices to new information. *International Economic Review, 10*(1), 1–21.

Fama, E. F. (1970). Efficient capital markets: A review of theory and empirical work. *Journal of Finance, 25*(2), 383–417.

Ferraro, O., & Veltri, S. (2011). The value relevance of intellectual capital on the firm's market value: An empirical survey on the Italian listed firms. *International Journal of Knowledge-Based Development, 2*(1), 66–84.

Firer, S., & Williams, S. M. (2003). Intellectual capital and traditional measures of corporate performance. *Journal of Intellectual Capital, 4*(3), 348–360.

Freeman, R. E. (1984). *Strategic Management: A Stakeholder Approach*. Boston, MA: Pitman.

Freeman, R. E., Rusconi, G., & Dorigatti, M. (2007). *Teoria degli Stakeholder*. Milan: Franco Angeli Editor.

Ghosh, S., & Mondal, A. (2009). Indian software and pharmaceutical sector IC and financial performance. *Journal of Intellectual Capital, 10*(3), 369–388.

Gigante, G., & Previati, D. (2011). A knowledge oriented approach to the investigation of Italian banks performances. *International Journal of Economics and Finance, 3*(5), 12–23.

Grossman, S., & Hart, O. (1986). The costs and benefits of ownership: A theory of vertical and lateral integration. *Journal of Political Economy, 94*(4), 691–719.

Gruppo Brembo (2005). Bilancio del valore tangibile e intangibile. Available at http://www.brembo.com/it/Investitori/reports/Documents/Reports%202005/tangibile-Intangibile2005_31-12-2005.pdf

Hall, R. (1992). The strategic analysis of intangible resources. *Strategic Management Journal, 13*(2), 135–144.

Hart, O. (1995) *Firms, Contracts, and Financial Structures*. Oxford: Oxford University Press.

Hart, O., & Moore, J. (1990). Property right and nature of the firm. *Journal of Political Economy, 98*(6), 1119–1158.

Hart, O., & Moore, J. (1994). A theory of debt-based on the inalienability of human capital. *Quarterly Journal of Economics, 109*(4), 841–879.

Healy, P. M., & Palepu, K. G. (2001). Information asymmetry, corporate disclosure, and the capital markets: A review of the empirical disclosure literature. *Journal of Accounting and Economics, 31*, 405–440.

Huang, C., & Wang, M.-C. (2008). The effects of economic value added and intellectual capital on the market value of firms: An empirical study. *International Journal of Management, 25*(4), 722–731.

Janosevic, S., Dzenopoljac, V., & Bontis, N. (2013). Intellectual capital and financial performance in Serbia. *Knowledge and Process Management, 20*(1), 1–11.

Javornik, S., Tekavcic, M., & Marc, M. (2012). The efficiency of intellectual capital investments as a potential leading indicator. *International Business and Economic Research Journal, 11*(5), 535–558.

Kamath, G. B. (2008). Intellectual capital and corporate performance in Indian pharmaceutical industry. *Journal of Intellectual Capital, 9*(4), 684–784.

Lev, B. (2001). *Intangibles: Management and Reporting*. Washington, DC: Brookings Institution Press.

Lev, B., & Radhakrishnan, S. (2003). "The measurement of firm-specific organization capital." NBER Working Paper, No. 9581. Cambridge, MA: National Bureau of Economic Research. Available at http://www.nber.org/papers/w9581

Lev, B., & Sougiannis, T. (1996). The capitalization, amortization and value-relevance of R&D. *Journal of Accounting and Economics, 21*, 107–138.

Lev, B., & Sougiannis, T. (1999). Penetrating the book-to-market black box: The R&D effect. *Journal of Business Finance and Accounting, 26*(3–4), 419–449.

Lev, B., & Zarowin, P. (1999). The boundaries of financial reporting and how to extend them. *Journal of Accounting Research, 37*(2), 353–385.

Lin, Y-Y. C., & Edvinsson, L. (2011). *National Intellectual Capital: A Comparison of 40 Countries*. New York, NY: Springer.

Maditinos, D., Chatzoudes, D., Tsairidis, C., & Theriou, G. (2011). The impact of intellectual capital on firm's market value and financial performance. *MIBES Transactions, 5*(1), 58–72.

Marr, B., Schiuma, G., & Neely, A. (2004). Intellectual capital—Defining key performance indicators for organizational knowledge assets. *Journal of Intellectual Capital, 10*(5), 551–569.

Mediobanca. (2012). *Indices and Data on Investments in Listed Securities.* Milan: Mediobanca Research.

MERITUM (2002). *Guidelines for Managing and Reporting on Intangibles (Intellectual Capital Report)*. European Union. Available at http://www.pnbukh.com/files/pdf_filer/MERITUM_Guidelines.pdf

Modigliani, F., & Miller, M. H. (1958). The cost of capital, corporation finance and the theory of investment. *American Economic Review, 48*(3), 261–297.

Mojtahedi, P. (2013). Intellectual capital accounting and its impact on organizational financial performance: Evidence from Malaysian firms. *Journal of Basic and Applied Scientific Research, 3*(3), 840–845.

Moore, J. (1992).The firm as a collection assets. *European Economic Review, 36*(2–3), 493–507.

Muhammad, N., & Ismail A. (2009). Intellectual capital efficiency and firm's performance: Study on Malaysian financial sectors. *International Journal of Economics and Finance, 1*(2), 206–212.

Nordika (2001). *Intellectual Capital—Managing and Reporting*. Oslo: Nordic Industrial Fund. Available at http://www.nordicinnovation.org/Global/_Publications/Reports/2001/nordika_report_-_final1.pdf

Ohlson, J. A. (1995). Earnings, books value, and dividends in equity valuation. *Contemporary Accounting Research, 11*(2), 661–687.

Ordóñez de Pablos, P. (2004). Measuring and reporting structural capital: Lessons from European learning firms. *Journal of Intellectual Capital, 5*(4), 629–647.

Petty, P., & Guthrie, J. (2000). Intellectual capital literature review: Measurement, reporting, and management. *Journal of Intellectual Capital, 1*(2), 155–175.

Pulic, A. (2000). MVA and VAIC™analysis on randomly-selected companies from FTSE 250. Retrieved July 12, 2011. Available at http://www.vaic-on.net

Pulic, A. (2004). Intellectual capital—Does it create or destroy value? *Measuring Business Excellence, 8*(1), 62–68.

Puntillo, P. (2009). Intellectual capital and business performance: Evidence from Italian banking industry. *Electronic Journal of Corporate Finance, 4*(12), 96–115.

Rajan, R. G., & Zingales, L. (2001). The firm as a dedicated hierarchy: A theory of the origins and growth of firms. *Quarterly Journal of Economics, 116*(3), 805–851.

Rehman, W., Rehman, C. A., Rehman, A., & Zahid, A. (2011). Intellectual capital performance and its impact on corporate performance: An empirical evidence from modaraba sector of Pakistan. *Australian Journal of Business and Management Research, 1*(16), 8–16.

RICARDIS (2006). *Reporting Intellectual Capital to Augment Research, Development and Innovation in SMEs.* Available at http://ec.europa.eu/invest-in-research/pdf/download_en/2006-2977_web1.pdf

Rusconi, G. (1988). *Il bilancio sociale d'impresa. Problemi e prospettive.* Milan: Giuffrè Editor.

Rylander, A., Jacobsen, K., & Roos, G. R. (2000). Towards improved information 67 disclosure on intellectual capital. *International Journal of Technology Management, 20*(5/6/7/8), 715–741.

Sharabati, Abdel-Aziz A., Jawad, S. N., & Bontis, N. (2010). Intellectual capital and business performance in the pharmaceutical sector of Jordan. *Management Decision, 48*(1), 105–131.

Sharpe, W. F. (1964). Capital asset prices: A theory of market equilibrium under conditions of risk. *Journal of Finance, 19*(3), 425–442.

Shiller, R. (1981). Do stock prices move too much to be justified by subsequent changes in dividends? *American Economic Review, 71*(3), 421–436.

Shiu, H.-J. (2006). The application of the value added intellectual coefficient to measure corporate performance: Evidence from technological firms. *International Journal of Management, 23*(2), 56–65.

Skandia (1998). *Human Capital in Transformation. Intellectual Capital Supplement.* Available at www.skandia.se

Sonnier, B. M., Carson, K. D., & Carson, P. P. (2008). Intellectual capital disclosure by traditional US companies: A longitudinal assessment. *Journal of Accounting and Organizational Change, 4*(1), 67–80.

Ståhle, P., Ståhle, S., & Aho, S. (2011). Value Added Intellectual Coefficient (VAIC): A critical analysis. *Journal of Intellectual Capital, 12*(4), 531–551.

Stewart, T. A. (1997). *Intellectual Capital: The Wealth of New Organizations.* London: Nicholas Brealey Publishing.

Sveiby, K. E. (1997). *The New Organizational Wealth: Managing & Measuring Knowledge Based Assets* (1st Edition). San Francisco, CA: Berrett-Koehler Publishers.

Tan, H. P., Plowman, D., & Hancock, P. (2007). Intellectual capital and financial returns of companies. *Journal of Intellectual Capital, 8*(1), 76–95.

Ting, W. K., & Lean, H. H. (2009). Intellectual capital performance of financial institutions in Malaysia. *Journal of Intellectual Capital, 10*(4), 588–599.

Trequattrini, R. (2008). *Conoscenza ed economia aziendale.* Naples: Esi.

Venugopal, D., & Subha, M. V. (2012). Intellectual capital and value creation efficiency—An empirical investigation into the intellectual capital and financial performance of Indian software industry. *European Journal of Social Sciences, 33*(1), 119–132.

Wang, M. S. (2011). "Intellectual capital and firm performance." Annual Conference on Innovations in Business & Management, The Center for Innovations in Business and Management, Practice, London UK. Available at http://www.cibmp.org/Papers/Paper566.pdf

Whiting, R. H., & Miller, J. C. (2008). Voluntary disclosure of intellectual capital in New Zealand annual reports and the "hidden value." *Journal of Human Resource Costing and Accounting, 12*(1), 26–50.

Zanda, G., Lacchini, M., & Oricchio, G. (1993). *La valutazione del capitale umano dell'impresa*. Turin: Giappichelli Editor.

Zéghal, D., & Maaloul, A. (2010). Analysing value added as an indicator of intellectual capital and its consequences on company performance. *Journal of Intellectual Capital, 11*(1), 39–60.

Zingales, L. (2000). In search of new foundations. *Journal of Finance, 55*(4), 1623–1653.

CHAPTER 7

An Assessment of the Accounting Perspective on Intellectual Capital and Some Results from the European Union

Michele Di Marcantonio and Marco Mattei

Introduction

Firms can be seen as a socio-technical system composed of assets, people, operations, etc. The social aspect is very important considering that people, with different expertise and needs, are always interacting with firms for various reasons and in various capacities (investors, suppliers, employees, etc.).

Among these persons who interact with firms every day are the firms' employees, also known as "human resources." We speak of human resources because employees—a general term referring to workers, directors, and stakeholders of the company—are, in all respects, like other assets (e.g., property, plants, and equipment), necessary in order to enable firms to achieve the business' purpose.

Traditionally, accounting theory has focused on tangible assets and on related productive processes, neglecting human capital. This was due to a context in which tangible assets appeared scarce when they were the target of growing demand. In more recent times, human resources have been investigated on a more in-depth basis, and many accounting experts have begun to study different assessment approaches in order to estimate a value that could be representative of this asset. This need emerged due to the growth of services businesses and has accelerated with development of the knowledge economy. Therefore, this change in context has originated the concept that the value of human resources is, in substance, the value of the firm.

Consistent with this concept, Burton A. Weisbrod in 1961 (p. 425) wrote that

> [t]he market mechanism places a value on those assets to which title can be transferred, and thus the market does evaluate land and capital goods in our economy. The market also provides rental values (wage rates) for labor but not capitalized values, and these are frequently essential for rational decision-making.[1] It would be useful if we could develop a substitute for the market evaluation of labor resources. This involves establishing a conceptual framework for estimating the value of assets in the form of human capital.

This view is, from an accounting perspective, very suitable because human resources are capable of affecting both cash flow and balance sheet values. In fact, since the 1980s, we cannot escape the fact that as a result of the dematerialization of services, which are characterized by a greater quantity of knowledge and information, a large part of firms' value has been shifting to the intangible assets area. More in particular, there are many businesses that are based on intellectual property (brands, patents, copyright, etc.) or, simply, on know-how that is related to a certain organization and quality of staff. In these businesses (e.g., high-tech sector), these elements are able to generate value in a greater amount than tangible or financial assets. Therefore, human resources should be investigated from an accounting perspective in order to better develop a financial statement that represents these resources.

In order to investigate the key issues related to this area, it is very useful to start from the concepts of human capital (HC) and intellectual capital (IC) developed by accounting experts. Subsequently, we shall summarize the current accounting treatment in order to raise some considerations on the adequacy of the accounting principles in representing these resources. On this point, we refer to the USA Generally Accepted Accounting Principles (US-GAAP) and International Accounting Standards—International Financial Reporting Standards (IAS-IFRS) principles.

Finally, after presenting the most widely used methods for measuring intellectual capital and human capital, in order to support our conclusion, we perform a quantitative analysis that assesses the impact of these resources on firm performances and their importance for investors. More in particular, we investigate whether the information on human resources is a relevant factor that influences the economic and financial performances of companies and the investment decisions of market operators. Thus, we believe that our results could be of interest to standard setters when they define what and how (the accounting treatment and disclosure) information on human resources should be provided by companies.

Human Capital and Intellectual Capital

Over the last few decades, accounting exponents have developed some different definitions concerning human capital (Leon, 2002). In particular, they have developed, not without some confusion at times, different definitions on human capital and intellectual capital. In all likelihood, this is because the term intellectual capital is also seen by some as being synonymous with intangible assets, invisible assets, knowledge assets, knowledge capital, information assets, human capital, and the hidden value of companies (Bontis, 2001; Tseng & Goo, 2005). Moreover, human capital and intellectual capital may have many similarities, but the latter is something more general and, in our view, includes the former. In fact, human capital is a general concept that we could summarize as the potential of employees themselves to generate more economic value for organizations in the future, which becomes surplus value over the returns of the other tangible and financial assets of the firm. However, intellectual capital means all intellectual material (knowledge, information, intellectual property, experience) that could be used in order to generate economic value.

In this chapter, we use the term "intellectual" to indicate employees who encapsulate the company's knowledge. As mentioned above, the concept of intellectual capital could be broadened to include all value creation activities performed by humans relating to the company (Chan, 2009a). More in particular, scholars have been advocating the inclusion of human capital and structural capital as part of intellectual capital (Andriessen, 2006; Bontis, 2004; Edvinsson, 1997; Guthrie, Petty, & Johanson, 2001). In other words, a significant number of scholars identify three main components of intellectual capital: human capital, customer (relation) capital, and structural capital (Edvinsson & Malone, 1997; Maditinos, Chatzoudes, Tsairidis, & Theriou, 2011; Mavridis & Kyrmizoglou, 2005; Ruta, 2009; Wall, 2005).

Furthermore, one of the most useful definitions of IC, offered by the Organisation for Economic Co-Operation and Development (OECD) in 1999, describes IC as the economic value of two categories of intangible assets of a company, namely structural and human capital. Whereas human capital refers to the staff and human resources within and external to an organization including suppliers and customers, structural capital comprises the tangible elements of an organization such as proprietary computer system, database, software, strategy, routines, procedures, and supply chains—also called organizational capital (Jashapara, 2004; Petty & Guthrie, 2000).

In 1997, Stewart defined intellectual capital as a composition of human capital (HC), structural capital (SC), and customer capital (CC). Similarly,

Roos, Roos, Dragonetti, and Edvinsson (1997) classified IC into SC and HC, which represent "thinking" and "nonthinking" assets. In other words, HC refers to knowledge, skills, and experiences that employees take with them when they leave the organization, while SC includes all nonhuman knowledge-based resources in the organization, which consist of databases, organizational charts, procedures and administrative processes, and strategies and generally consist of everything that creates higher value for the organization rather than its physical aspect.

Another distinction has been suggested by Brooking (1996), who identifies four components of IC: market, human centered, intellectual property, and infrastructure assets.

The difference between these classification systems is that they assume different levels of aggregation of the elements of intellectual capital. Most other classifications (e.g., Petrash, 1996; Sveiby, 1997, 2001) distinguish among external structure (customer and supplier relations), internal structure (patents, concepts, computers, and administrative systems), and human capital (people's capacity to act in various situations, including skills, experience, education values, and motivation).

Consistent with Roos et al. (1997), Meritum (2002, pp. 10–11) gives the following definition for the component of IC:

> Human capital is defined as the knowledge that employees take with them when they leave the firm. It includes the knowledge, skills, experiences and abilities of people. Some of this knowledge is unique to the individual, some may be generic. Examples are innovation capacity, creativity, know-how and previous experience, teamwork capacity, employee flexibility, tolerance for ambiguity, motivation, satisfaction, learning capacity, loyalty, formal training and education. Structural capital is defined as the knowledge that stays within the firm at the end of the working day. It comprises the organizational routines, procedures, systems, cultures, databases, etc. Examples are organizational flexibility, a documentation service, the existence of a knowledge centre, the general use of Information Technologies, organizational learning capacity, etc. Some of them may be legally protected and become Intellectual Property Rights, legally owned by the firm under separate title. Relational capital is defined as all resources linked to the external relationships of the firm, with customers, suppliers or R&D partners. It comprises that part of Human and Structural Capital involved with the company's relations with stakeholders (investors, creditors, customers, suppliers, etc.), plus the perceptions that they hold about the company. Examples of this category are image, customers loyalty, customer satisfaction, links with suppliers, commercial power, negotiating capacity with financial entities, environmental activities, etc.

Therefore, in sum, there are two aspects of intellectual capital:

(1) one referring to patents, intellectual property, brands, and trademarks; and
(2) one referring to knowledge, information, and experience.

On this point, it should be noted that the second aspect forms much of the intellectual capital today (Chan, 2009a, 2009b; Gan & Saleh, 2008; Gavious & Russ, 2009).

Finally, independently and at different times also over recent decades, a number of frameworks have been developed. These are designed in order to satisfy the need to better classify and study the components of IC. Many of these frameworks are conceptually similar; however, the major distinctions are the basic assumptions and classifications that lead to different levels of aggregation of the intellectual capital elements.

Some of these frameworks are the balance scorecard by Kaplan and Norton (1992), the classification of resources by Haanes and Lowendahl (1997), the intangible assets monitor by Sveiby (1997), the Skandia value scheme by Edvinsson and Malone (1997), and the three categories of "knowledge" by the Danish Confederation of Trade Unions (DCTU, 1999).

The Concept of Intellectual Capital under the Accounting Standards

Based on the above considerations, while IC is becoming increasingly important, accounting for intellectual capital is, nowadays, a controversial issue, in particular if we are referring to human capital. In fact, generally, traditional accounting statements appeared unable to reflect the value created by intangibles (Canibano, Garcia-Ayuso, & Sanchez, 2000; Chen, Cheng, & Hwang, 2005).

In spite of it being accepted among researchers (e.g., Flamholtz, 2005) that "accounting for the worth of employees has implications for both managers and investors" (Roslender & Dyson, 1992, p. 319), many researchers (Edvinsson & Malone, 1997; Pulic, 1998, 2000; Stewart, 1997; Sveiby, 2000) have underlined that traditional measures of firm's performance, which are based on accounting principles (i.e., IAS-IFRS, US-GAAP), may not represent human resources adequately in the financial statements.

Moreover, also under the accounting standards perspective, there is some confusion regarding the terms intangibles and intellectual capital. In particular, IFRS 3 (International Financial Reporting Standard 3) on business combinations and IAS 38 (International Accounting Standard 38) on intangible assets define intangible assets as identifiable nonmonetary assets without physical substance (IAS 38 par. 8). On this point, it may be very useful to note that IAS 38 never refers to IC, including HC, in a way that is strictly consistent with the concept presented in the introduction. In particular, paragraph 9 of IAS 38 explains that

> Entities frequently expend resources, or incur liabilities, on the acquisition, development, maintenance or enhancement of intangible resources such as scientific or technical knowledge, design and implementation of new processes or systems, licenses, intellectual property, market knowledge and trademarks (including brand names and publishing titles). Common examples of items encompassed by these broad headings are computer software, patents, copyrights, motion picture films, customer lists, mortgage servicing rights, fishing licenses, import quotas, franchises, customer or supplier relationships, customer loyalty, market share and marketing rights.

In fact, according to IASB (2004), IC consists of "non-financial fixed assets that do not have financial substance but are identifiable and controlled by the entity through custody and legal rights." In addition, paragraph 69 of IAS 38 provides that "... Other examples of expenditure that is recognized as an expense when it is incurred include: ... b) expenditure on training activities." Furthermore, under IFRS 3 requirements, although in a business combination there could be items that present characteristics similar to the other identifiable intangible assets (trademarks, patents, etc.), there are intangible assets that cannot be recognized separately from goodwill. In particular, this situation may occur, frequently, when employees are highly specialized. In fact, a buyer may assign a value to the existence of highly specialized employees, which allows the buyer to continue the firm's activity without interruptions during the business combination process. However, the IAS-IFRS system, due to fact that these skills cannot be separately identified among other assets, requires that they should be recognized within the goodwill.

Clearly, if we refer to the concepts presented above, these requirements cannot fit the concepts underlying both intellectual capital and human capital. In addition, the US-GAAP also requires the immediate and full expensing of compensation costs (see ASC 350, Intangibles—Goodwill and Other).

Both these accounting systems provide for this treatment because they are concerned about the reliability and objectivity of the capitalization of such costs. However, although these accounting systems treat the cost related to IC as a current expense, there are many studies that demonstrate that these amounts provide useful information about an unrecorded intangible asset (Bell, Landsman, Miller, & Yeh, 2002).

It is useful to note that, many years ago, some academics argued that the spending on employees should not be treated as an expense in the year because some employee expenditures may generate returns over a period of time that exceeds a single year (Brummet, Flamholtz, & Pyle, 1968; Flamholtz, 1972;

Lev & Schwarz, 1971). In particular, Brummet et al. (1968) proposed treating the expenditure on human resources as "capital rather than consumption" or as "asset rather than expenses," especially due to the future services potential of employees. In this study, multiple techniques, including the historical cost (acquisition cost), the cost to replace firm's existing human resources and the economic value (replacement cost), and the present value of the portion of firm's future earnings attributable to human resources (economic value), have been proposed to measure HC. Flamholtz (1971, 1972), focusing upon measurement of an individual's value of a firm, has proposed a model for the economic valuation of human resources based on individuals, as individuals become the primary focus in many of the organizational decisions such as selection, training, placement, and job design. Under this, expected states of service life of person in terms of service level and the service group has been taken into account and has estimated the present monetary equivalent of the expected services as the HC value of an individual. Lev and Schwartz (1971) proposed a model for individual valuation that, in order to estimate the value of HC, sums the values of persons calculated using the accounting concept of "service potential" as the principle. In particular, the sums of discounted future earnings of the employees, according to the earnings profile of each, have been treated as the HC of the firm. However, Flamholtz (1972) has criticized this work for the lack of relevance and utility to decision-makers, highlighting that significant applications and implications for management and investors have not been considered. On this point, Lev and Schwartz (1972) note the nonexistence of a well-defined and empirically valid set of decision models used by investors.

The failure to achieve, from an accounting perspective, a shared method for HC has led researchers to change their view (Roslender, 1997; Roslender & Dyson, 1992). In particular, Roslender and Dyson (1992) wrote about "shifting away from the narrow economic-accounting perspective of the past to a broader social scientific perspective," because previous attempts to put persons in the balance sheet have been diverted to generating softer accounting information.

Finally, it may be very useful note also that, though many studies have attempted to develop a human resource accounting system, the involvement of firms in this practice is mostly limited to qualitative disclosures of such information (Abeysekera, 2006; Abeysekera & Guthrie, 2004; Ax & Marton, 2008; Hussain, Khan, & Yasmin, 2004; Subbarao & Zeghal, 1997). In particular, Abeysekera (2006, 2008) and Abeysekera and Guthrie (2004) show that many firms do not even use the terms HC or IC in their annual reports, other than merely providing a qualitative description on the people component whenever necessary.

Measurements

The new economy is a knowledge-based economy. The forces of globalization have highlighted the fact that knowledge and communication have become the most critical resources for an organization. In other words, successful companies' most important assets are intangible (e.g., Edvinsson & Malone, 1997; Lev, 2001; Stewart & Ruckdeschel, 1998). On the basis of the foregoing, there is a clear need to recognize the intangibles, in particular IC. On this point, it could be very useful to recall that if one cannot measure, one cannot manage (Liebowitz & Suen, 2000). This is consistent with Lord Kelvin,[2] who once said:

> When you can measure what you are speaking about and express it in numbers, you know something about it; but when you cannot express in numbers, your knowledge is of a meagre and unsatisfactory kind. It may be the beginnings of knowledge, but you have scarcely, in your thoughts, advanced to the stages of a science.

This stresses the importance of the concept of measurement.

Previously, we have summarized the lack of a generally accepted concept about IC and HC, particularly when scholars depart from the general definition in order to identify some specific elements/components of these.

As regards the measurement concept, we are no more fortunate here. In fact, many years before accounting theory created the double-entry bookkeeping system, although in some inventories assets were recognized and denominated with words such as "Martha our slave,"[3] nowadays there is no generally accepted methodology for valuing intangible assets, including IC and HC.

However, on the basis of Luthy (1998) and Williams (2001), Sveiby (2002) suggests that measurement approaches for intangibles, including intellectual capital and, consequently, human capital, fall into four categories. In addition, these categories may be aggregated by financial or nonfinancial methods. The former include market capitalization and direct intellectual capital methods and the latter include return-on-assets and scorecard methods (Tan, Plowman, & Hancock, 2008). Thus, the financial methods are as follows:

- Market capitalization methods (MCMs). Under these methods, the value of the intellectual capital or intangible assets is calculated as the difference between a firm's market capitalization and the book value of its equity. One widely used model is the VAIC™ (Value Added Intellectual Capital) developed by Pulic (Pulic, 1998, 2000)—a model that can be applied considering also purely accounting-dependent variables. This model has been developed in order to quantify the efficiency of the employed potential of a company, financially as well as intellectually. More in particular, Pulic, in his models, developed the VAIC™ as the sum of the value added capital employed coefficient (VACA), the value added human capital coefficient (VAHU), and the value added structural capital coefficient (STVA), as an aggregate measure of corporate intellectual efficiency. Subsequently, this model has been utilized in many studies in different contexts, particularly with the objective to assess the impact of HC on firms' financial performance and the capital market performance (Chan, 2009a, 2009b; Chen et al., 2005; Nazari & Herremans, 2007; Tan et al., 2007).

- Direct intellectual capital (DIC) methods. These methods estimate the monetary value of intangible assets by identifying their various components. Once these components are identified, they can be directly evaluated, either individually or as an aggregated coefficient.

The nonfinancial methods are not related to firms' financial market performance—where, by the latter term, we refer to a measure connected with the evolution of share market prices, hence strictly for listed companies—and, frequently, one is not able to assign a financial value for the intellectual assets in an objective manner. They are as follows:

- Scorecard methods (SCMs). The various components of intangible assets or intellectual capital are identified, and indicators and indices are generated and reported in scorecards or as graphs. These methods are similar to the DIC methods, except that they make no estimate about the monetary value of the intangible assets.
- Return-on-assets (ROA) methods. An ROA method is based on the balance sheet ratio that is the average pre-tax earnings of company for a period of time divided by the average tangible assets of the company. This ratio is compared with its industry average, and the difference is multiplied by the company's average tangible assets to calculate average annual earnings from the intangibles. Dividing the above average earnings by the company's average cost of capital or an interest rate, one can derive an estimate of the value of its intangible assets or intellectual capital.

As mentioned above, considering that human resources constitute one of the main success factors for a company—since, due to their know-how, which is often included in the product or service offered on the market, they should have a significant influence on the ability of companies to achieve corporate profits—we are interested in analyzing their actual impact on firms' performance and their value relevance by using empirical data and some of the main econometric models well known in literature. To this end, we took to market capitalization methods for a reference: the VAIC™ model developed by Pulic, for measuring the impact of IC on firms' performances; and another widely known model recently applied by Gavious and Russ (2009), for assessing the value relevance of intellectual capital. The choice of these market methods is aimed at verifying the validity of the capital market theory for IC, since, in general, it presumes that capital market participants use *all* relevant available information to make their investment decisions (Beaver, 1981; Fama, 1991; Fama, Fisher, Jensen, & Roll, 1969; Malkiel & Fama, 1970); this implies that traded values should reflect the available information on the relevant firm. Recent studies have demonstrated that markets are characterized by a "semi-strong" form of efficiency, reflecting all publicly available information (Beaver, 1981; Fama, 1991; Fama et al., 1969; Malkiel & Fama, 1970); hence, we expect that market quotes should also incorporate the disclosed information on human resources of firms. These models are separately discussed in the following two sections respectively.

The Impact of Intellectual Capital on Firms' Performance: The VAIC™ Model

Data

The model we present in this chapter was tested using a sample of listed companies that operated in the European area during the period from 2002 to 2012 (the "Period").

The sample was determined by selecting all the companies that were included in the European Union equity index "Market Europe" (mnemonic: "G#LTOTMKEU") published by Thomson Reuters Datastream during the Period. At the date of the research, throughout the entire Period, the Market Europe index was comprised of 2,264 companies; thus, a total of 24,904 observations were collected for each type of data (stock price, net income, etc.) needed to run the analyses.

Both market and accounting data were collected on an annual basis on the 31st of December of each year of the Period using the Bloomberg and Thomson Datastream databases, with all economic values expressed in euros. For each variable of the model, extreme values are excluded from the group of observations through a Winsorization procedure, eliminating the values that are below the 2.5 percent percentile and above the 97.5 percent percentile.

Table 7.1 Structure of the selected Sample

Year	*2003*	*2004*	*2005*	*2006*	*2007*	*2008*	*2009*	*2010*	*2011*	*2012*	*Total*
Listed firms	*2,264*	*2,264*	*2,264*	*2,264*	*2,264*	*2,264*	*2,264*	*2,264*	*2,264*	*2,264*	*22,640*
Austria	4	4	5	5	5	4	4	7	4	1	43
Belgium	4	3	7	8	7	6	5	8	3	1	52
Denmark	9	8	9	10	8	9	7	9	6	3	78
Finland	9	11	13	18	17	15	15	18	15	4	135
France	14	20	23	29	28	28	25	25	20	4	216
Germany	16	20	30	24	25	36	25	37	25	7	245
Greece	1	2	1	2	2	1	1	2	1	0	13
Ireland	3	2	2	2	4	3	2	5	0	0	23
Italy	7	11	13	11	12	10	9	10	6	1	90
Luxembourg	0	1	1	1	1	1	1	1	1	0	8
Netherlands	5	7	9	10	11	8	12	16	9	4	91
Poland	0	0	0	0	1	1	2	2	0	0	6
Portugal	0	0	0	0	0	0	0	0	1	0	1
Spain	3	5	8	5	7	5	6	6	6	0	51
Sweden	18	25	26	22	21	21	22	26	14	12	207
United Kingdom	24	47	54	54	56	55	60	62	31	17	460
Total Selected firms	117	166	201	201	205	203	196	234	142	54	1,719

Note: This table provides the structure of the Sample organized by year and by country, showing the number of companies included in the Market Europe equity index (the Listed firms) during the Period and the number of observations with available data selected using the search criteria (the Selected firms).

Finally, the observations that do not have the necessary data to apply to all the models considered in this chapter are excluded.

Table 7.1 presents the structure of the selected sample (the "Sample") organized by year and by country, showing the number of companies included in the equity index previously specified (the "Listed" firms) and the number of observations with available data selected using the search criteria previously specified (the "Selected" firms). The reference period goes from 2003 to 2012, excluding 2002 because the examined models include growth variables determined as a difference between the values observed in year t and the ones observed in year $t-1$. The number of Selected observations (included in the Sample) is 1,719, out of 22,640 total Listed firms.

In addition to the general Sample, we also identify two subsamples on the basis of the industry sector of each company. To this aim, we consider the industry classification available in the Thomson Reuters Datastream database (the Industry Classification Benchmark, coded "ICBIN") provided for each element of the Sample. According to Bontis et al. (2000), we split the Sample into two groups, distinguishing between non-services industries (subsample "Non-Services") and services industries (subsample "Services"), basing the distinction on the ICBIN sector of each firm. In particular, we include in the Non-Services subsample the companies that operate in the following sectors of the ICB classification: basic materials, consumer goods, industrials, and oil and gas. The companies that operate in the other sectors of the ICB classification, which are consumer services, financials, health care, technology, telecommunications, and utilities, are included in the Services subsample.

Methodology

In order to assess the impact of IC on business performance, we first need to define a measure of performance to be used as the dependent variable of the model. To this aim, according to Chu, Chan, Yu, Ng, and Wong (2011) and Hofer (1983), financial performance measures represent the dominant model in examining business performance. In prior researches (Chan, 2009a, 2009b; Chu et al., 2011; Firer & Stainbank, 2003; Firer & Williams, 2003), the productivity and the profitability of companies have been measured using a large number of accounting-based and market-based measures. In our study, we focus on four measures of business performances, namely the market-to-book value (M/B), that is, the ratio of the total market capitalization to the book value of equity; the return on assets (ROA), that is, the ratio of the net income to the book value of total company assets; the asset turnover (ATO), calculated as the ratio between total revenues and the total book value of assets; and the return on equity (ROE), that is, the ratio of net income to the book value of equity.

In our study the impact of IC on business performances was measured by using the Value Added Intellectual Coefficient (VAIC™) introduced by Pulic in 1998. The VAIC™ is a method aimed at measuring and managing the efficiency of a company in the creation of value based on intellectual (capital) efficiency or intellectual resources (Pulic, 2000). Employees are considered as valuable contributors to a company's performance, and the objective of the model is to measure their productivity in terms of impact on the business performance. In particular, especially for knowledge-based companies characterized by a high incidence of the human capital on the total value of the organization, Pulic's objective is to measure the intellectual work efficiency similar to what Taylor did with physical work (Pulic, 2008). The VAIC™ model has been widely applied in a large number of research studies as a universal indicator of the efficiency of each component of the IC based on the concept of added value.

The calculations of the VAIC™ model are based on the following figures:

- human capital (HC), which is often estimated by using employee-related expenditures;
- structural capital (SC), which is determined as the difference between the added value produced by the firm (VA) and the HC, thus representing the share of VA after deducting investments in HC;
- capital employed (CE), which is interpreted as financial capital, that is the book value of net assets.

The VA is the value added by all the resources of the company during the Period and it is calculated as the difference between the income and the expenditures that it generates. According to the formula proposed by Pulic (2005), for each reference company i and year t, the VA equals to

$$\text{VA} = P + C + D + A \tag{7.1}$$

where P is the operating profit, C are the personnel costs (salaries and social costs), D are the depreciation expenses, and A are the amortization expenses of the company. Alternatively, VA can be determined as follows (Muhammad & Ismail, 2009):

$$\text{VA} = \text{OUTPUT} - \text{INPUT} \tag{7.2}$$

where, for each reference company i and year t, OUTPUT represents the total income from all the products and services sold during the relevant period and INPUT is the aggregate value of all the expenses (except labor, taxation, interests, dividends, and depreciation) incurred by the company during the relevant period.

Based on this formulation, Riahi-Belkaoui (2003) proposed an additional formula for calculating VA, which can be derived from the following relation:

$$R = S - B - \text{DP} - W - I - D - T \tag{7.3}$$

where, for each reference company i and year t, R is the (annual) change in retained earnings, S is net sales revenue, B is bought-in materials and services (cost of goods sold plus all expenses, except labor, taxation, interests, dividends, and depreciation), DP is depreciation, W is employees' salaries and wages, I is interest expenses, D is the dividends paid to shareholders, and T is the corporate taxes. According to equation 7.3, the (annual) change in retained earnings is determined as the difference between sales revenue, on one hand, and costs and dividends, on the other hand. Therefore, Equation 7.3 can be rearranged to calculate the value added by the firm:

$$\mathrm{VA} = S - B = \mathrm{DP} + W + I + D + T + R \tag{7.4}$$

where, for each reference company i and year t, each variable assumes the same meaning considered for Equation 7.3.

On the basis of these definitions and assumptions, VAIC is calculated as the sum of the following three efficiency indicators:

- capital employed efficiency (CEE) = VA/CE;
- human capital efficiency (HCE) = VA/HC;
- structural capital efficiency (SCE) = SC/VA.

Hence:

$$\mathrm{VAIC} = \mathrm{CEE} + \mathrm{HCE} + \mathrm{SCE} = \frac{\mathrm{VA}}{\mathrm{CE}} + \frac{\mathrm{VA}}{\mathrm{HC}} + \frac{\mathrm{SC}}{\mathrm{VA}} \tag{7.5}$$

As an intermediate result, the efficiency of intellectual capital (ICE) can be calculated as the sum of HCE and SCE, hence VAIC = CEE + ICE.

We test the VAIC™ model examining the relationship between market-to-book value (M/B), the return on assets (ROA), the asset turnover (ATO), and the return on equity (ROE), on a side, and the aggregate value of VAIC (models 1, 2, 3, and 4 shown in Table 7.2), on the other side. Furthermore, we examine the relationship between the same independent variables (M/B, ROE, ATO, and ROE) and the individual components of VAIC (models 5, 6, 7, and 8 shown in Table 7.2). To this aim, we define eight ordinary least squares (OLS) regression models, whose structure is presented in Table 7.2.

Empirical Results

Table 7.3 shows descriptive statistics for the variables included in the OLS regression models presented in Table 7.2, distinguishing between the main Sample, the subsample Non-Services, and the subsample Services.

Table 7.4 shows Pearson correlation coefficients and their statistical significance (the p-value, in brackets) for the variables included in the OLS regression models shown in Table 7.2 for the main Sample of observations.

The OLS regressions are performed using the models defined in Table 7.2, on the basis of data calculated as specified in the subsection "Data." Besides the basic tests (F-statistics, adjusted R^2, t-statistics), for each multivariate

Table 7.2 The VAIC™ models

Model number	*Model structure*
1	$M/B_t^i = \beta_0 + \beta_1 VAIC_t^i + \varepsilon_t^i$
2	$ROA_t^i = \beta_0 + \beta_1 VAIC_t^i + \varepsilon_t^i$
3	$ATO_t^i = \beta_0 + \beta_1 VAIC_t^i + \varepsilon_t^i$
4	$ROE_t^i = \beta_0 + \beta_1 VAIC_t^i + \varepsilon_t^i$
5	$M/B_t^i = \beta_0 + \beta_1 CEE_t^i + \beta_2 HCE_t^i + \beta_3 SCE_t^i + \varepsilon_t^i$
6	$ROA_t^i = \beta_0 + \beta_1 CEE_t^i + \beta_2 HCE_t^i + \beta_3 SCE_t^i + \varepsilon_t^i$
7	$ATO_t^i = \beta_0 + \beta_1 CEE_t^i + \beta_2 HCE_t^i + \beta_3 SCE_t^i + \varepsilon_t^i$
8	$ROE_t^i = \beta_0 + \beta_1 CEE_t^i + \beta_2 HCE_t^i + \beta_3 SCE_t^i + \varepsilon_t^i$

Note: This table provides the structure of the VAIC™ models used to assess the impact of intellectual capital on business performance, namely on market-to-book value (M/B), return on assets (ROA), asset turnover (ATO), and return on equity (ROE) ratios, for each reference company *i* and year *t* of the selected samples of observations. Models 1, 2, 3, and 4 are characterized by a single explanatory variable (plus the intercept), constituted by the VAIC, while models 5, 6, 7, and 8 are characterized by three explanatory variables (plus the intercept), constituted by the single components of VAIC (CEE, HCE, and SCE).

Table 7.3 Descriptive statistics of the variables included in the VAIC™ models shown in Table 7.2

Group	*Sample*			*Non-Services*			*Services*		
Variable	*Obs*	*Mean*	*Std. Dev.*	*Obs*	*Mean*	*Std. Dev.*	*Obs*	*Mean*	*Std. Dev.*
M/B	1,719	2.637	1.541	1,187	2.471	1.404	532	3.007	1.755
ROA	1,719	0.064	0.042	1,187	0.064	0.040	532	0.066	0.047
ATO	1,719	0.863	0.383	1,187	0.956	0.357	532	0.655	0.357
ROE	1,719	0.180	0.112	1,187	0.181	0.115	532	0.177	0.106
VAIC	1,719	3.352	2.755	1,187	3.007	2.147	532	4.121	3.662
CEE	1,719	0.522	0.267	1,187	0.519	0.240	532	0.529	0.320
HCE	1,719	2.393	2.689	1,187	2.088	2.070	532	3.075	3.625
SCE	1,719	0.437	0.193	1,187	0.400	0.179	532	0.518	0.200

Note: This table presents descriptive statistics for the main Sample, the subsample Non-Services, and the subsample Services of the variables used to measure the impact of intellectual capital on business performances. For each company of the sample, data were collected from 2002 to 2012 on an annual basis at the date of December 31 of each year. M/B (market-to-book value), ROA (return on assets), ATO (asset turnover), and ROE (return on equity) are the dependent variables respectively of the OLS regression models [1; 5], [2; 6], [3; 7] and [4; 8] shown in Table 7.2. VAIC is the explanatory variable of models 1, 2, 3, and 4, while CEE, HCE, and SCE are the explanatory variables of the models 5, 6, 7, and 8 shown in Table 7.2.

Table 7.4 Pearson correlation coefficients for the main Sample

Variable	*M/B*	*ROA*	*ATO*	*ROE*	*VAIC*	*CEE*	*HCE*	*SCE*
VAIC	0.037	0.121	−0.225	0.083	1.000			
	(0.126)	(0.000)	(0.000)	(0.001)				
CEE	0.306	0.315	0.326	0.134	−0.203	1.000		
	(0.000)	(0.000)	(0.000)	(0.000)	(0.000)			
HCE	0.004	0.078	−0.231	0.056	0.996	−0.272	1.000	
	(0.874)	(0.001)	(0.000)	(0.020)	(0.000)	(0.000)		
SCE	0.051	0.204	−0.457	0.211	0.676	−0.490	0.670	1.000
	(0.036)	(0.000)	(0.000)	(0.000)	(0.000)	(0.000)	(0.000)	

Note: This table shows the Pearson correlation coefficients for the main Sample for the variables used to examine the impact of intellectual capital on business performances. Below the value of coefficients, in brackets, is shown the *p*-value of each correlation. See Tables 7.2 and 7.3 for variables' definitions.

regression we calculate the variance inflation factor ("VIF"), as an indicator of multicollinearity. For each explanatory variable *k* we report the value of the coefficient β_k and its *t*-statistic (below the value of each coefficient, in brackets), indicating with "***" the estimates that are significant at a level of confidence of 99 percent, with "**" the estimates that are significant at a level of confidence of 95 percent, and with "*" the estimates that are significant at a level of confidence of 90 percent.

With reference to the models with VAIC as explanatory variable (numbers 1, 2, 3, and 4), Table 7.5 provides the results of the OLS regressions' estimates and significance tests for the whole Sample.

Table 7.5 OLS regressions (models 1, 2, 3 and 4) for the main Sample

Group	*Sample*			
No. of model	*1*	*2*	*3*	*4*
Dep. variable	*M/B*	*ROA*	*ATO*	*ROE*
β_0 (intercept)	2.568***	0.058***	0.968***	0.169***
	(0.000)	(0.000)	(0.000)	(0.000)
β_1 (VAIC)	0.021	0.002***	−0.031 * **	0.003***
	(0.126)	(0.000)	(0.000)	(0.001)
R^2 adjusted	0.08%	1.41%	5.03%	0.63%
n	1,719	1,719	1,719	1,719
F-statistic	2.350	25.600	91.920	11.820
	(0.126)	(0.000)	(0.000)	(0.001)

Note: ***, significant at the 0.99 level; for each coefficient, *p*-values are shown below in brackets. See tables 7.2 and 7.3 for variables' definitions.

Similarly, always with reference to the models with VAIC as explanatory variable (numbers 1, 2, 3, and 4), Table 7.6 provides the results of the OLS regressions' estimates and significance tests for the subsamples Non-Services and Services.

Consistently with prior studies (Chu et al., 2011; Gan & Saleh, 2008; Muhammad & Ismail, 2009; Shiu, 2006), the empirical results show that for the whole Sample of observations the VAIC coefficient is statistically significant at a level of confidence of 99 percent for all the financial reporting performance indicators, namely ROA, ATO, and ROE. On the contrary, significance is not reached for the performance indicator M/B, which differs from ROA, ATO, and ROE as it is determined (also) on the basis of a market quote of the companies. Similar results are obtained for the subsample Non-Services, for which VAIC is always significant at 99 percent confidence level for the accounting performance indicators, namely ROA, ATO, and ROE, and at 90 percent for the M/B ratio. Differently, the models applied to the Services subsample are significant at a level of confidence of 99 percent only for model number 3 (ATO).

With reference to the models with the single components of VAIC as explanatory variables, namely CEE, HCE, and SCE (model numbers 5, 6, 7, and 8), Table 7.7 provides the results of the OLS regressions' estimates and significance tests for the whole Sample.

Similarly, always with reference to the models with CEE, HCE, and SCE as explanatory variables (numbers 5, 6, 7, and 8), Table 7.8 provides the results of the OLS regressions' estimates and significance tests for the subsamples Non-Services and Services.

The breakdown of VAIC in its single addends allows us to examine the quantitative impact and the significance of each of its components on the selected business performance indicators. A common result for all the samples of observations is the relevant increase of the value of the F-statistics and adjusted R^2 in comparison to the univariate models with VAIC, as well as a differentiation between the explanatory variables in terms of value and, in some cases, sign of the coefficients. The CEE ratio is significant in 100 percent of cases, while HCE and SCE are significant at a level of confidence of 99 percent in most cases. The low levels of VIF indicate that the models do not present problems of multicollinearity among the explanatory variables.

In summary, consistently with previous research (Chu et al., 2011), our results evidence that the impact of IC (VAIC and also its separate components) is not consistent among samples and business performance indicators in terms of both significance and sign of coefficients. On this point, it should be noticed that, with reference to the VAIC™ model developed by Pulic (1998, 2000), Chen et al. (2005) show that the firm's intellectual capital has a positive impact on its market value and financial performance, both current

Table 7.6 OLS regressions (models 1, 2, 3 and 4) for subsamples Non-Services and Services

Group	*Non-Services*				*Services*			
No. of model	*1*	*2*	*3*	*4*	*1*	*2*	*3*	*4*
Dep. variable	*M/B*	*ROA*	*ATO*	*ROE*	*M/B*	*ROA*	*ATO*	*ROE*
β_0(intercept)	2.36***	0.053***	1.046***	0.162***	3.095***	0.064***	0.726***	0.171***
	(0.000)	(0.000)	(0.000)	(0.000)	(0.000)	(0.000)	(0.000)	(0.000)
β_1(VAIC)	0.037*	0.003***	−0.03***	0.006***	−0.021	0.001	−0.017***	0.001
	(0.052)	(0.000)	(0.000)	(0.000)	(0.307)	(0.257)	(0.000)	(0.257)
R^2 adjusted	0.23%	3.30%	3.16%	1.38%	0.01%	0.05%	2.91%	0.05%
n	1,187	1,187	1,187	1,187	532	532	532	532
F−statistic	3.780	41.450	39.720	17.600	1.050	1.290	16.920	1.290
	(0.052)	(0.000)	(0.000)	(0.000)	(0.307)	(0.257)	(0.000)	(0.257)

Note: ***, significant at the 0.99 level; and *, significant at the 0.90 level; for each coefficient, *p*-values are shown below in brackets. See Tables 7.2 and 7.3 for variables' definitions.

Table 7.7 Multivariate OLS regressions (models 5, 6, 7, and 8) for the main Sample

Group	*Sample*			
No. of model	*5*	*6*	*7*	*8*
Dep. variable	*M/B*	*ROA*	*ATO*	*ROE*
β_0(intercept)	0.281*	−0.032 * **	1.14***	0.001
	(0.065)	(0.000)	(0.000)	(0.898)
β_1(CEE)	2.551***	0.089***	0.18***	0.137* * *
	(0.000)	(0.000)	(0.000)	(0.000)
β_2(HCE)	−0.057***	−0.003***	0.018***	−0.008***
	(0.001)	(0.000)	(0.000)	(0.000)
β_3(SCE)	2.659***	0.129***	−0.948***	0.288***
	(0.000)	(0.000)	(0.000)	(0.000)
R^2 adjusted	15.02%	28.17%	22.97%	13.67%
n	1,719	1,719	1,719	1,719
F-statistic	102.210	225.530	171.790	91.650
	(0.000)	(0.000)	(0.000)	(0.000)
VIF	1.790	1.790	1.790	1.790

Note: ***, significant at the 0.99 level; and *, significant at the 0.90 level; for each coefficient, *p*-values are shown below in brackets. See Tables 7.2 and 7.3 for variables' definitions.

and future. However, evidence indicates that the VAIC™ model also generates contradictory results in different contexts where Chan (2009a, 2009b) revealed an overall lack of association between IC and financial performance in the Hong Kong context. Nor did the analysis through breakdown provide any statistical support for the relationship between efficiency indicators and organizational performance (Chan, 2009b). The negative association between HC efficiency and productivity, as well as that between HC efficiency and market valuation indicate that investors hold a negative view of companies that have relatively high employee-related expenditure. However, this indicator warrants further examination of the subject since this reasoning might arguably vary in different socioeconomic contexts.

The Value Relevance of Intellectual Capital

Some studies have examined the influence that accounting information, particularly on human resources, can have for users and investors. Here, by value relevance, we refer to Barth (2000), Barth and Clinch (1998), and Barth, Beaver, and Landsman (2001), who observed that an accounting entry has value relevance when it is associated with some measure of the market value of the company.

Table 7.8 Multivariate OLS regressions (models 5, 6, 7, and 8) for subsamples Non-Services and Services

Group	*Non-Services*				*Services*			
No. of model	*5*	*6*	*7*	*8*	*5*	*6*	*7*	*8*
Dep. variable	*M/B*	*ROA*	*ATO*	*ROE*	*M/B*	*ROA*	*ATO*	*ROE*
β_0(intercept)	−0.272*	−0.05***	1.02***	−0.046***	2.073***	−0.011	0.978***	0.029
	(0.099)	(0.000)	(0.000)	(0.001)	(0.000)	(0.230)	(0.000)	(0.191)
β_1(CEE)	3.027***	0.101***	0.289***	0.186***	1.517***	0.079***	0.208***	0.097***
	(0.000)	(0.000)	(0.000)	(0.000)	(0.000)	(0.000)	(0.000)	(0.000)
β_2(HCE)	−0.122***	−0.006***	0.008	−0.014***	0.007	0	0.023***	−0.004**
	(0.000)	(0.000)	(0.190)	(0.000)	(0.792)	(0.997)	(0.000)	(0.018)
β_3(SCE)	3.563***	0.183***	−0.578***	0.397***	0.212	0.069***	−0.975***	0.21***
	(0.000)	(0.000)	(0.000)	(0.000)	(0.716)	(0.000)	(0.000)	(0.000)
R^2 adjusted	21.46%	40.61%	15.10%	20.31%	6.21%	18.20%	30.27%	7.38%
n	1,187	1,187	1,187	1,187	532	532	532	532
F-statistic	108.990	271.320	71.330	101.740	12.720	40.380	77.840	15.100
	(0.000)	(0.000)	(0.000)	(0.000)	(0.000)	(0.000)	(0.000)	(0.000)
VIF	1.840	1.840	1.840	1.840	1.950	1.950	1.950	1.950

Note: ***, significant at the 0.99 level; **, significant at the 0.95 level; and *, significant at the 0.90 level; for each coefficient, *p*-values are shown below in brackets. See Tables 7.2 and 7.3 for variables' definitions.

The objective of our analyses is to assess the value relevance of IC with reference to listed companies operating in the European Union (EU) in recent years. For our purposes, the determination of the historical impact of intellectual capital on stock prices—and the choice of the EU context—is aimed at assessing whether the ideal objective of IAS-IFRS-compliant financial statements (i.e., provide relevant information for investment decisions (Dumontier & Raffournier, 2002), similar to US-GAAP) has actually been achieved. This is considered with reference to the socioeconomic context in which these accounting principles are mainly applied. In other words, our analyses seek to determine whether the information on intellectual capital included in EU companies' financial statements is a relevant factor in influencing market operators' investment decisions.

Data

In order to make all the analyses of this chapter consistent, the value relevance of intellectual capital was assessed on the basis of the same sample of observations considered for determining the impact of IC on firm performances.

As specified above, in fact, the sample described in the previous "Data" subsection was selected by excluding the observations lacking the necessary data to apply to *all* the models considered in this chapter, hence considering also the variables that are necessary for assessing the value relevance of IC. Consequently, for details on the criteria used to select the sample of observations considered for running the analyses, see the previous "Data" subsection.

Methodology

The assessment of the value relevance of IC was conducted using a model based on the valuation structure proposed by Feltham and Ohlson (1999), Gavious and Russ (2009), and Ohlson (1995, 1999). The explanatory variables are defined as in Gavious and Russ (2009), except for the measure of value of the intellectual capital, which was determined following the Pulic (1998, 2000) model for VAIC.

The model that we employ is the following:

$$\begin{aligned} MV_t^i = \beta_0 + \beta_1 BV_t^i + \beta_2 AbE_t^i + \beta_3 NegAbE_t^i + \beta_4 R\&D_t^i + \beta_5 Capex_t^i \\ + \beta_6 SalesGr_t^i + \beta_7 Div_t^i + \beta_8 SC_t^i + \beta_9 HC_t^i + \varepsilon_t^i \end{aligned} \tag{7.6}$$

For each reference company *i* and date (December 31 of year *t*), all the variables of the model reported in Equation 7.6 are deflated by year-end total ordinary shares outstanding.

MV is the market value of equity. BV is book value of equity. AbE represents the abnormal earnings calculated as the difference between net income (NI) and the product rBV_{t-1}, where r is the expected rate of return on book value of equity and BV_{t-1} is the book value of equity of year $t - 1$. The value of r was determined based on two alternatives used in prior researches: (1) r was determined using as a proxy the earnings-price ratio E/P (e.g., Cheng & McNamara, 2000; Fama & French, 1992; Gavious & Russ, 2009; Swartz, Swartz, & Firer, 2006), calculated for each reference company i and year t. As evidenced by Gavious and Russ (2009), the advantage of using this surrogate for the cost of capital is that the E/P ratio is able to capture the risk and growth of companies. (2) When the necessary data for calculating the earnings-price ratio were not available, r was set at 12.00 percent, which is considered the long-term return on equities (Barth, Beaver, Hand, & Landsman, 1999; Bell et al., 2002; Dechow, Hutton, & Sloan, 1999; Gavious & Russ, 2009). NegAbe is set equal to AbE when AbE ≤ 0, and to 0 otherwise. R&D is the expenditures on research and development. Capex is capital expenditures. SalesGr is the annual change in sales. Div is the dividends paid by the company. The last two explanatory variables, that is, SC and HC, are respectively the structural capital and human capital; thus, their aggregate value represents the intellectual capital of the company. As previously specified, in order to make all the analyses of this chapter consistent, the variables SC and HC assume the same values considered for applying the VAIC™ model, for which details are provided in the previous "Methodology" subsection.

Empirical Results

Table 7.9 shows descriptive statistics for the variables included in the OLS regression model reported in Equation 7.6, distinguishing between the main Sample, the subsample Non-Services, and the subsample Services. We observe that, on average, the mean values of the variables related to the non-services industries are higher than the ones related to the services industries.

Table 7.10 shows Pearson correlation coefficients and their statistical significance (the p-value, in brackets) for the variables included in the OLS regression model reported in Equation 7.6 for the main Sample of observations.

The OLS regressions are performed using the model defined in Equation 7.6, on the basis of data calculated as specified in the subsection "Data." Similarly to the multivariate analyses of the VAIC™ model, besides the basic tests (F-statistics, adjusted R^2, T-statistics), for each regression we calculate the variance inflation factor (VIF), as an indicator of multicollinearity.

Table 7.9 Descriptive statistics of the variables included in the OLS regression model of Equation 7.6

Group	*Sample*			*Non-Services*			*Services*		
Variable	*Obs.*	*Mean*	*Std. Dev.*	*Obs.*	*Mean*	*Std. Dev.*	*Obs.*	*Mean*	*Std. Dev.*
MV	1,719	22.027	20.676	1,187	23.749	21.978	532	18.185	16.817
BV	1,719	10.557	11.315	1,187	12.037	12.555	532	7.253	6.807
AbE	1,719	0.844	1.075	1,187	0.916	1.164	532	0.683	0.821
NegAbE	1,719	−0.026	0.147	1,187	−0.035	0.174	532	−0.006	0.046
R&D	1,719	0.633	1.144	1,187	0.696	1.221	532	0.493	0.936
Capex	1,719	1.568	2.170	1,187	1.756	2.237	532	1.148	1.948
SalesGr	1,719	1.693	4.114	1,187	2.070	4.525	532	0.852	2.828
Div	1,719	0.634	0.631	1,187	0.652	0.616	532	0.594	0.661
SC	1,719	4.079	4.370	1,187	4.558	4.728	532	3.009	3.194
HC	1,719	6.582	8.510	1,187	7.824	9.182	532	3.811	5.906

Note: This table presents descriptive statistics for the main Sample, the subsample Non-Services, and the subsample Services of the variables used to assess the value relevance of intellectual capital. MV, the market value of equity, is the dependent variable of the multivariate OLS regression model. For each company of the sample, data were collected from 2002 to 2012 on an annual basis at the date of December 31 of each year, and all the variables are deflated by year-end total ordinary shares outstanding. BV is the book value of equity. AbE represents abnormal earnings. NegAbe is set equal to AbE when AbE ≤ 0, and to 0 otherwise. R&D is the expenditures on research and development. Capex is capital expenditures. SalesGr is the annual change in sales. Div is the dividends paid by the company. SC is the structural capital. HC is the human capital.

Table 7.11 provides the results of the OLS regressions' estimates and significance tests for the whole Sample, for subsample Non-Services, and for subsample Services.

The results show a high level of significance (F-statistics) and explanatory power (adjusted R^2) of the model for all the examined samples of observations. The low levels of the VIF indicate that the explanatory variables do not present problems of multicollinearity.

Most of the regressors are significant at a level of confidence of 99 percent or 95 percent for all the samples (BV, AbE, Capex, SC, HC, intercept), while the significance is not constant among the samples for the variables R&D, SalesGr, and Div. The variable NegAbE is significant in none of the examined cases. For our purposes, it is relevant to notice that structural capital and human capital are always significant at a level of confidence of 99 percent; hence, with reference to the examined European companies that were listed between 2002 and 2012, the information on intellectual capital results value is relevant for investors that operate on the stock markets.

The analysis of coefficients' signs shows that, consistently with expectations, stock prices are positively correlated with the book value of equity, the

Table 7.10 Pearson correlation coefficients for the main Sample

Variable	*MV*	*BV*	*AbE*	*NegAbE*	*R&D*	*Capex*	*SalesGr*	*Div*	*SC*	*HC*
MV	1.000									
BV	0.788	1.000								
	(0.000)									
AbE	0.786	0.463	1.000							
	(0.000)	(0.000)								
NegAbE	0.058	−0.184	0.280	1.000						
	(0.016)	(0.000)	(0.000)							
R&D	0.446	0.513	0.275	−0.077	1.000					
	(0.000)	(0.000)	(0.000)	(0.001)						
Capex	0.551	0.703	0.394	−0.133	0.387	1.000				
	(0.000)	(0.000)	(0.000)	(0.000)	(0.000)					
SalesGr	0.358	0.374	0.378	−0.041	0.169	0.381	1.000			
	(0.000)	(0.000)	(0.000)	(0.091)	(0.000)	(0.000)				
Div	0.761	0.691	0.618	0.017	0.374	0.511	0.282	1.000		
	(0.000)	(0.000)	(0.000)	(0.486)	(0.000)	(0.000)	(0.000)			
SC	0.759	0.817	0.643	−0.079	0.472	0.831	0.439	0.684	1.000	
	(0.000)	(0.000)	(0.000)	(0.001)	(0.000)	(0.000)	(0.000)	(0.000)		
HC	0.562	0.672	0.335	−0.164	0.672	0.628	0.320	0.480	0.686	1.000
	(0.000)	(0.000)	(0.000)	(0.000)	(0.000)	(0.000)	(0.000)	(0.000)	(0.000)	

Note: This table shows the Pearson correlation coefficients for the main Sample for the variables used to examine the value relevance of intellectual capital. Below the value of coefficients, in brackets, is shown the *p*-value of each correlation. See Table 7.9 for variables' definitions.

abnormal earnings, the paid dividends, and the human capital. Betas' signs are not constant among samples for the variables R&D, Capex, and SalesGr, showing negative values for the main sample and for the Non-Services group and positive values for the Services subsample.

It is interesting to note that the value of the coefficient of HC is always positive and higher for the firms that operate in the services industry; this evidence is consistent with the fact that, on average, the importance of employees' knowledge is higher for firms that are characterized by a higher incidence of the workers' "value" than the value of its tangible capital on the total value of the firm. On the contrary, stock prices' result negatively correlated with SC. A possible explanation of this evidence is the fact that, with reference to the European listed companies, market operators interpret investments in structural capital as a cost rather than an added value that is part of the whole intellectual capital of a company.

Our results are consistent with previous studies that demonstrated the existence of a positive association between the disclosed human capital

Table 7.11 OLS regressions of the model reported in Equation 7.6 for the main Sample, for subsample Non-Services and for subsample Services

Group	*Sample*	*Non-Services*	*Services*
Dep.variable	*MV*	*MV*	*MV*
β_0 (intercept)	2.184***	1.826***	2.085***
	(0.000)	(0.000)	(0.000)
β_1 (BV)	0.968***	0.944***	1.072***
	(0.000)	(0.000)	(0.000)
β_2 (AbE)	10.238***	9.308***	14.54***
	(0.000)	(0.000)	(0.000)
β_3 (NegAbE)	0.124	0.877	2.91
	(0.931)	(0.562)	(0.651)
β_4 (R&D)	−0.009	−0.712 **	1.357***
	(0.967)	(0.013)	(0.001)
β_5 (Capex)	−0.412 **	−0.598 ***	0.626**
	(0.013)	(0.005)	(0.019)
β_6 (SalesGr)	−0.203 ***	−0.249 ***	0.012
	(0.000)	(0.000)	(0.918)
β_7 (Div)	4.501***	6.147***	0.479
	(0.000)	(0.000)	(0.485)
β_8 (SC)	−0.52 ***	−0.313 **	−1.431 ***
	(0.000)	(0.022)	(0.000)
β_9 (HC)	0.189***	0.196***	0.274***
	(0.000)	(0.000)	(0.000)
R^2 adjusted	86.15%	87.19%	85.58%
n	1,719	1,719	1,719
F-statistic	1,188.510	898.010	351.070
	(0.000)	(0.000)	(0.000)
VIF	3.150	3.420	3.170

Note: ***, significant at the 0.99 level; and **, significant at the 0.95 level; for each coefficient, *p*-values are shown below in brackets. See Table 7.9 for variables' definitions.

information and share prices; hence, market participants incorporate this available information in their investment decisions (Abdel-Khalik, 2003; Abdolmohammadi, 2005; Acland, 1976; Anam, Fatima, & Majdi, 2011; Bell et al., 2002; Gamerschlag, 2013; Gamerschlag & Möller, 2011; Lev, 2001; Uyar & Kiliç, 2012; Vafei, Taylor, & Ahmed, 2011; Wyatt, 2008).

Conclusions

In this study we have tried to further underline the importance of concepts related to human resources from an accounting perspective. In fact, intellectual capital, including human capital, is increasingly recognized as an important strategic asset for sustainable corporate competitive advantages.

However, we know that, due both to different cultural factors and different expertise characterizing different accounting exponents, interpretations on this issue vary. In particular, nowadays, both academics and other accounting exponents are approaching this topic with growing interest and addressing different aspects in a way that often departs from previous studies. This has generated a picture of the situation that is not completely clear, although all studies that have been performed on the intellectual capital and human capital have pointed out the importance of these factors for firms.

In addition, in spite of some of the most popular accounting standards which keep a significant part of intellectual capital from being recognized in financial statements, investors still grasp and take into account the invisible value of the intellectual capital. Our analyses highlight the importance of human capital in enhancing firm performance form both an economic perspective and a financial perspective. In particular, with reference to the SC and HC variables, the model used for assessing the value relevance of intellectual capital presents a higher level of consistency in terms of statistical significance and sign of betas in comparison with the VAIC™ model, as the latter shows that the impact of IC is not constant among samples and business performance indicators in terms of both significance and sign of coefficients.

Further investigation should be conducted in order to develop, *imprimis*, a conceptual framework that may be shared by different accounting exponents (researchers, standard setter, auditor, etc.) and possibly compliant for different countries. This might be the first step toward developing both a shared evaluation method for human resources and, eventually, a different accounting treatment that is capable of better representing these resources for the purposes of financial reporting.

Notes

1. For an excellent statement of the importance of additional analysis in this area of human capital, see Schultz (1961).
2. Thomson (1891, p. 80).
3. More in particular, during the fourteenth century, the idea that a person could be exchanged was widely accepted in some parts of the word. So, persons were assimilated and treated as a firm's assets. At that time, unfortunately, this was normal, and there were no measurement problems because there were also markets and relative prices (Myers & Flowers, 1974).

References

Abdel-Khalik, A. R. (2003). Self-sorting, incentive compensation and human capital assets. *European Accounting Review, 12*(4), 661–697.

Abdolmohammadi, M. J. (2005). Intellectual capital disclosure and market capitalization. *Journal of Intellectual Capital, 6*(3), 397–416.

Abeysekera, I. (2006). The project of intellectual capital disclosure: Researching the research. *Journal of Intellectual Capital, 7*(1), 61–77.

Abeysekera, I. (2008). Motivation behind human capital disclosure in annual reports. *Accounting Forum, 32*, 16–29.

Abeysekera, I., & Guthrie, J. (2004). Human capital reporting in a developing nation. *British Accounting Review, 36*, 251–268.

Acland, D. (1976). The effects of behavioural indicators on investor decisions: An exploratory study. *Accounting, Organizations and Society, 1*(2), 133–142.

Anam, O. A., Fatima, A. H., & Majdi, A. R. H. (2011). Effects of intellectual capital information disclosed in annual reports on market capitalization: Evidence from Bursa Malaysia. *Journal of Human Resource Costing and Accounting, 15*(2), 85–101.

Andriessen, D. (2006). On the metaphorical nature of intellectual capital: A textual analysis. *Journal of Intellectual Capital, 7*(1), 93–110.

Ax, C., & Marton, J. (2008). Human capital disclosures and management practices. *Journal of Intellectual Capital, 9*(3), 433–455.

Barth, M. E. (2000). Valuation-based accounting research: Implications for financial reporting and opportunities for future research. *Accounting and Finance, 40*(1), 7–32.

Barth, M. E., Beaver, W. H., Hand, J. R., & Landsman, W. R. (1999). Accruals, cash flows, and equity values. *Review of Accounting Studies, 4*(3–4), 205–229.

Barth, M. E., Beaver, W. H., & Landsman, W. R. (2001). The relevance of the value relevance literature for financial accounting standard setting: Another view. *Journal of Accounting and Economics, 31*, 77–104.

Barth, M. E., & Clinch, G. (1998). Revalued financial, tangible, and intangible assets: Associations with share prices and non-market-based value estimates. *Journal of Accounting Research, 36*, 199–233.

Beaver, W. H. (1981). Market efficiency. *Accounting Review, 56*(1), 23–37.

Bell, T. B., Landsman, W. R., Miller, B. L., & Yeh, S. (2002). The valuation implications of employee stock option accounting for profitable computer software firms. *Accounting Review, 77*(4), 971–996.

Bontis, N. (2001). Assessing knowledge assets: A review of the models used to measure intellectual capital. *International Journal of Management Reviews, 3*(1), 41–60.

Bontis, N. (2004). National intellectual capital index: A United Nations initiative for the Arab region. *Journal of Intellectual Capital, 5*(1), 13–39.

Bontis, N., Keow, W. C. C., & Richardson, S. (2000). Intellectual capital and business performance in Malaysian industries. *Journal of Intellectual Capital, 1*(1), 85–100.

Brooking, A. (1996). *Intellectual Capital.* International Thomson Business Press and Indiana University.

Brummet, R. L., Flamholtz, E. G., & Pyle, W. C. (1968). Human resource measurement—A challenge for accountants. *Accounting Review, 43*(2), 217–224.

Canibano, L., Garcia-Ayuso, M., & Sanchez, P. (2000). Accounting for intangibles: A literature review. *Journal of Accounting Literature, 19*, 102–130.

Chan, K. H. (2009a). Impact of intellectual capital on organisational performance: An empirical study of companies in the Hang Seng Index (Part 1). *Learning Organization, 16*(1), 4–21.

Chan, K. H. (2009b). Impact of intellectual capital on organisational performance: An empirical study of companies in the Hang Seng Index (Part 2). *Learning Organization, 16*(1), 22–39.

Chen, M. C., Cheng, S. J., & Hwang, Y. (2005). An empirical investigation of the relationship between intellectual capital and firms' market value and financial performance. *Journal of Intellectual Capital, 6*(2), 159–176.

Cheng, C. A., & McNamara, R. (2000). The valuation accuracy of the price-earnings and price-book benchmark valuation methods. *Review of Quantitative Finance and Accounting, 15*(4), 349–370.

Chu, S. K. W., Chan, K. H., Yu, K. Y., Ng, H. T., & Wong, W. K. (2011). An empirical study of the impact of intellectual capital on business performance. *Journal of Information and Knowledge Management, 10*(1), 11–21.

DCTU (1999). "Your knowledge—Can you book it?" Paper presented at the International Symposium Measuring and Reporting Intellectual Capital: Experiences, Issues, and Prospects, OECD, Amsterdam, June.

Dechow, P. M., Hutton, A. P., & Sloan, R. G. (1999). An empirical assessment of the residual income valuation model. *Journal of Accounting and Economics, 26*(1), 1–34.

Dumontier, P., & Raffournier, B. (2002). Accounting and capital markets: A survey of the European evidence. *European Accounting Review, 11*(1), 119–151.

Edvinsson, L. (1997). Developing intellectual capital at Skandia. *Long Range Planning, 30*(3), 366–373.

Edvinsson, L., & Malone, M. S. (1997). *Intellectual Capital: Realizing Your Company's True Value by Finding Its Hidden Brainpower*. New York, NY: Harper Business.

Fama, E. F. (1991). Efficient capital markets: II. *Journal of Finance, 46*(5), 1575–1617.

Fama, E. F., Fisher, L., Jensen, M., & Roll, R. (1969). The adjustment of stock prices to new information. *International Economic Review, 10*(1), 1–21.

Fama, E. F., & French, K. R. (1992). The cross-section of expected stock returns. *Journal of Finance, 47*(2), 427–465.

Feltham, G. A., & Ohlson, J. A. (1999). Residual earnings valuation with risk and stochastic interest rates. *Accounting Review, 74*(2), 165–183.

Firer, S., & Stainbank, L. (2003). Testing the relationship between intellectual capital and a company's performance: Evidence from South Africa. *Meditari Accountancy Research, 11*(1), 25–44.

Firer, S., & Williams, S. M. (2003). Intellectual capital and traditional measures of corporate performance. *Journal of Intellectual Capital, 4*(3), 348–360.

Flamholtz, E. (1971). A model for human resource valuation: A stochastic process with service rewards. *The Accounting Review, 46*(2), 253–267.

Flamholtz, E. (1972, August). Human resource accounting: A review of theory and research. *Academy of Management Proceedings, 1972*(1), 174–177.

Flamholtz, E. (2005). Conceptualizing and measuring the economic value of HC of the third kind corporate culture. *Journal of Human Resource Costing and Accounting, 9*(2), 78–93.

Gamerschlag, R. (2013). Value relevance of human capital information. *Journal of Intellectual Capital, 14*(2), 325–345.

Gamerschlag, R., & Möller, K. (2011). The positive effects of human capital reporting. *Corporate Reputation Review, 14*(2), 145–155.

Gan, K., & Saleh, Z. (2008). Intellectual capital and corporate performance of technology-intensive companies: Malaysia evidence. *Asian Journal of Business and Accounting, 1*(1), 113–130.

Gavious, I., & Russ, M. (2009). The valuation implications of human capital in transactions on and outside the exchange. *Advances in Accounting, 25*(2), 165–173.

Guthrie, J., Petty, R., & Johanson, U. (2001). Sunrise in the knowledge economy: Managing, measuring and reporting intellectual capital. *Accounting, Auditing and Accountability Journal, 14*(4), 365–384.

Haanes, K., & Lowendahl, B. (1997). In H. Thomas (Ed.), *The Unit of Activity: Towards an Alternative to the Theories of the Firm, Strategy, Structure and Style.* Copenhagen: Wiley.

Hofer, C. W. (1983). ROVA: A new measure for assessing organizational performance. *Advances in Strategic Management, 2*, 43–55.

Hussain, D. M., Khan, A. R., & Yasmin, I. (2004). The nature of voluntary disclosures on human resources in the annual resources of Bangladeshi companies. *Dhaka University Journal of Business Studies, 25*(1), 221–231.

IASB (2004). *Issues Standards on Business Combinations, Goodwill and Intangible Assets.* London: International Accounting Standards Board.

Jashapara, A. (2004). *Knowledge Management: An Integrated Approach.* Harlow, UK: Pearson Education.

Kaplan, R. S., & Norton, D. P. (1992). The balanced scorecard: Measures that drive performance. *Harvard Business Review, 70*(1), 71–79.

Leon, M. V. S. (2002). Intellectual capital: Managerial perceptions of organisational knowledge resources. *Journal of Intellectual Capital, 3*(2), 149–166.

Lev, B. (2001). *Intangibles: Management, Measurement and Reporting.* Washington, DC: Brookings Institution Press.

Lev, B., & Schwartz, A. (1971). On the Use of the Economic Concept of Human Capital in Financial Statements. *Accounting Review, 46*(1), 103–112.

Liebowitz, J., & Suen, C. Y. (2000). Developing knowledge management metrics for measuring intellectual capital. *Journal of Intellectual Capital, 1*(1), 54–67.

Luthy, D. H. (1998, August). "Intellectual capital and its measurement." Available at http://www.apira2013.org/past/apira1998/archives/pdfs/25.pdf

Maditinos, D., Chatzoudes, D., Tsairidis, C., & Theriou, G. (2011). The impact of intellectual capital on firms' market value and financial performance. *Journal of Intellectual Capital, 12*(1), 132–151.

Malkiel, B. G., & Fama, E. F. (1970). Efficient capital markets: A review of theory and empirical work. *Journal of Finance, 25*(2), 383–417.

Mavridis, D. G., & Kyrmizoglou, P. (2005). Intellectual capital performance drivers in the Greek banking sector. *Management Research News, 28*(5), 43–62.

Meritum Project (2002). Canibano, L., Garcia-Ayuso, M., Sanchez, P., & Chaminade, C. (Eds.), *Guidelines for Managing and Reporting on Intangibles (Intellectual Capital Report).* Madrid: Airtel-Vodafone Foundation. Available at www.uam.es/meritum

Muhammad, N. M. N., & Ismail, M. K. A. (2009). Intellectual capital efficiency and firm's performance: Study on Malaysian financial sectors. *International Journal of Economics and Finance, 1*(2), 206–212.

Myers, M. S., & Flowers, V. S. (1974). A framework for measuring human assets. *California Management Review*, summer, *XVI*(4), 5–16.

Nazari, J. A., & Herremans, I. M. (2007). Extended VAIC model: Measuring intellectual capital components. *Journal of Intellectual Capital, 8*(4), 595–609.

Ohlson, J. (1995). Earnings, book value, and dividends in security valuation. *Contemporary Accounting Research, 11*, 661–687.

Ohlson, J. A. (1999). On transitory earnings. *Review of Accounting Studies, 4*(3–4), 145–162.

Petrash, G. (1996). Dow's journey to a knowledge value management culture. *European Management Journal, 14*(4), 365–373.

Petty, R., & Guthrie, J. (2000). Intellectual capital literature review: Measurement, reporting and management. *Journal of Intellectual Capital, 1*(2), 155–176.

Pulic, A. (1998). "Measuring the performance of intellectual potential in knowledge economy." Paper presented at the 2nd World Congress on Measuring and Managing Intellectual Capital, McMaster University, Hamilton, ON.

Pulic, A. (2000). VAIC™—An accounting tool for IC management. *International Journal of Technology Management, 20*(5), 702–714.

Pulic, A. (2005). Value creation efficiency at national and regional levels: Case study—Croatia and the European Union. In Bounfour, A., & Edvinsson, L. (Eds.), *Intellectual Capital for Communities* (pp. 197–211). Oxford: Butterworth-Heinemann.

Pulic, A. (2008). The principles of intellectual capital efficiency—a brief description. *Inspired by Knowledge in Organisations, 182*(6), 67–93.

Riahi-Belkaoui, A. (2003). Intellectual capital and firm performance of US multinational firms: A study of the resource-based and stakeholder views. *Journal of Intellectual Capital, 4*(2), 215–226.

Roos, J., Roos, G., Dragonetti, N. C., & Edvinsson, L. (1997). *Intellectual Capital: Navigating in the New Business Landscape*. London: Macmillan Press.

Roslender, R. (1997). Accounting for the worth of employees: Is the discipline finally ready to respond to the challenge. *Journal of Human Resource Costing and Accounting, 2*(1), 9–26.

Roslender, R., & Dyson, J. R. (1992). Accounting for the worth of employees: A new look at an old problem. *British Accounting Review, 24*, 311–329.

Ruta, C. D. (2009). HR portal alignment for the creation and development of intellectual capital. *International Journal of Human Resource Management, 20*(3), 562–577.

Schultz, T. W. (1961, March). Investment in human capital. *American Economic Review, 51*, 1–17.

Shiu, H. J. (2006). Application of the VAIC method to measures of corporate performance: A quantile regression approach. *Journal of American Academy of Business, 8*(2), 156–160.

Stewart, T., & Ruckdeschel, C. (1998). *Intellectual capital: The new wealth of organizations.* Doubleday/Currency, University of Michigan.

Stewart, T. A. (1997). *Intellectual Capital: The Wealth of New Organizations.* London: Nicholas Brealey Publishing Ltd.

Subbarao, A. V., & Zeghal, D. (1997). Human resource information disclosure in annual reports: An international comparison. *Journal of Human Resource Costing and Accounting, 2*(2), 53–73.

Sveiby, K. (2000). *Intellectual Capital and Knowledge Management.* Available at www.sveiby.com.au

Sveiby, K. E. (1997). *The New Organizational Wealth: Managing and Measuring Knowledge-Based Assets.* San Francisco, CA: Berrett-Koehler Publishers.

Sveiby, K. E. (2001). A knowledge-based theory of the firm to guide in strategy formulation. *Journal of Intellectual Capital, 2*(4), 344–358.

Sveiby, K. E. (2002). "Methods for measuring intangible assets." Available at www.sveiby.com/articles/IntangibleMethods.htm

Swartz, G. E., Swartz, N. P., & Firer, S. (2006). An empirical examination of the value relevance of intellectual capital using the Ohlson (1995) valuation model. *Meditari Accountancy Research, 14*(2), 67–81.

Tan, H. P., Plowman, D., & Hancock, P. (2008). The evolving research on intellectual capital. *Journal of Intellectual Capital, 9*(4), 585–608.

Thomson, W. (1891). *Popular Lectures and Addresses*, vol. I. London: MacMillan.

Tseng, C. Y., & James Goo, Y. J. (2005). Intellectual capital and corporate value in an emerging economy: Empirical study of Taiwanese manufacturers. *R&D Management, 35*(2), 187–201.

Uyar, A., & Kiliç, M. (2012). Value relevance of voluntary disclosure: Evidence from Turkish firms. *Journal of Intellectual Capital, 13*(3), 363–376.

Vafei, A., Taylor, D., & Ahmed, K. (2011). The value relevance of intellectual capital disclosures. *Journal of Intellectual Capital, 12*(3), 407–429.

Wall, A. (2005). The measurement and management of intellectual capital in the public sector: Taking the lead or waiting for direction? *Public Management Review, 7*(2), 289–303.

Weisbrod, B. A. (1961). The valuation of human capital. *Journal of Political Economy, 69*(5), 425–436.

Williams, S. M. (2001). Is intellectual capital performance and disclosure practices related? *Journal of Intellectual Capital, 2*(3), 192–203.

Wyatt, A. (2008). What financial and non-financial information on intangibles is value-relevant? A review of the evidence. *Accounting and Business Research, 38*(3), 217–256.

CHAPTER 8

Human Capital Assessment: A Labor Accounting or a Management Control Perspective?[1]

Paola Demartini and Paola Paoloni

Introduction

Literature on human capital suggests that organizations need to recruit and retain talents. This view is based on the awareness that knowledge, skills, and expertise are embedded in individuals, who are in the end responsible for the creation and utilization of knowledge for learning and improvements (Argyris & Schon, 1978).

As a result of increased attention placed on human capital, accountants are interested in designing reliable indicators for human resources' skill, competence, and behavior, which are intangible, perishable, and difficult to store and protect (Mouritsen, 2004).

For the above-mentioned reasons, many aspects of the measurement of intangibles are still contentious, such as the inadequacy of traditional economic tools in financial management and measurement. One of the challenges for management, therefore, is the search for a model to enhance, measure, and manage human capital assets, which, being "firm specific" and difficult to imitate, are the key value drivers that can be relied on to gain a competitive advantage over time.

In our chapter we highlight that in the field of accounting the researcher's main effort is to assess how the contribution of employees added to the firm's asset value and performance. Thus, human capital assessment is functional to find out a link between human resources attributes, such as skill, competence, and behavior, and value created for shareholders and, in a more comprehensive perspective, for stakeholders of a company. Furthermore, we will discuss that within the accounting discipline, there are two main streams for human capital assessment: one related to labor accounting and the other to management accounting. While both have the same ontological aim, which is to visualize and to measure the contribution of the workforce, the former endeavors to suggest a metric for the reporting of human asset value in financial reporting, the latter to find out indicators for managerial decision-making to mobilize and manage human resources in order to increase the company's value.

From a methodological point of view, our investigation is the result of an ongoing research project carried out together with the management of two selected large high-tech companies; that is, it takes an "action research" perspective. While care should be taken in generalizing any of the findings, our research outcome aims to highlight that the contribution of the management control process is to establish relationships between strategic challenges, operations, and indicators associated with human capital, as a main component of intellectual capital (Murthy & Guthrie, 2009).

Developing a more complete understanding of strategy implementation requires the integration of insights from macro (i.e., organization) to micro levels (i.e., individuals) (Hitt, Beamish, Jackson, & Mathieu, 2007, p. 1386). The micro approach is rooted in psychology and focuses on understanding the thoughts, feelings, and actions of individuals. The macro approach is rooted in sociology and economics; it focuses on understanding organizations and markets.

Most management research investigates phenomena by examining them at single levels of analysis (e.g., individuals, groups, organizations, industry, region, etc.). However, in the last years, researchers are developing more complex understandings of phenomena by using a multilevel lens, which aids in understanding the context in which behavior occurs and illuminates the different consequences traversing levels of social organizations (Verma & Dewe, 2008).

Thus, we deem it important to investigate the behavioral dynamic of strategy implementation processes in regard to "mechanisms of transmission" such as leadership, relationships between managers and employees, incentives, and so on. Yet, in this chapter we will address the question of how a new performance measurement focused on intellectual capital and human capital indicators will help managers to intervene into processes of value creation within the two selected companies. This chapter contributes to the developing literature on human capital accounting in practice by using two case studies to compare experience in intellectual capital measuring control and management. Our research is consistent with the third stage of intellectual capital accounting research (ICAR), focusing on enablers and boundaries for implementation of intellectual capital models within the companies, thus filling the gap between theory and practices (Guthrie, Ricceri, & Dumay, 2012).

Finally, the chapter proceeds as follows. In the next section a literature review on human capital measurement is presented. The section thereafter outlines the research methodology, and the findings of the analysis are presented in another following section. Finally, a discussion and conclusion follow in the last section.

A Literature Review on Human Capital Assessment

The literature review will take into account two main streams of research on human capital assessment. The first stream directly refers to the labor accounting research, which has been developed in an attempt to resolve some limitation of the financial reporting that does not disclose the contribution of employees to the asset value of the firm. The second stream refers to a management accounting perspective. More specifically, in recent years, several authors interested in intellectual capital (IC) research have tried to specify the key human capital dimensions in order to figure out the human resources contribution on firm performance and market value.

A Labor Accounting Perspective

Generally speaking, literature on human capital suggests that organizations need to recruit and retain talents. This view is based on awareness that knowledge, skills, and expertise are embedded in individuals, who are in the end responsible for the creation and utilization of knowledge for learning and improvements (Argyris & Schon, 1978).

As a result of increasing attention placed on human capital, accountants are interested in designing reliable indicators for human capital.

Since the 1960s and 1970s, human resource accountants have wanted to explain how the contributions of employees added to the asset value of the firm. The chief issue within human resources accounting is that human assets have a largely uncertain future service life.

Lev and Schwartz suggested that the value of an employee is the present worth of their remaining earnings from employment (1971). Flamholtz (1974), Morse (1973), Friedman and Lev (1974), and Lau and Lau (1978) developed a stochastic valuation model to measure system dynamics and estimate expected service life. Other authors, such as Steffy and Maurer (1988), suggested the replacement cost method, where costs incurred in recruiting,

Table 8.1 Human capital measurement according to labor accounting literature

Some authors	*Measurement of employees' value*
Lev and Schwartz (1971)	Present worth of remaining earnings from employment
Morse (1973)	Present net worth of benefits employees create for the company
Steffy and Maurer (1988)	Replacement cost

selecting, compensating, and training employees reflect the expected value of successful job performance.

Table 8.1 provides an overview of the above-mentioned studies focusing on measurement of employees' value.

The development of human resource accounting as a field demonstrated the high interest in that topic. However, in the 1980s, interest in the area waned for the main reason that accounting standards did not allow for the direct reporting of human assets value in financial reporting.

A Management Accounting Perspective

In the second half of the last century, there was an increasing awareness that accounting information should be appropriate to the needs of managers for managerial decision-making, and management accounting developed as it became recognized that accounting information could be useful for both planning and control.

Argyris (1952) was one of the first writers to examine the "impact of budgets on people," and later, in the 1960s and early 1970s, a considerable amount of behavioral accounting research was undertaken. Its objective was to demonstrate how the design of a performance measurement can impact on the behavior of organizational participants, their level of job satisfaction, and their individual performance and the performance of the organization as a whole. However, over recent years, the implementation of performance measurement systems does not seem to be a significant focus of current behavioral accounting research.

Recently, several authors interested in intellectual capital (IC) research (Berkowitz, 2001; Edvinsson & Malone, 1997; Murthy & Guthrie, 2009; Roos, Roos, Edvinsson, & Dragonetti, 1998; Sàenz, 2005) have tried to specify key human capital dimensions and assess their characteristics using financial and nonfinancial measures in order to figure out the human resources contribution on firm performance and market value.

The main ways of measuring human capital are presented in Table 8.2, while an interesting view of human capital indicators proposed in the literature is elaborated in Martensson (2009).

Table 8.2 Human capital measurement according to intellectual capital literature

Key dimensions	*Measurement (examples)*
Workforce profile	Age, diversity, pay level, promotion rate
Competencies	Measuring competency levels, skills database, tracking competencies and training investments
Employee attitude/engagement	Attitude, engagement, and commitment survey
Productivity measures	Revenue per employee, operating cost per employee, added value per employee
Output measures	Units produced, customer served, customer satisfaction; innovativeness

Albeit the measurement or valuation of human capital is an area of great interest to some academics, there is a lack of agreement as to what should be included in the set of metrics.

Generally speaking on intellectual capital assessment, Mouritsen (2006), based on the Latourian theoretical distinction between ostensive and performative definition of reality (Latour, 1986), recognized two basic research streams—IC ostensive versus IC performative—and, consequently, two related but different roles of measurement. According to the IC-ostensive research stream, knowledge and strategy are linked through causal mapping and related to effects on value creation. Thus, measurement is "essence," useful to discover value-generating assets not visible in the firm's balance sheet.

On the other hand, the IC-performative research stream recognizes that IC is a representation of knowledge resources, whose transformative qualities emerge in application. Thus, measurement is "convention," useful to understand the idiosyncratic qualities of IC and to interpret its role within a specific organizational context.

According to the IC-performative perspective we deem that discovering and measuring intangible assets is not the accounting scholar's main goal but there is an additional *management control agenda* where information about intangibles is an input to management activities (Mouritsen & Larsen, 2005, p. 372).

This means that, to be useful, IC information should be relevant and reliable for internal or external stakeholders interested in its assessment and, above all, it should be consistent with their interest and their cognitive process. Thus, there is no best portfolio of measurement metrics to be identified (Roslender & Fincham, 2004, p. 9), but the issue addressed in this chapter is how firm-specific information on intellectual capital will help managers to intervene in processes of organizational knowledge development, sharing, and application. More specifically, this chapter aims to highlight how two high-tech companies can develop a reporting aiming to increase human resources in skill and competence by the management and mobilizing of firm-specific strategic intangibles functional to the creation of value.

In our research, an interventionist approach (Dumay, 2010) to researching and implementing an IC sustainability framework has been followed.

Research Methodology

The Selection of the Two Companies

The selection of two companies, of which one belongs to the aerospace and defense sector and the other to the renewable energy sources sector, is consistent with our research aims. In fact, in this sector there are large global competitors selling products and services that incorporate a high value of high technology, which stems not only from the financial capital of the firms but also from their human, structural, and relation-based capital spheres and sustainability.

In particular, we decided to focus on the case of two large companies whose headquarters are located in Italy. The selection of these entities is consistent with our research scope. In recent years both the companies' top management has demonstrated its interest in increasing the company's IC-promoting innovation, increasing patents and trademarks, strengthening personnel competences, and enabling community and academic relationships.

This allowed us in both cases to be involved in a company project aiming to identify, measure, and manage intangible resources. Our analysis also offers a picture of how managers can intervene in processes of knowledge development, sharing, and application within the firm.

Accordingly, we suggest that it could be useful both for researchers and for practitioners working together as a joint research team to implement an IC approach into the company management system. Researchers could increase their comprehension of the managers' evaluation of IC framework usefulness. Practitioners could increase their knowledge of IC tools developed by academics, meanwhile improving their awareness of how these fit the company's needs.

Therefore, it is extremely important to define our role as researchers inside the company, which is not comprised of researchers just observing phenomena, nor as consultants, but rather is driven by "action research" principles.

Action Research

Action research attempts to combine the process of research and action based on what Shein (1987) describes as a key assumption—that one can never really understand any human system without trying to change it. Thus, a key aim of action research is to increase both researchers' and practitioners' understanding. Reason and Bradbury (2006, p. 1) define action research as a process that "... seeks to bring together action and reflection, theory and practice, in participation with others, in the pursuit of practical solutions to issues of pressing concern to people."

The researcher is seen to act on a situation in concert with the host organization, observes process and outcome, and analyzes findings in view of the relevant literature. This methodology reflects not only upon the observations of the researcher, but also on the impact the interventions have in the organization. The main benefit for researchers is the ability to develop insights into the implementation of new management innovations in organizations; for practitioners the benefit is to gain the assistance and knowledge of academics as a resource in the implementation process (Dumay, 2010).

There is not an agreed set of methodological protocols, or rules, shared by all researchers; however, action research usually begins with the establishment of initial contact between the action researcher and representatives of the organization. This early stage of research, often called the *entry stage*, entails the identification of perceived ongoing problems within the organization: Who "the client/stakeholder" is, and who will participate in the research, how, where, and when?

During the entry stages of the action research process, either the organization or the researcher can take the initiative in presenting the problem. The action research mode involves a close collaborative relationship, in which there is a mutual agreement at each stage of the action research sequence in order to contribute both to the practical concerns of people and to the goal of social science. Diagnosis is a pivotal stage in action research because the researcher may introduce a conceptual scheme and theories to organizational members that enable them to reinterpret how they understand their situation. The aim is to develop an organization's members' understanding and to co-determine and plan possible interventions.

Analysis and Findings

Context

In the following, some information about the sector in which the entities operate and the two companies' management is provided.

The Aerospace and Defense Sector and Company Management
Players in the aerospace and defense sector are generally large, integrated multinational companies that are highly diversified in terms of both the products they manufacture and their geographical presence. This scale makes it difficult for new companies to enter the market, a problem further exacerbated by the high capital outlay and expertise needed for market success to be achieved. Rivalry in this market is strong. Expertise and knowledge is crucial to the success of companies, as the work is highly specialized. Companies in the industry are compelled to adhere to strict regulations involving national security, export restrictions and licensing for military goods, accounting rules, and safety requirements.

The analyzed company, which we will call "Defence Ltd.," designs and develops large systems for homeland protection: systems and radars for air defense, battlefield management, naval defense, air and airport traffic management, and coastal and maritime surveillance.

The Renewable Energy Sources Sector and Company Management
Structural changes in the energy sector, accompanied by the liberalization of relevant markets, have been taking place in many developing and advanced countries in recent years. The growing demand for electricity and the ongoing climate debate increase the level of interest in technology for generating electricity from renewable energy sources.

The selected company, which we will call "Energy Ltd.," promotes the development of renewable energy sources in Italy by granting support for and organizing awareness campaigns on the environmentally sustainable and responsible use of electricity. In particular, the company fosters sustainable development by providing support for the renewable electricity generation and by taking action to encourage the awareness of environmentally efficient energy uses. The sole shareholder of the selected entity is the ministry of economy and finance, which exercises its rights in consultation with the ministry of economic development.

The Entry Stage

Alvesson and Deetz (2000, p. 17) said that the task of "insight" is to demonstrate "our commitment to the hermeneutic, interpretive and ethnographic goals of local understandings closely connected to an appreciative of the lives of real people in real situations." So, insight from a critical interventionist perspective involves trying to understand the impact of practice on both people and the organizations to which they belong.

The early stage of research, the so-called entry stage, entails the identification of perceived ongoing problems within the organization, who "the manager/stakeholder" is, who will participate in the research, and how, where, and when.

Thus, the first issue is the identification of the main users of IC information. In both the analyzed case studies, the primary IC information user identified is the company's top management. Although the disclosure of IC information to external stakeholders is a further important aim, it was not included here as the entry stage mainly focused on the managerial decision-making process.

The joint research group was composed of at least three professionals involved in the project and three academics. At the entry stage the main role of the researchers was to introduce the IC conceptual scheme and theories to organizational members (thus enabling them to reinterpret how they understand their company), whereas the main role of the practitioners was to assess their usefulness in practice.

The main goal of the research group, supervised by a senior professor, was the proposal to the company's top management of a model for the measurement and management of the company's intangibles. Such a model could therefore be integrated into managerial practices in support of the decision-making process.

During the entry stage of the action research process, either the manager or the researcher can take the initiative in presenting the problem. In a consulting context the client usually presents the problem, and in "basic" research the researcher generally asks for access to investigate a problem in which he or she is interested. The essential difference between the action research approach and others lies in the former's close collaborative relationship: a mutual agreement characterizes each stage of the action research sequence, thus contributing both to practical concerns and to the body of knowledge.

Diagnosis

Diagnosis forms a pivotal stage in action research; it implies an understanding of the organizational context, an analysis of the practical problems and of the faced challenges. Diagnosis entails also the proposal of ideas concerning how to change the organization.

In this case, the "researcher" and "practitioner" create a model to evaluate the measurement and management of the company's intangible assets, which can be integrated into the managerial practices in order to support the firm's decisions.

Visualizing the Company's Intellectual Capital

All information gathered about the sector and the company profiles help us understand why it was vital for the two selected companies to focus their attention on intangible resources.

In fact, growing competition in innovation and new technology force these companies to increase both intangible stock and the effectiveness and the efficiency of its use.

As a first step we carried out the company's intellectual capital visualization (Demartini & Paoloni, 2013a, b). According to prevailing literature, intellectual capital is categorized into three subcomponents, namely human capital, structural capital, and relational capital (Bontis, 1998; Roos et al., 1997; Sveiby, 1997). Human capital is defined as the individual's knowledge, experiences, capabilities, skills, creativity, and behavior; structural capital consists of the nonhuman storehouses of knowledge in an organization that are embedded in systems, databases, and programs. Finally, relational capital consists of all the knowledge embedded in relationships with external parties such as customers, suppliers, partners, and other external stakeholders.

In our research, the "researcher" and "practitioner" create a model to evaluate the measurement and management of the intangible assets of the company, which can be integrated in managerial practices supporting company decisions. The starting point is the mapping of the intangible resources present in the business that must be reinforced, or the resources that must be acquired in response to the management's suggestions, supporting the strategic objectives of the company (Figures 8.1 and 8.2).

It was therefore necessary to create a strategic map of the firm-specific intangible resources. The joint research group started from the company strategic plan and then gathered qualitative information from several meetings with the top management. Final mapping received the endorsement of the companies' CEOs.

Thus, the approach used is that of "an initiative": in other words, starting from the strategic plan, each project envisaged in the strategic plan that has an impact on IC undergoes calculation, evaluation, and reporting. Even in this case, the traditional vision of IC is used, with the three areas represented by structural capital, relational capital, and human capital.

As far as human capital is concerned, it is interesting to highlight that in both cases skills, competence, and behaviors are considered the main assets to focus on.

Then increasing the effectiveness and the efficacy of intangibles, it implies an additional management control perspective, where information about intellectual capital is an input to management activities.

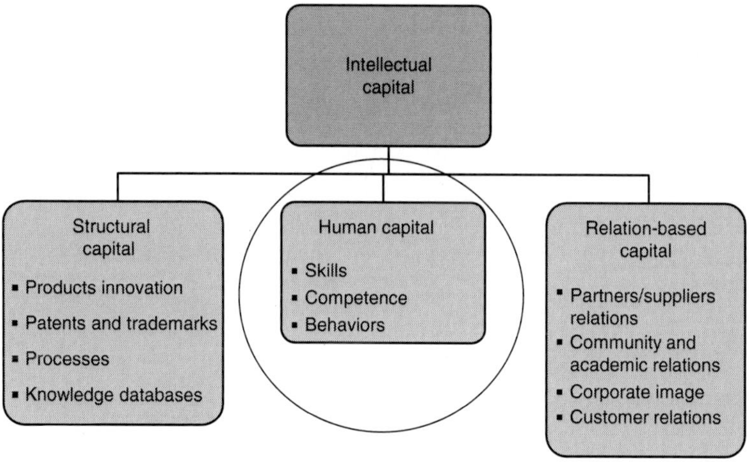

Figure 8.1 Case study: "Defence Ltd."—Visualizing IC

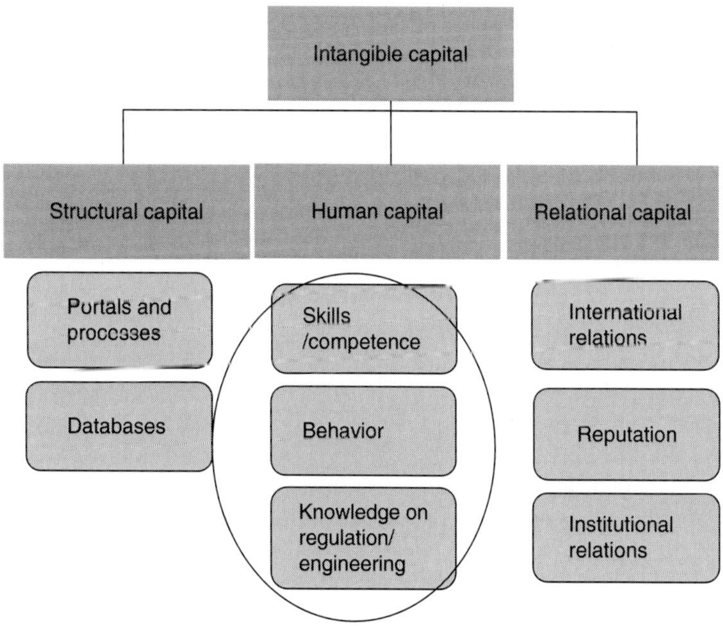

Figure 8.2 Case study: "Energy Ltd."—Visualizing IC

As suggested in the academic literature (Demartini & Paoloni, 2011), analyzing how to manage IC in a knowledge-intensive business is concentrated on the human capital assets' identification, measurement, and management.

Consequently, for the purpose of this chapter, in the following we will highlight the business challenges (i.e., projects, or initiatives), included in both the companies' strategic plans, related to the increase of skills and competence of the company's human resources. All other projects analyzed by the research group but not directly referred to human capital will not be addressed.

A Management Control Perspective

Case Study: "Defence Ltd."

In the Defence Ltd. company, the new management control process was applied to an innovative initiative at the company: a corporate training school (called "Academy") was launched to enhance the firm's corporate culture while sustaining its growth.

First of all it is vital to establish what the managers aim to achieve and the company's intangible resources they want to strengthen.

The Academy has been created to manage corporate knowledge development as well as to coordinate and foster technology innovation and scientific research. In particular, the initiative stems from the need to combine (a) professional, human, and technical know-how and expertise consolidated over years, via transmission from one generation to another; (b) the continuous growth of the know-how the company needs to maintain its leadership in the sector.

The Academy has been conceived as a strategic tool able to provide corporate human resources with advanced training, preserve and strengthen the system and engineering knowledge, as well as promote the dissemination of corporate culture. This approach allows for close cooperation with universities and research institutions.

The use of internal teachers allows for the creation of a close relationship between students and teachers, with positive development of mentoring and coaching, while ensuring at the same time knowledge development and its transfer to new generations. In addition, a specific training program can be created together with external teachers to further knowledge on advanced topics.

The Academy's impact on all the three components of IC (i.e., human capital, structural capital, and relational one) is evident.

A corporate school can increase employees' skills and expertise; meanwhile, the wide range of courses constitutes a knowledge depository that can be updated over the time. Finally, the Academy is an opportunity to foster relationships with universities and research institutions, while it increases the company's reputation with clients, partners, and other stakeholders.

However, without a dynamic approach to IC development, even an interesting initiative such as the launch of the Academy can fail to foster knowledge resources within the company. Thus, a corporate training school should be managed through an *intangibles management control process*.

As far as the Academy is concerned, the strategic plan defines the school's goals and related initiatives to be realized within the year. Then, performance indicators are used to measure the impact of Academy initiatives on the company's IC (Table 8.3).

Table 8.3 Case study: "Defence Ltd."—Management challenges and performance indicators

Management challenges	*Initiatives*	*Indicators to measure the impact on IC*
Transfer of knowledge from one generation to another Development of business skills and competence Integration of complementary expertise	Corporate training school, called "Academy"	*Structural capital* No. of training programs (by expected outcomes, i.e., required professional profiles/skills, etc.) No. of courses (by know-how/discipline/subject, etc.) No. of online/on-video courses Innovation index of training programs *Human capital* Learning tests *Relational capital* No. of universities and research institutions involved in training initiatives No. of customers/partners/other stakeholders to whom training service has been offered

Case Study: "Energy Ltd."

In the "Energy Ltd." company, the new management control process was applied to the goal defined in the strategic plan as development of business skills through training initiatives and projects on the field.

The above-mentioned objective entails the following management challenge and its related actions to be implemented:

- development of business skills through training initiatives for employees of the whole group while the enhancement of business skills should also be realized through promotion of renewable energies.

The above-mentioned challenge implies the two following *initiatives*:

- provision of learning experiences to ensure the development of professional and managerial employees in keeping with the needs of the business, and
- participation by the company staff at conferences and seminars for the promotion of renewable energy sources.

A set of qualified indicators could help the management in monitoring if the planned initiatives were successful in increasing the company's IC in its two components: human and relational capital (Table 8.4).

Table 8.4 Case study: "Energy Ltd."—Management challenges and performance indicators

Management challenges	*Initiatives*	*Indicators to measure the impact on IC*
Development of business skills through training initiatives and projects on the field	Provision of qualified learning experiences	*Human capital* Hours of training provided • Number of training hours • % of turnover invested in training • Expenses in training of total investments • Hours of managerial training • Number of hours of training given to managers/executives • Learning coverage • Percentage of employees who have received at least one day of training • Investment per capital in training • Total costs in training/no employees

Active participation by the company staff at conferences and seminars	*Relational capital—Reputation/corporate image indicators* • Training events/information • Number or events promoted in the year • Conferences organized • Number or conferences organized/trade fairs in the year • Membership in associations/ organizations

Discussion and Concluding Remarks

This chapter aims at highlighting how two high-tech companies can develop a reporting aiming to increase human resources in skill and competence by the management and mobilizing of related firm-specific intangibles.

The opportunity to be involved in a joint research group allowed us to follow the process of choosing a useful IC approach/tool. As this project is ongoing, the following discussion considers only the first step of the diagnosis phase concerning the planning of a new management control process and performance system.

The IC perspective considers the human, structural, and relational capital as assets of the company and, therefore, examines how they can be best developed according to the managerial strategy.

In the two selected case studies, the application of an IC management control process coherent with the strategic plan's main goals represents an organizational innovation for management, while in the meantime it offers an important reporting tool for the whole firm.

As Mouritsen and Larsen (2005) point out, there is an additional *management control agenda* wherein information about IC is an input to management activities. This means to be able to understand the relationships existing between measurement on the one side and operational activities, strategies, and context on the other.

Thus, we deem that it is extremely important for managers to be aware of the mechanism that allows a certain initiative to increase specific intangibles (operational side) and what intangibles are crucial to strengthen for increasing the competitive advantage of a firm (strategy side) within a particular context.

Following the IC-performative research approach (Mouritsen, 2006), this chapter suggests a new approach addressing that intangibles are dynamic resources worthwhile to be measured from a managerial perspective.

For the above-mentioned reasons, key performance indicators (financial or nonfinancial) do not provide sufficient information for management decisions when they are not integrated in a narrative knowledge (Mouritsen, Larsen, & Bukh, 2001).

This supports also Dumay (2009a, b), who suggests a good narrative on IC is more useful for the firm in terms of efficient IC management than a forced algorithm giving a numerical value. Finally, thanks to our methodological approach, that is, "action research," we were witnesses to the process that involved the managers of the analyzed companies in planning activities for 2013.

As always, the observations and conclusions reached here are limited to these cases and are based on the authors' interpretations of facts. Therefore, care should be taken in generalizing any of the findings.

The authors' future research will continue to monitor the way in which the company manages, measures, and reports on its IC. This type of longitudinal research should continue to provide insights into managing, measuring, and reporting IC over time.

Note

1. While the research project is common, sections "Introduction," "A literature review on human capital assessment," "Action research," and "A management control perspective" of this chapter are to be attributed to Paola Demartini, and sections "The selection of the two companies," "Context," "The entry stage," and "Visualizing the company's intellectual capital" to Paola Paoloni. Conclusions are shared.

References

Alvesson, M., & Deetz, S. (2000). *Doing Critical Management Research.* London: Sage

Argyris, Chris. "The Impact of Budgets on People (Controllership Foundation, (1952)." ArgyrisThe Impact of Budgets on People1952 (1952).

Argyris, C., & Schon, D. A. (1978). *Organizational Learning: A Theory of Action Perspective.* Reading, MA: Addison-Wesley.

Berkowitz, S. J. (2001). Measuring and reporting human capital. *Journal of Government Financial Management, 50*, 12–17.

Bontis, N. (1998) "Intellectual capital: an exploratory study that develops measures and models", Management Decision, Vol. 36 Iss: 2, pp.63–76

Demartini, P., & Paoloni, P. (2011), Assessing human capital in knowledge intensive business services, *Measuring Business Excellence, 15*(4), pp 16–26

Demartini, P., & Paoloni, P. (2013a). Implementing an intellectual capital framework in practice. *Journal of Intellectual Capital, 14*(1), pp.69–83.

Demartini, P., & Paoloni, P. (2013b). Awareness of your own intangible assets. *Journal of Intellectual Capital,* Vol *14*(3), pp. 360–375.

Dumay, J. C. (2009a). Intellectual capital measurement: A critical approach. *Journal of Intellectual Capital, 10*(2), 190–210.

Dumay, J. C. (2009b). Reflective discourse about intellectual capital: Research and practice. *Journal of Intellectual Capital, 10*(4), 489–503.

Dumay, J. C. (2010). A critical reflective discourse of an interventionist research project. *Qualitative Research in Accounting and Management, 7*(1), 46–70.

Edvinsson, L., & Malone, S. (1997). *Intellectual Capital: Realizing Your Company's True Value by Finding Its Hidden Brainpower.* New York, NY: Harper Collins.

Flamholtz, E. G. (1974). *Human Resource Accounting.* Encino, CA: Dickenson.

Friedman, A., & Lev, B. (1974). A surrogate measure for the firm's investment in human resources. *Journal of Accounting Research, 12*(2), 235–250.

Guthrie, J., Ricceri, F., & Dumay, J. (2012). Reflections and projections: A decade of intellectual capital accounting research. *British Accounting Review, 44*, 68–82.

Hitt, M. A., Beamish, P. W., Jackson, S. E., & Mathieu, J. E. (2007). Building theoretical and empirical bridges across levels: Multilevel research in management. *Academy of Management Journal, 50*(6), 1385–1399.

Latour, B. (1986). The power of association. In J. Law (Ed.), *Power Actions and Belief: A New Sociology of Knowledge* (pp. 160–172). London: Routledge and Kegan Paul.

Lau, A. H., & Lau, H. (1978). Some proposed approaches for writing off capitalised human resource assets. *Journal of Accounting Research, 16*, 80–102.

Lev, B., & Schwartz, A. (1971, January). On the use of the economic concept of human capital in financial statements. *Accounting Review, 48*, 103–122.

Martensson, M. (2009). Recounting counting and accounting: From political arithmetic to measuring intangibles and back. *Critical Perspectives on Accounting, 20*(7), 835–846.

Morse, W. J. (1975, April). Toward a model for human resource valuation: A comment. *Accounting Review, 50*, 345–347.

Mouritsen, J. (2004). Measuring and intervening: How do we theorise intellectual capital management? *Journal of Intellectual Capital, 5*(2), 257–267.

Mouritsen, J. (2006). Problematising intellectual capital research: Ostensive versus performative IC. *Accounting, Auditing and Accountability Journal, 19*(6), 820–841.

Mouritsen, J., & Larsen, H. T. (2005). The 2nd wave of knowledge management: The management control of knowledge resources through intellectual capital information. *Management Accounting Research, 16*, 371–394.

Mouritsen, J., Larsen, H. T., & Bukh, P. N. (2001). Intellectual capital and the "capable firm": Narrating, visualising and numbering for managing knowledge. *Accounting, Organizations and Society, 26*(7/8), 735–762.

Murthy, V., & Guthrie, J. (2009). Past present and possible future developments in human capital accounting: A tribute to Jan-Erik Gröjer. *Journal of Human Resource Costing and Accounting, 13*(2), 125–142.

Reason, P., & Bradbury, H. (2006). *Handbook of Action Research: The Concise Paperback Edition.* London: Sage Publications.

Roos, J., Roos, G., Edvinsson, L., & Dragonetti, N. C. (1997). *Intellectual Capital: Navigating in the New Landascape*. New York, NY: New York University Press.

Roslender, R., & Fincham, R. (2004). IC: Who counts, controls? *Accounting and the Public Interest, 4*(1), 1–24.

Sàenz, J. (2005). Human capital indicators, business performance and market-to-book ratio. *Journal of Intellectual Capital, 6*, 374–384.

Shein, E. (1987). *The Clinical Perspective in Field Work*. Newbury Park, CA: Sage Publications.

Steffy, B. D., & Maurer, S. D. (1988). Conceptualising and measuring the economic effectiveness of human resource activities. *Academy of Management Review, 13*, 271–286.

Sveiby, K. E. (1997). *The New Organizational Wealth: Managing and Measuring Knowledge-Based Assets*. San Francisco, CA: Berrett-Koehler.

Verma, S., & Dewe, P. (2008). Valuing human resources: Perceptions and practices in UK organizations. *Journal of Human Resource Costing and Accounting, 12*, 102–123.

Index

Printed and bound by CPI Group (UK) Ltd, Croydon, CR0 4YY